NEW YORK F

CW00614018

Studies in Twentieth-Century Literature

Series Editor:
Stan Smith, Professor of English, University of Dundee

Published Titles:
Rainer Emig, *Modernism in Poetry: Motivation, Structures and Limits*
Lee Horsley, *Fictions of Power in English Literature: 1900–1950*
Peter Brooker, *New York Fictions: Modernity, Postmodernism, The New Modern*

New York Fictions
Modernity, Postmodernism, The New Modern

Peter Brooker

Longman
London and New York

Longman Group Limited,
Longman House, Burnt Mill,
Harlow, Essex CM20 2JE, England
and Associated Companies throughout the world.

*Published in the United States of America
by Longman Publishing, New York*

© Longman Group Limited 1996

All rights reserved; no part of this publication may be
reproduced, stored in a retrieval system, or transmitted
in any form or by any means, electronic, mechanical,
photocopying, recording, or otherwise without either the
prior written permission of the Publishers or a licence
permitting restricted copying in the United Kingdom issued
by the Copyright Licensing Agency Ltd.,
90 Tottenham Court Road, London W1P 9HE.

First published 1996

ISBN 0 582 09955 2 CSD
ISBN 0 582 09954 4 PPR

British Library Cataloguing-in-Publication Data

A catalogue record for this book is
available from the British Library

Library of Congress Cataloging-in-Publication Data

Also available

Set by 5 in 10/12 Bembo
Produced by Longman Singapore Publishers (Pte) Ltd
Printed in Singapore

To my mother, Gwendoline Brooker,
and in memory of my father,
Kenneth Henry Brooker (1916–93)

'Time for dinner boys, let's go eat' – Lyle Lovett

Contents

Contents

Acknowledgements

There are some people I would like to thank for encouraging me in writing this book. First of all thanks to Liz for simply everything, including yet another winning epigraph. Thanks to Joe and Will for background vocals. Thanks to Peter Nicholls who read a version of the chapter on Doctorow and advised me where to tighten it up, and thanks to *Borderlines* for accepting a tightened-up version. Thanks to Les and Elizabeth for the Thai dinners and for bringing the Ishmael Reed; thanks to Arlyn for the Vietnamese dinner and for telling me I didn't have to do everything as she left for Mongolia. Thanks to the British Academy and the University of Greenwich for a travel grant and sabbatical time to work at Harvard in 1992; thanks to Nene College for research money for a visit to New York and Columbia University in 1994. Thanks to Martin and Martha Meisel in London and Columbia, New York. Thanks to the green pastures of Harvard and the grey miles of the M1 for their high- and low-grade inspiration and thanks, above all, to the Brooklyn Bridge.

Peter Brooker
London and New York, 1994.

The publishers are grateful to the following for permission to reproduce copyright material:

Bloodaxe Books Ltd for an extract from *Penniless Politics* by Douglas Oliver (1994); Criterion Music Corporation for a lyric line from 'Church' by Lyle Lovett © 1995 Michael H Goldsen, Inc./Lyle Lovett (ASCAP), All rights reserved; Faber & Faber Ltd/New Directions Publishing Corp. for the poem 'N.Y.' by Ezra Pound from *Collected Shorter Poems* (UK title)/*Personae* (US title) © 1926 by Ezra Pound.

CHAPTER ONE

Introduction: 'Companion Cities of the Other Side'

THE CITY FROM LONDON BRIDGE

'Tell me about New York', he said. 'I don't get there anymore.
When I think of cities where I lived, I see great cubist paintings.'
Don DeLillo, *Mao II*

In Brooklyn you can take a driving test in Russian.

First a confession. On seeing the New York skyline Fritz Lang felt he was seeing the face of the future. We all know pretty much what he saw. For whether it is seen from the harbour, the heavens, or the canyons of Wall Street, the image of New York has world-wide currency. Its views and visions are lodged in some global *musée imaginaire*, a collective dream which tells over our desires and fears in the way Italo Calvino has said that modern cities do.[1] But New York has been more of a dream than other cities. Cinema audiences viewing the future in Lang's *Metropolis* have had little trouble in recognising New York as its inspiration. For here was the city of modernity, a constellated symbol of the New, at once inheritor of the first sighting of the new world by Vespuccio in the 1500s and harbinger of the utopia or dystopia the twentieth century would become. And even if, in the event, New York has been in some ways overtaken by the decentred sprawl of Los Angeles or the newer finance capital of Tokyo, it retains in its consistently mixed potential the uncompleted narrative of the century.

In 1987 the magazine *Dissent* devoted an entire number to reflections on New York City (following an earlier survey in 1961). The contributors deal frankly with cases of political corruption, the administration's compliance with real estate values and big money

1

speculators. They see poverty, homelessness, apathy, ethnic tension and racism, the failure of the Jewish intellectual class to sustain its traditional critical role and the lack of any opposition or coalition that would work effectively for social change. But invariably, in the midst of these many failings, each essay in the magazine trusts in some revival; a hope built on the idea of the city's historic character and destiny and most often invested in its new immigrants. In one such contribution, Philip Kasinitz concludes:

> At its best New York has historically shown the potential for a public life that emphasises equality without requiring conformity. It is a mode of politics in which diversity is welcome, and perhaps even rewarded. This ideal has seldom been achieved in practice, particularly where nonwhite people are concerned. It also contains the danger that the various component parts will seal themselves off in opposition to the whole . . . . Still the idea of different people coming together in the public sphere is a central part of the city's cultural history.[2]

As here, so elsewhere in the collection, the sound of postmodern buzz words (fragmentation, pluralism, diversity) might seem to jar with the modernist idiom of social equality, a unifying public sphere and reformist urban planning. In fact, though this is suggestive of the difficulties of the present transitional moment, these tensions, between versions, one might say, of democratic libertarianism and Republicanism have been familiar since the eighteenth century. And it is indeed the spell and paradox of New York City, as of the nation, that amid signs of disintegration, lack of hope and the end of things it retains the promise of an always unrealised potential. New York is always new, abidingly modernist and already postmodern.

And so to my confession. I know the New York skyline and the grid of Manhattan streets like the back of my hand. I've seen the city a million times. I've even sung the city. I 'know' New York, I mean, as an image and compelling cultural myth, at once beacon of hope and newness and warning nightmare; both Celestial and Gotham City. And all thanks to photographs, poems, postcards, films, fictions, memoirs, monographs, cop shows and comic books. What I 'know' are some of its representations. Perhaps we can expect no more in the way of knowledge in a society of the image. But how can this be enough? How can I claim that having seen the photographs of Alfred Stieglitz, having seen *On the Town* as boy and man, and Woody Allen movies in two countries, having read *Last Exit to Brooklyn* and *American Psycho* gives me any proper basis for writing a book in some way about New York City, even a book about books about the city? I might as well think I could write about the United States or the twentieth century.

As I stood in another city waiting for a late train on London Bridge station thinking these thoughts, I realised that of course I could do better than this, that maps and surveys, a long shelf of social, economic and cultural histories meant I 'knew' New York better than I 'knew' London where I have lived for over twenty years. Also, I had visited it three times. I had actually walked the streets, taken the subway, done the sights. I would write the conclusion to this book there. So why the inverted commas around what I 'knew'? Because (the confession returns) my knowledge was the knowledge of a dreamer, an out-of-date futurist, critic, movie-goer and doer of books: a Londoner and at best a visitor, in short an outsider.

Opposite me, no more than four feet from the other side of the train line, stood the blackened brick wall of an office building. Amazingly there were lights on inside the building, though no sign of office workers. A confused image of Melville's *Bartleby the Scrivener* came to mind. His clerk's desk looked out upon the black wall of a neighbouring building on Wall Street. Often his situation and perspective has been taken to represent one key relationship to the city; a life lived low down at eye-level, staring at its brute deprivations. I climbed aboard the train and stared at the office wall, even closer now, through the smeared window pane. Who now, I thought, over a century later, could know the inner life of such an existence at such a time, outside of Melville's fiction? Weren't native New Yorkers strangers to the city's past? And what native New Yorker did not have parents or grandparents or great grandparents who had been immigrants; strangers themselves before the city and its promise dimmed with familiarity?

It was dark as I walked home from the station. No place for a woman to walk alone, I thought. But then a young woman passed me carrying a pair of sturdy heeled boots. Somebody waited opposite in the shadows. Two black youths, their hoods up, laughed outside the corner off-licence. An Asian child ran from her house to the shop, clasping some change. Some white teenagers jump-started a car, swearing loudly. A small thin man in a cloth cap and tight jacket, a cigarette held between his thumb and forefinger, walked a boxer dog. At home a new Chinese restaurant had delivered a take-away menu, including fish and chips. A neighbour's car had been broken into. The TV News reported on the Sarajevo cease-fire, on the Winter Olympics, on espionage at the highest level in the CIA, on the Hebron massacre. An average day's miscellany. Much the same extremes of international and local drama and inconsequence might be experienced in any suburb of any major Western city. Give or take a change of iconography and scheduling I could easily imagine a transatlantic double coming to a similar end of a similar day in a Brooklyn suburb.

There are two points here. Sometimes it does indeed seem as if the new space–time co-ordinates of postmodernism have concertinaed the globe to the point where you don't need to leave your TV set or go further than your local identikit supermarket and mall to know all about it. At worst this is a deadening entrapment that might come to comprise postmodernism's unique addition to the rings of hell. At best it is a mixed blessing. But it is also false to accept this new uniformity of consumption and media-information and the kind of plentiful sameness it produces as the sole leading feature of the postmodern condition, when it is accompanied by (and can be a consoling reaction to) the display, again locally and internationally, of more manifest difference and disparity between haves and have-nots than ever before.

This double play of plenitude and poverty suggests strong structural similarities between London and New York, and this helps us take some measure too of their differences. In the 1980s New Right administrations guided both cities through boom to immediate and unrelieved recession. The streets of both cities are occupied by a new population of the homeless; crack is a problem in the schools; the long-term inhabitants feel a common and increased threat of local violence and attacks upon property and the person; racism is on the increase; old enmities have resurfaced and new ethnic groups are especially scapegoated. In both cities, the bottom third of the population lives in poverty. Half the manufacturing jobs of forty years ago have been lost, and over 80 per cent of all jobs are now in the service sector.

Even within this narrative of late capitalism, however, there are differences, stemming from the cities' different administrative and economic structures and their different political histories. The Left, for example, makes regular use of London streets and parks for mass demonstrations, and would probably argue still for a city-wide governing body such as the defunct GLC. Liberal opinion in New York, by contrast, is agitated by singular incidents with little evidence of public political gatherings or sustained mass campaigning. Common social themes are also played out differently. London, notably, does not experience anything like the level of shootings and murders that are in New York a regular and barely reported daily occurrence. (In 1990 there were 2,200 recorded murders in the city. The victims are often random, and include children, five of whom were killed by stray bullets in this same year.)[3] Very few Londoners will have ever seen a hand-gun, though many will have experienced an IRA bomb attack, and all commuters have learned to build security alerts into their regular timetables. Again, though both cities are racially diverse (London is the most polyglot city in the world with 180 home languages), recent immigration has meant that New York is no longer a majority white ethnic city. In London, by contrast the non-white population is calculated at 15 per cent.[4]

The cities are like transatlantic companions running in parallel dimensions, and there is a way of knowing one by knowing the other's sameness and difference. But does this count for lived experience as well as for the mutating structural features they exhibit under late capitalism? This is to raise the query once more of my own perspective and authority as author. We 'know', so it is said, what we directly experience. 'I know Brooklyn', a New Yorker tells me, 'and you know South London'. 'Yes, of course' I answer, 'but . . . .' Because it is just as obvious that I do not live the lives of my neighbours, nor any of those I saw and heard walking home on the evening of thinking about this introduction. They are more or less strangers to me, perhaps even more strange than Herman Melville or Bartleby the Scrivener. Similarly in New York, for Jean Baudrillard at least, there is 'mind-boggling' solitude, with no relationship between the city's inhabitants beyond the 'inner electricity which results from the simple fact of their being crowded together'.[5]

This might indeed describe one level of common experience in the postmodern city, and help mark the boundaries of the kind of knowledge derived from direct personal acquaintance with people and places. On one side of our minimal coexistence in city crowds and public places there is the full but circumscribed familiarity of immediate relationships in households and demarcated neighbourhoods. Beyond this our mental maps conduct us along favoured, safe routes outside the neighbourhood and across the city, or some of it. But on the other side of stark coexistence there is estrangement: the look of the unknown, and the risk and threat this brings. To take just one example of what this might mean: in the largely Italian district of Bensonhurst in Brooklyn, some older, first-generation immigrants have never moved beyond the two or three blocks marking the neighbourhood, and never learned to speak English. (This is common of course among other groups in other cities, including London.) In August 1989, a black youth venturing into Bensonhurst to look at a used car was gunned down by white youths. Commenting on these youths, who carried baseball bats and a 3.2 caliber gun on the night of the murder, one elderly inhabitant said 'They were good boys. They were defending the neighbourhood.'[6] We should be wary therefore. Lived experience is a way of 'knowing', certainly, but it is no guarantee of authenticity or wisdom. The known is always coupled with the unknown and this relationship can swing in its inherent risk from the worst complacency to wide curiosity. The look of the unknown can spark prejudice to the point of racism and murder, or produce the breakthrough of uncommon knowledge. Both lived relationships and the unseen, less directly comprehended structural features mentioned above are composed in this way of the same and the different. The best we can know and accept of other lives and other cities is therefore a combination of this sort, not the non-relationship of pure difference, but of a 'changing same' over time and physical distance. The contemporary city presents us with this challenge and opportunity, and New York City has above all represented and sought to meet and provide for both as its historic mission: 'a public life that emphasises equality without requiring conformity . . . a model of politics in which diversity is welcome, and perhaps even rewarded'. It's worth remembering at the same time how this statement continues, blocking in the fuller picture of failure and inequality, but also how it again revives, to repeat the hope of a multicultural public sphere.

It is one thing to live this experiment in New York City itself, to witness and help make it succeed, and another to live inside the contradictory idea of the city, both with and without knowledge. The reflections which follow upon the representations of New York in literary and other narratives are the result. To read the city's fictions over the twentieth century in this way, with the estranging gaze, both knowing and innocent of the cultural visitor, is a relationship of sorts between self and other. New patterns of immigration marking the newness of New York now mean that its inhabitants experience this in acute ways. The 'double-consciousness' and 'twoness' of the Negro, which W.E.B. Du Bois remarked upon at the beginning of the century, has multiplied.[7] In one important sense this describes the transition from modernity to postmodernity, from an internalised binary logic in which the terms were never equal to heterocultural modes in which there are intra- and inter-ethnic divisions and assimilations in a general culture whose centre is felt to be melting. The history of the twentieth century, Du Bois predicted, would be the history of the colour line. In fact it has become the history of colour lines, overlapping and criss-crossing other lines of class and gender and sexual difference. In its postmodern, late capitalist phase, the United States has produced societies, both its own and those under its global influence, of hybrid, newly hyphenated, borderline identities, structured in relations of power. I want to discuss some of the fictions that represent this experience below. One less recognised example of this formation, however, across the white Atlantic has been 'Anglo-American'. However mixed and presently unstable this cultural identity is, it still plainly occupies a relatively privileged, if dependent position in relation to the hegemonic culture of the United States. It is from within this cultural position, as a London-based, white-Anglo-male-left literary academic that I attempt to read the twentieth-century fictions of New York. This is at once a position of familiarity and estrangement, as I've suggested, but one which is also brought now, like the modernist perspective it echoes, to a point of self-estrangement. As such, it serves in itself to introduce the forms of the 'new modern'.

THE NEW MODERN

From its beginnings in the last quarter of the nineteenth century European modernism was linked with the environment and conditions of the city, both ancient and modernising, in Vienna, Berlin, Paris, Dublin, London and New York.[8] At the same time it was associated, in Baudelaire's famous description, with the fleeting and fragmentary, and even more importantly with disparity and division. 'By "modernity"', wrote Baudelaire, 'I mean the ephemeral, the fugitive, the contingent, the half of art whose other half is the eternal and the immutable.'[9]

The social equivalent of this separation of part and whole in the aesthetic realm was alienation and estrangement; an experience George Simmel in his own classic modern essay of 1903, 'The Metropolis and Mental Life', saw as characteristic of modern city life.[10] Simmel, and others after him, in particular Louis Wirth, concluded that the bombardment of conflicting impressions in large and densely populated urban environments produced city inhabitants who were at once blasé and reserved. The new citizens were individually sophisticated but limited to transitory, segmental and utilitarian social relations, and given thus to attitudes of relativism and anomie.[11] One role which the new environment made available to the modern artist, though more to men than to women, was that of Baudelaire's *flâneur*, the window-shopping stroller who could observe the physiognomy of the urban crowd while remaining unobserved in the city's new anonymous public places.[12] Many premodernist and modernist writers (Conrad, James, Ford Madox Ford, Pound, Eliot, Joyce, Gertrude Stein, Jean Rhys, for example), but with the different exclusions and openings historically decided by gender, were also exiles and expatriates. The new metropolitan centres were an attractive cultural magnet for such figures, the object of enthusiasm and disappointment which allowed a paradoxical mobility and freedom of association in the midst of anonymity, and made possible the artistic groupings, coteries, and friendships which were so vital a part of the modernist formation. These small associations of emigré artists who advertised themselves as movements in little magazines and in the new form of the manifesto were also very importantly at odds with establishment taste and business culture, even as they thrived within its general bounds. (Eliot, as one example, made a fascinating temporary accommodation with the city's commercial interests and an uncompromising reconciliation with religious orthodoxy if not with the literary establishment, which rather accommodated itself to him.)

The modernist attitude was in these respects one of dissent from bourgeois attitudes and values. Beyond this, however, we have to recognise a plurality of modernisms which sought to innovate on different artistic and cultural fronts, and to understand too the process by which a selective modernism came to represent a standard and orthodoxy and thus marginalise other work.[13] For if the orthodox high modernism, as it became, of Eliot and Pound (to choose its key expatriate American examples) was an innovative, formally experimental and critical literature which dissented from contemporary literary and cultural liberal–humanist norms, this has until fairly recently obscured (or been read so as to obscure) other literatures which in turn dissented from its own constructed hegemony. These other modernisms would include in the United States writers and artists such as H.D. (Hilda Doolittle), Gertrude Stein, Mina Loy, William Carlos Williams, Hart Crane, Charles Demuth and Charles Sheeler, Stuart Davis, Alfred Stieglitz and Georgia O'Keeffe, many of them New York-based, as well as the writers, essayists, musicians and performers of the Harlem

Renaissance. A further, much noticed and then forgotten example would be John Dos Passos. These artists contracted a different relation with, and sometimes rejected, traditional European- or more narrowly English-based models in the name of an indigenous racial or national affiliation, or on occasion with the consciousness of a broader cosmopolitanism which looked to the European avant-garde and to Soviet art. Mayakovsky, Eisenstein, Kafka, George Grosz, Brecht, Kurt Weill and Marcel Duchamp, on the other side of this relation, might be numbered amongst avant-garde artists fascinated by the imagined or actual fact of modernity expressed especially by New York City. And as some of these names also remind us, modernism was often characterised by an enthusiasm and ready appropriation of the new achievements in engineering and technology displayed in the city.

In some ways these latter trends, in an odd reversal, might be thought of, in retrospect at least, as 'anti-modern', as Milan Kundera has chosen to designate certain non-canonic tendencies in European writing.[14] Unlike the reactionary dissent associated with high modernism, these other American modernisms also inclined, as did the European avant-garde, towards libertarian anarchist, populist and Left positions sympathetic towards early Bolshevism, Spanish Republicanism and Communism. In terms of Baudelaire's definition above, an awareness of contingency was coupled with different, antagonistic notions of artistic, philosophical and social order and unity. If this returns us to the sense of a common impulse in modernism we have to recognise we are talking less about the achieved fact of order (as different in conception as the names Bertolt Brecht and Ezra Pound imply), then an aspiration or commitment to it, very often expressed in terms of its provisionality or failure.

We might still think of all this as predominantly European in its orientation. One of the main questions I want to pose below, therefore, is what dilutions, negations or expansions this tradition has undergone in the passage from earlier periods of American radicalism, including the most overt influence of Marxism in the 1930s, to the period of postwar, postmodernity when the hegemony of European models has been directly challenged.

Raymond Williams's account of modernism and the metropolis emphasises the diversity and mutual antagonism of modernist projects, as I think we must, and associates their emergence especially with the consolidated transition of major cities into metropolitan

centres.[15] These expanded, open environments, he says, brought
with them the combined anonymity and mobility, emancipation
and licence mentioned above. Williams's account therefore shares
an understanding of the conditions of the modern city with the
classical essays of Simmel, Louis Wirth and others. But he clarifies
some of the confusions of this tradition. As Gerd Hurm reports,
classical urban theory attributed the experience of the modern city
by turns to a money economy, an evolutionary process, or to the
autonomous physical features of size, density and heterogeneity. It
therefore 'muddled the relationship between cause and effect', he
says.[16] Williams associates the double moment of artistic modernism
and the modern city more clearly with capitalist development, with
'the imperial and capitalist metropolis as a specific historical form,
at different stages: Paris, London, Berlin, New York' (p. 93). Most
importantly, while attitudes towards the city in literature remained
unaltered, says Williams, modernist artists turned their attention in
innovative and newly self-conscious ways to matters of language and
form. This again focuses in a new way the influential description of
urban experience as overstimulating, liberating, and anonymous: a
view which in academic work largely derives from this same tradition
in sociology, though its idea of a generic urban experience has been
more recently recognised as the generalisation of an outside observer's
or of middle-class perceptions than an objective description. In the
present context we can say that this perspective approximates closely
to the perceptions of visiting and emigré writers and artists who were
in much the situation of the social type Hurm says it represents:
'the newcomer, traveler, or transient urbanite'.[17] Williams extends
this point:

> The most important general element of the innovations in
> [modernist] form is the fact of immigration to the metropolis,
> and it cannot too often be emphasised how many of the major
> innovators were, in this precise sense, immigrants. At the level
> of theme, this underlies, in an obvious way, the elements of
> strangeness and distance, indeed of alienation, which so regularly
> form part of the repertory. But the decisive aesthetic effect
> is at a deeper level. Liberated or breaking from their national
> or provincial cultures, placed in quite new relations to those
> other native languages or native visual traditions, encountering
> meanwhile a novel and dynamic common environment from
> which many of the older forms were obviously distant, the artists
> and writers and thinkers of this phase found the only community
> available to them: a community of the medium; of their own
> practices.
>
> (pp. 91–2).

The attention to form as malleable rather than settled, to language as if it were a second language and as therefore conventional and arbitrary, made it 'more evident as a medium . . . than as a social custom', says Williams, and thus a prime means of artistic community. The fractured, multilingual, cross-cultural discourse characterising modernist forms can therefore be seen to derive from a particular social situation and perspective upon the urban metropolis. Hence the characteristic modernist attitude of estrangement (as of the newcomer or transient) *vis-à-vis* the 'common' experience, whether this was understood as the dominant or the popular. Modernism therefore registered an experience of the modern as fragmented and relativistic in its very verbal texture; although, given its different ideological projects, it might either celebrate or deplore this, or seek to remedy it in the 'other half' of Baudelaire's modern art.

But this is still to over-generalise the modernist relation to the modern city. Williams suggests that we need to think first of the 'metropolis', and of this in its historical stages in Paris, London, Berlin, New York – where the experience of the newcomer and observer could be quite different, and new art could meet with quite different degrees of welcome and resistance. In New York as the last-named in this series, the proximity of immigrant and modernist perspectives could be especially telling. Twenty-seven million immigrants, largely from Southern and Eastern Europe, entered the United States between 1880 and 1930, otherwise the age of advancing modernisation and of modernism. As Werner Sollers comments in a discussion of ethnicity and literary form in the United States: 'ethnicisation and modernisation often go hand in hand'.[18] And New York, we might add, served historically as the gateway to both.

In the metropolis of the late twentieth century, says Williams, marked changes in the now globalising reach of mass media and cultural technologies make the categories 'modern' and 'modernism' in their habitual cultural and historical uses anachronistic or residual, if still in some quarters hegemonic. What lies beyond this moment, in the 'present beyond "the modern"', as he puts it, is uncertain (pp. 84–5). Crucially, however, Williams does not speak of an abrupt and absolute break into 'postmodernity' (nor does he use this description). He writes rather of an intensification of the earlier diversity of modernism, and of a 'deadlock' and 'cultural stasis' in which the one thing that is clear is that the universals of the earlier period, in art and ideas, including its conception of itself as universal and absolute, 'belong to a phase of history which was both creatively preceded and creatively succeeded' (p. 93).

Williams's conclusions coincide with a scepticism within urban theory on the notion of a generic urban mind or culture and a new emphasis instead, of the kind Gerd Hurm adopts, on 'the fragmentation and diversity of the ways in which the modern city may be experienced depending on the class, gender, and ethnicity of the urbanite'.[19] A formulation such as this expresses an intensification of the 'immigrant' perspective associated with modernism, but extends and further differentiates its social base (in terms of class and gender as well as ethnicity) as befits the composition of the contemporary city, rather than simply generalising the earlier perspective.

The anti-universalism of these positions, and the intensified diversity they point to, are often associated with postmodernism. In a way the postmodern therefore appears to bring forward the contingent and fragmented side of Baudelaire's 'modern' without its yearning for the universal and eternal. This can give rise to two common simplifications, however, one of which Williams's essay is already effectively a reply to. In the first, the language of difference becomes a way of ignoring the role of ideology and the persistence of forms of oppression, inequality and marginalisation, or a way of tolerating these as examples of the new pluralism. The authors of the volume, *Breaking Boundaries*, draw attention, for instance, to the way that Latina writers have had to question and unmask the labelling of themselves as 'different'. And 'like "difference"', they add,

> the much used concept of 'diversity' also becomes a euphemism for racism when it is imposed by outsiders . . . . If diversity is perceived *only* in racial or ethnic terms, without questioning the relations of, and to, power structures, then it also becomes a celebration of oppression and continues the marginalisation of the 'diverse' people in question by assigning them a framed space and date in which to perform.[20]

Diversity can therefore be made to mean diversity for others and sameness for those protected by invisible, taken-for-granted norms. Secondly, even where an awareness of ethnicity and postmodern hybridity is allied to a progressive political perspective and strategy, one which would expose and critique such norms, it can be weakened by a demonising view of modernity and modernism as postmodernism's absolute Other. Henry Giroux, for example, speaks of postmodernism as 'a culture and politics of transgression . . . a challenge to the boundaries in which modernism has developed its discourses of mastery, totalization, representation, subjectivity and history'.[21] For Giroux, the modern is branded as totalising, Eurocentric, implicitly racist and the enemy of popular culture. In a not dissimilar vein, Philomena Mariani introduces the postmodern contributors to the volume *Critical Fictions* as 'unearthing what was previously unseen by the God's-eye-view of the modernist gaze'. 'The realities of critical fiction', she says, 'are multiple, chaotic, inclusive, hybridised, undomesticated, unpurified; often polemical, anti-universal.'[22] Here modernism is universalist, masculinist, and presumably the opposite on every count to the list of postmodern attributes.

Critical or oppositional postmodernism also has a further aspect in these accounts, however, since, although the terms are sometimes confused, it is not simply 'anti-modernist' but also 'anti-modern'; that is to say, opposed to the Enlightenment project and specifically to Marxism. In Giroux's judgement Marxism appeals to 'the modernist logic of essentialism in which reason and history seem to move according to some inner logic outside the play of difference and plurality'. The effect, he says, is that 'class struggle becomes the all-embracing category that relegates all other struggles, voices, and conflicts to simply a distraction in the march of history'.[23] In her account, Mariani polemicises against those who feel 'nostalgia for the surety of master narratives – Family, Nation, God, Progress, or even Class Struggle' – since this 'veils a desire to escape the complexity of historical and cultural realities exposed by oppositional postmodern practices'.[24]

We do not need to be defenders of Marxism to see that there are inconsistencies in these formulations. One lies in their recourse, as in much postmodern thinking, to the anti-essentialism and 'the category of difference' associated with deconstruction. Yet deconstruction does not countenance absolute rejection any more than absolute affirmation; it talks not of turning the page (of philosophy), but of reading in a new way, of setting the concepts that underlie a metaphysics of presence 'under erasure'; that is to say, of simul-taneously writing and unwriting but not simply and absolutely of cancelling these concepts. Deconstruction, in short, is a method of critique. Derrida's comments on the relation of deconstruction and Marxism have emphasised this further:

> . . . the deconstruction of the metaphysics of the 'proper', of logocentrism, linguisticism, phonologism, the demystification or the de-sedimentation of the autonomic hegemony of language . . . would have been impossible and unthinkable in a pre-Marxist

space. Deconstruction has never had any sense or interest, in my
view at least, except as a radicalization, which is to say also in
the tradition of a certain Marxism, in a certain spirit of Marxism.
There has been then, this attempted radicalization of Marxism called
deconstruction.[25]

Secondly, though Giroux in his essay might choose to see Marxism
as universalist, teleological, as simplifying difference and struggle
to the 'reductionist logo-centrism' of class struggle,[26] it is clear
that his own vision of a newly democratic subject and public
realm depends on the vocabulary and principles of Enlightenment
modernity ('the very fate of our society as a democratic nation is a
risk', he writes, and elsewhere invokes 'the principles of liberty,
justice and equality' derived from 'political modernism').[27] More
precisely, it is clear that his thinking is indebted, in the 'spirit' of
Marxism, to Chantal Mouffe's neo-Gramscian project for radical
democracy.[28] Significantly too, Mouffe talks in the passage quoted
by Giroux of the need 'to *deepen* the democratic revolution' (my
italics), of 'modifying' the identities of democratic forces so as to
establish an equivalence between their struggles, in a description
that names workers as well as women, immigrants and consumers
amongst those engaged in this political project.

The appeal to postmodernism as a way of naming the 'present
beyond "the modern"', in Williams's phrase, can therefore fall foul of
a simplified view of its own radicalism. But this is not to say that there
can be a return to modernism, or that this has not been employed as an
exclusive orthodoxy, nor to deny that the Enlightenment tradition has
been brought to serve cruel, partisan and imperialist purposes, or that
Marxism has been associated with the most stultifying masculinist
regimes. Rather it is to say that modernism and the modern
project have to be understood in terms of both the conservative
and oppressive, and open and liberating forms that have been launched
in their names, and that we have, in the same way, to recognise both
conservative and progressive forms of postmodernism. The task for a
critical and oppositional postmodernism of the type Giroux, Mariani
and others describe is more appropriately therefore to deconstruct the
black and white binaries that have constructed cultural modernism as
a selective hegemonic tradition than to reinforce them. Proposals for
a radical democracy depend, similarly, we might argue, on rethinking
and renewing modern political traditions, on fully taking up Mariani's
call to 'the traditional left to reexamine its most fundamental precepts',
rather than in abandoning them. As one British contributor to these
debates has written: 'The postmodern question consists in asking

what can count as rationality now?' To answer this question 'means articulating a politics capable of constituting a "we" which is not essentialist, fixed, separatist, divisive, defensive or exclusive. Clearly the structures and forms of such a politics must be capable of representing both the diversity and the desire of contemporary politics.'[29]

A newly constituted, rational public sphere of the kind such thinkers imagine will continue to 'make it new' in the famous modernist dictum. Much also that is described as 'critical' or 'oppositional', or as 'post-structural postmodernism',[30] is vital to the creation of such a new public sphere and idea of citizenship. I am led to suggest the term 'new modern' as a description of this moment and in discussing some of the fictions of New York City as a way of combining these innovative and critical impulses but as confirming neither. The main reasons for preferring this description to 'postmodernism', whatever supporting adjective is brought to it, are those I have already implied. In literary and cultural debate, 'postmodernism' is too often associated with the merely stylistic features of self-conscious play and parody for it to serve the broader radicalising purpose ascribed to it. In this mode postmodernism is generally explained as the result of changed psychic, technological and cultural worlds which have made any assumptions of a unified subjectivity and any reference to a 'real' rather than constructed or simulated world impossible. In a further move its anti-essentialism provokes a suspicion or abandonment of the modern project and the resources it has supplied of a stable ethical position or cultural and political critique. At its most extreme, postmodernism therefore becomes a celebratory or fatalistic aestheticism, a self-ratifying denial of any effective cultural politics. The description 'new modern' by contrast, I hope, retains the sense of a world of lived social, cultural and economic relations which this postmodernism denies, along with a recognition of the material effects of advanced media and information technology (the continuing experience of 'modernisation' in the modern city), with all due sense of how problematised representation, identity, forms of critique and politically motivated action have become in this ever 'new', ever more complex environment. I propose this study and search in the 'spirit' of modernism, since the 'new modern' cannot in my reckoning come simply and dramatically 'after' (in the sense that the prefix 'post' is often understood) but only from 'within' the modern.[31]

The essays which follow are an attempt to reflect further on these criteria and distinctions, less in the theoretical form they deserve perhaps, than in a series of case studies of New York fiction from the 1850s to the present. I can introduce this fiction here and elaborate further on the idea of the 'new modern' by way of two examples from writers I consider in later chapters.

Ishmael Reed's writing is often described as postmodernist. Its dominant mode is parody; it scrambles and scatters discourses, mixing fact with fiction and fantasy, contemporary reference with ancient oral tales, the folk with the popular and erudite, the styles of philosophical discourse and television cartoons, writing with drawing and photographs. 'We salute the postmodernists and we have a coalition with them', says Reed.[32] The 'we' of this statement is in the first instance an African–American community on behalf of whom Reed draws on older oral traditions and non-literary cultural forms, discovering resources from within and behind the modernist, realist and classical texts that have comprised the European-based literary mainstream.

Reed's writing therefore connects postmodern style with contemporary postcolonial or multiculturalist agendas. Yet where the first can often describe a literature of pastiche detached from reference, critique and history, and the second an opposition to European philosophical and cultural traditions, their combination in Reed produces a broad, politicised and critical eclecticism. He writes: 'I'm not going to abandon Western values. I want to mix things up a little. Multiculturalism has been around since the imagists, but now this is becoming the standard. This will be the trend of the twenty-first century, as more people come to this country and no longer feel the need to abandon their culture. That's what the fight is about.'[33] Like other sometime 'postmodernist' writers (Toni Morrison, E.L. Doctorow), Reed also seeks, indeed assumes, a critical and constructive relation to the past and a cultural function within a changing history. 'I'm concerned', he says, 'about doing a take on the present and perhaps saying something about the past and the future';[34] and elsewhere, 'The black writer [practising 'necromancy'] lies in the guts of old America, making readings about the future.'[35]

In short, a hybridity of creative forms is linked in Reed's thinking to a comparable social vision of 'the United States as a mosaic, instead of black versus white'.[36] A bricolage of the old and new, of the high and low, the modern and the postmodernist, the European and the American, the American and the African–American, as well as other new ethnic groups and languages is seen to serve a critical cultural purpose.[37]

Reed here outlines the dialogic forms and purposes of the 'new modern' as I understand it. But this is still to think in general, even ideal terms, when it is important to avoid setting a model or ideal. I have wanted to stress above that there is no uniform modernism or postmodernism, nor generic urban identity. Instead, there are dominant and alternative conceptions or images of these, bound up in the operations of power, privilege, protest and change (which may of course seek to homogenise and stabilise perceptions). By the 'new modern' I mean a politicised, deconstructive take on the modern past. As such it is a strategy in the making rather than an achieved position, one which I see certain writers as prefiguring in the late nineteenth and early twentieth centuries and as more intently engaged with in the late twentieth century. Thinking about this writing in relation to the city means, as elsewhere, tracking the forms of a 'changing same'. The physical and social history of New York as one such 'changing same' presents a contradictory narrative of abundance and deprivation, energy and enervation, stability and discontinuity, and perhaps above all, to borrow from Raymond Williams's discussion above, of intensifying diversity. Literature, as always, confirms, reveals, rejects and interrogates the many processes this describes, according to its own modes and position within the culture. Which is to say of course that literature does not have a uniform identity or function either.

The literatures of European modernism knew and reflected upon, and sometimes imagined, cities displaying the early features of modernisation (planned environments, new municipal and commercial building, the growth of suburbs, arcades, bridges, towers in new materials, new systems of transport and communication). But it is not to European cities that we or modernist artists looked for the fullest and fastest expression of modernisation. This was New York, compared with which Joyce's Dublin was a neighbourly and still knowable community. The Dublin of *Ulysses* in 1904 had electric trams and streetlighting, a national newspaper, advertising, the public buildings and parks, middle-class and slum areas which marked the physical environment of the modern city, but, aside from the blessing of the largest brewery in the world, it had little significant industry or commerce, and no cinema (Joyce's attempt to introduce one in 1909 failed). Nor was there a skyscraper in sight. If it was a modern city it was not an emerging metropolis. In New York, by contrast, the signs of advancing modernisation in architecture, engineering, commerce and communications began to appear in a flurry and in earnest in the middle and late nineteenth century. (I consider these and some literary responses to them in the following section.) Interestingly, this period is the subject also of the contemporary novel *The Waterworks*, the most recent novel, at the time of writing, by E.L. Doctorow, who I also consider below.

The Waterworks is set in the period of New York's first wave of modernisation after the civil war, a world full of the newness of rotary presses, steam engines, gas-lamps 'when there was nothing to stop progress' when 'Nowhere else in the world was there such an acceleration of energies', and the city seemed to build itself overnight.[38]

The story, told by McIlvaine, a newspaper editor, follows the search of his freelance, Martin Pemberton, for his father, a corrupt businessman and slave-trader. Pemberton senior, though officially buried, is twice seen by his son, once in a carriage passing through the city and secondly by the reservoir. Coming to terms with the past in the form of a ghostly or absent father is a familiar theme in Doctorow's work.[39] Here it is mediated through McIlvaine's reflections at a later date on what kind of story he is telling and what access he has to a retreating past. His analogy is with the early modern form of the newspaper, eight wide pages of 'seven word-packed columns of simultaneous descent'. In his own present-day news story, however, 'the sense is not in the linear column', not in 'linear thinking' but transmitted via a disrupted chronology which promises 'that finally all the columns will be joined to be read across the page' (pp. 111, 141). 'The way enlightenment comes', McIlvaine confides, '. . . is in bits and pieces of humdrum reality, each adding its mosaic bit of glitter to the eventual vision' (p. 85). He narrates the story accordingly, to capture 'the knowledge that comes with estrangement', in a version of the modernist method of collaged simultaneity. Both these concerns are overtaken, however, by an interest in the figure of Dr Wrede Sartorius, a German immigrant, wartime colonel and surgeon in the United States. (His Latin name, McIlvaine tells us, signifies the self-aggrandising transformation of 'trade people who wanted to elevate themselves socially'; thus 'the tailor became Sartorius', p. 124.) Sartorius is employed by Augustus Pemberton and the crooked municipal officials of the Tweed Ring to ensure their longevity. His brilliance as a surgeon is extended to experiments on bone marrow transplants, blood transfusions, electrotherapy and even heart transplants, using the bodies of young city vagrants, the city's freaks and mentally ill.

Sartorius is personally indifferent to all but the potential of medical science and the 'amoral energies' of life, pursuing the 'afflicted and grotesque' of existence to 'the truly unreasoning thing it is' (pp. 180, 192). He is modernity's contingency, its Nietzschean excess and driving force to the businessmen's wished-for eternal life, and in Doctorow's terms a figure, like Wilhelm Reich elsewhere, of the tragic radical, ahead of his time, and doomed in the logic of his inspiration to his eventual isolation in an insane asylum. (He is murdered in the asylum, but before his death takes the inmates and himself as models for the observation of Nature's endless, wasteful profusion and self-transformation, p. 233.) The ambivalent genius of modernist rationality embodied in Sartorius and the corrupt coupling of science and capital is expressed also in the Croton Waterworks itself: both a marvel of industrial engineering, vital to the city's hygiene and its protection from fire, but the scene too of the drowning and abduction of a child, and, as it transpires, the site of the sanatorium where Sartorius sustains the lives of the ghostly municipal chiefs.

What in the present context can we learn from this novel? It is about change, the contradictions and coincidences in early modernity of corruption and progress, about fathers and sons, access to the past and its representation in narrative. The novel probes these tensions within and across eras. A new regime under an honest Police Commissioner is on the point of succeeding the corrupt reign of the Tweed ring; the wheels of modernity are set to turn once more, and there is a promise that a stronger moral perspective will govern public affairs. In the terms of its internal nineteenth-century narrative this is an important reform, but the novel also consistently speaks to a later period, sometimes in the narrator's direct address to ourselves in the present time of simultaneous composition and reading. It asks therefore to be read as a parable. But how? Does Doctorow mean to show us our own society and the promise of a new improved public sphere? If so, the novel falls short of contemporary concerns. The questions it has raised of the treatment of children – said to be a yardstick of a civilised society – of urban poverty, mental and public health, in the end lie dormant; women are assigned no positive independence beyond the roles of fiancée, wife and helpmeet, and ethnicity is never more than a sketchy feature of the background.

Is this a failure on Doctorow's part? Or is it a mistake to read and judge this novel (or any novel) according to a particular cultural agenda and the expectations this sets? Am I asking writers to conform to a ready-made idea of the 'new modern'? In truth, neither writers nor readers can avoid a political or cultural agenda in an historical novel or elsewhere. Increasingly urban life and sensibility are felt to have gone beyond the older descriptions and spatial metaphors and to have become decentred and illegible. We look to social scientists, urban geographers and others to name and analyse this condition, to find new forms and vocabularies for reading the text of urban life. Amongst those others are contemporary novelists. Early literary modernism had, for its part, evolved new forms for expressing a new urban experience: the prose poem, the imagist text which caught a passing moment, and the technique of stream of consciousness which was a way of showing the city as a kind of internalised walking–talking itinerary.[40] My question is, therefore, a question to contemporary literary fiction. What ways does it find to name and inscribe the structures of feeling and meaning in this contemporary moment? What questions does it frame about this 'what comes next' which is neither modernism nor postmodernism. As an allegorical text of the social themes of the late twentieth-century city Doctorow's *The Waterworks* appears incomplete. Yet we realise, I think, that the novel is of interest precisely in its incompleteness, in the sense it gives of a lack of achieved result or of confident prediction. For the ending of the novel is above all a pause, a hiatus in historical time and the march of modernity. It is in this halting gesture, I think, that Doctorow's novel tells us something about the new modern.

Doctorow's companion prose essay to the novel, 'The Nineteenth New York' suggests this ending is analogous to the moment of public silence that accompanied Abraham Lincoln's death.[41] The narrator refers early on to Walt Whitman, the bard of Lincoln's death, as a familiar New York contemporary. His verses were for the most part foolish, says McIlvaine, save for the three 'confessional lines about his city':

> Somehow I have been stunned. Stand back!
> Give me a little time beyond my cuffed head
>   and slumbers and dreams and gaping . . .

(p. 10)

Much of the novel questions the one-dimensional optimism of Whitman's encomiums on America's modernity. Its characters, by contrast, like Pemberton and his painter friend, Harry Wheelwright, have 'the same conflicted mind' caught between 'critique and the necessity of earning a living, side by side' (p. 93). But the sense of Whitman's lines is recalled again in the novel's close, or pause, when the city's machinery is brought to rest on a Winter Sunday, as if 'frozen in time . . . a glitter and godstunned' (p. 246). The reaction to the sweep of modernity this captures is that of the stunned bystander, or, we might say, the immigrant, or newcomer and traveller described above, with whom the modernist artist shared a social situation and perspective. The moment of being taken aback, of taking a breath, as McIlvaine says of Whitman's lines, of taking 'a little time' in the lines themselves, expresses the jolt of modernist estrangement and distance upon the familiar. Thus the hesitant rhythms of the narrative, heavily punctuated throughout by the three dots that link and halt its progress, come into their full meaning in this pause that doubles as ordinary rest day and historical watershed.

Thus the narrative mimes the revolving energies of modernity in motion and brought to a standstill, but also the memory and a taking stock of this process. All of the major characters are described as living at this kind of distance from their contemporary society. Martin Pemberton's generation, again, are said to make 'little social enclaves of irony', and when he is under Sartorius's influence he is most conscious of feeling 'like a foreigner in my own country . . . estranged, a born alien, disynchronous with my times' (pp. 2, 190). Even the incorruptible police captain Edmund Donne whose help McIlvaine enlists is an 'odd misplaced policeman' (p. 84).

The narrator once more gives controlling expression to this sense of displacement. As a newspaper editor he presided over a medium for the 'municipally dissociated' (p. 83). Now, at the time of narration, the reporter is less a first-time witness than a time-traveller reporting his own memories in the weave of the story. In the past he sees moments 'that are something like breaks or tears in moral consciousness, as caesuras break the chanted line'. Through this breach the eye sees 'a companion life [. . .] parallel in time, but within a universe even more confounding than our own' (p. 213). To his future readers, as he reaches out to the perspective of Doctorow's prose essay McIlvaine shows a New York that 'You may think [. . .] stands to your New York City today as some panoramic negative print, inverted in its lights and shadows [. . .] a companion city of the other side' (p. 56). In this gathering estrangement, at the point of mid-modernity, in the pause of his tale, McIlvaine bridges modernity's earlier and later phases.

Finally, the divided view, possible at a tear on the cusp of history, occurs in the present time of Doctorow's composition and our reading. As such it reminds us of Raymond Williams's sense of cultural stasis and uncertainty at the end of modernism, or more precisely of its discredited universalism. In Doctorow's nineteenth-century story history picks up and goes on. And this must therefore be the implication for the later and present periods. 'You may think you are living in modern times, here and now', says McIlvaine, 'but that is the illusion of every age. We did not conduct ourselves as if we were preparatory to your time' (p. 9). The modern moment by implication is the present moment, always unstoppably now. Yet by the same token every period will define its newness as going beyond and after the last modern, since this is what makes it new.

Descriptions of the late twentieth century tell us the postmodern is indeed unlike the modern. In a world of pastiche and simulation, instantaneous global information, recycled newness and nostalgia, there is no stability of aesthetic or moral reference, or creditable space for historical reflection or critique. So the more familiar account runs. I think, however, that Williams and Doctorow give us another sense of what this difference is. In other words they give us a different sense of history.

'Modernism', says David Harvey, 'reminding us of Baudelaire's definition, could only speak to the eternal by freezing time and all its fleeting qualities'.[42] For those committed to the agenda of the modern project (to a belief in moral consciousness, social betterment, rationality), but alert to its dark side and fallacious universals, the moment of stasis is temporary. It is an 'illusion' only, Doctorow's final sentence confirms, that 'the entire city of New York would be forever encased and frozen' (p. 246). Cold stillness descends upon the city's operations in the precise ellipsis, as it were, that modernism's frozen universals melt into social and historical time. Modernity breaks then in a rush of intensified diversity into its new phase, in both the late nineteenth and late twentieth centuries. This sense of the critical hesitation of history in Williams and in Doctorow's novel expresses an attitude of scepticism and expectancy, therefore, given neither to immutable universals nor to unrelieved contingency. It describes neither modernist nor postmodernist positions in their customary uses, so much as an estranged perspective upon both, the stereoscopic look in Doctorow's narrative through the rent in history which shows the past to the present, or seeks in Williams's words, 'a present beyond "the modern"'. It is the sense, we might say, of being between moderns. To see what this second modern might be both writers interestingly turn to the history of the first. I take this as a cue for the chapter which follows.

NOTES

1. Italo Calvino, *Invisible Cities* (New York: Harcourt Brace Jovanovich, 1978; London: Pan, 1979), p. 36.
2. 'The City's "New Immigrants"', *Dissent*, Fall 1987, reprinted as *In Search of New York* (New Jersey: Transaction Publishers, 1989), p. 99.
3. *New Statesman*, 25 January 1991: 19, 22.
4. Ibid.: 24.
5. Jean Baudrillard, *America* (London: Verso, 1988), p. 15.
6. *The New York Times*, 1 Sept. 1989, A1: 12.
7. W.E.B. Du Bois, *The Souls of Black Folk* (Chicago: A.C. McClurg & Co., 1903). Quoted *Black Voices. An Anthology of Afro–American Literature*, ed. Abraham Chapman (New York and Scarborough, Ontario: Mentor, 1968), p. 496.
8. See the essays in Malcolm Bradbury and James McFarlane (eds), *Modernism 1890–1930* (Harmondsworth: Penguin, 1976), especially Part One, 3. Also Edward Timms and David Kelley (eds), *Unreal City. Urban Experience in Modern European Literature and Art* (New York: St Martins Press; Manchester: Manchester University Press, 1985), and the discussion in David Harvey, *The Condition of Postmodernity* (Oxford: Basil Blackwell, 1989), especially pp. 25–7 and the chapters 'Modernity and Modernism' and 'Postmodernism in the City'.
9. 'The Painter of Modern Life' (1863), in *The Painter of Modern Life and Other Essays*, trans. and ed. Jonathan Mayne (London: Phaidon Press, 1964; published as a Da Capo Paperback, 1986), p. 13.
10. See Georg Simmel, 'The Metropolis and Mental Life'; also in particular Louis Wirth, 'Urbanism as a Way of Life' in Richard Sennett (ed.) *Classic Essays on the Culture of Cities* (New Jersey: Prentice-Hall, 1969), pp. 47–60 and pp. 143–64. We should note that Simmel's essay responded to contemporary urban life in Berlin and that those who followed his work in the United States, notably Robert Park and Louis Wirth, produced their findings in the context of the larger industrial city of Chicago.
11. See especially Wirth, pp. 152–8.
12. As Janet Wolff has pointed out, 'the solitary and independent life of the *flâneur* was not open to women' in the new city. At least not in the late nineteenth century. As Liz Heron shows in relation particularly to Dorothy Richardson and her novel *The Pilgrimage*, young women were able in the new century to claim the city as their own, even to claim parts of the city at night. The situation of the modern 'new woman' nevertheless remained an ambiguous combination of independence and oppression, signalled by the association, of which men were clearly exempt, between the role of the bohemian city stroller and the occupation of street walker – Janet Wolff, '"The Invisible *Flâneuse*", Women and the Literature of Modernity' in *The Polity Reader in Cultural Theory* (Cambridge: Polity Press, 1994), p. 208, and Liz Heron, *Streets of Desire* (London: Virago, 1993), pp. 1–9.

13. See my 'Introduction: Reconstructions' to *Modernism/Postmodernism* (Harlow: Longman, 1992), especially pp. 5–10.
14. Milan Kundera, *The Art of the Novel* (London: Faber, 1986), p. 141.
15. 'The Metropolis and The Emergence of Modernism' in Brooker (ed.) op. cit., pp. 83–93. Further page references are given in the text.
16. Gerd Hurm, *Fragmented Urban Images. The American City in Modern Fiction from Stephen Crane to Thomas Pynchon* (Bern, New York, Paris: Peter Lang, 1992), p. 54. See his discussion of the insights and failings of this 'grand urban theory' of the modern city, pp. 45–72.
17. Ibid., p. 56.
18. Werner Sollers, *Beyond Ethnicity. Consent and Descent in American Culture*, (New York and Oxford: Oxford University Press, 1986), p. 246.
19. Gerd Hurm, op. cit., Preface, pp. vii–viii. We might note that Jane Jacobs' celebrated attack on the forms and effects of postwar urban modernism in *The Death and Life of American Cities* accuses architects and planners of failing to respect and provide for the 'spontaneous *self-diversification* among city populations'. My italics, quoted Harvey, op. cit., p. 75.
20. Eliana Ortega and Nancy Saporta Sternbach, 'At The Threshold of the Unnamed: Latina Literary Discourse in the Eighties' in Asunción Horno-Delgado, Eliana Ortega, Nina M. Scott, Nancy Saporta Sternbach (eds), *Breaking Boundaries. Latina Writing and Critical Readings* (Amherst: The University of Massachusetts Press, 1989), p. 13.
21. Henry Giroux, 'Postmodernism as Border Pedagogy: Redefining the Boundaries of Race and Ethnicity' in Joseph Natoli and Linda Hutcheon (eds), *A Postmodern Reader* (New York: State University of New York Press, 1993), p. 461.
22. Philomena Mariani, 'God is a Man' in Philomena Mariani (ed.), *Critical Fictions. The Politics of Imaginative Writing* (Seattle: Bay Press, 1991), p. 12.
23. Giroux, op. cit., p. 459.
24. Mariani, op. cit.
25. Jacques Derrida, 'Spectres of Marx', *New Left Review*, 205 (May/June, 1994): 56.
26. Giroux, op. cit., p. 458.
27. Ibid., pp. 454, 456–7, and see p. 479.
28. Ibid., pp. 466, 480–1.
29. Wendy Wheeler, 'Nostalgia Isn't Nasty: The Postmodernising of Parliamentary Democracy' in Mark Perryman (ed.), *Altered States* (London: Lawrence and Wishart, 1994), p. 105. See other essays in this volume and also in the British context the contributions to Judith Squires (ed.), *Principled Positions. Postmodernism and the Rediscovery of Value* (London: Lawrence and Wishart, 1993).
30. This last is a description adopted by Robert Siegle in a wish to avoid the de-politicised uses of 'postmodernism', *Suburban Ambush. Downtown Writing and the Fiction of Insurgency* (Baltimore: Johns Hopkins University Press, 1989), pp. xvi, 395–401.
31. This formulation might suggest some indebtedness to Lyotard's description of the postmodern as 'undoubtedly a part of the modern', as modernism in its permanently 'nascent state'. I do indeed want

to suggest that the 'postmodern' functions to interrogate, critique and surpass an established and orthodox modernism and thus give rise to the new, but I do not follow Lyotard in his view of the modern project as entirely discredited and defunct (a judgement summed up, he says, by the name 'Auschwitz') nor, at all points, in the association of the postmodern with the sublime ('the unrepresentable in presentation itself') since this commits art and intellectual work too exclusively to an avant-garde project. See 'Answering the Question: What is Postmodernism?' and 'Note on the Meaning of "Post-"' in Docherty (ed.), *Postmodernism. A Reader* (London: Harvester, 1993), pp. 44, 46, 48. Nor do I intend to endorse the idea of the 'uncompleted modern project' associated with Habermas. My view is that the 'modern' is at an end: that is why it makes sense to think of a 'present beyond "the modern"', in Raymond Williams's phrase, or of a 'new modern'.

32. 'Interview with Ishmael Reed', by Liam Kennedy et al., *Over Here*, 9: 2 (Winter, 1989): 87.
33. Kevin Bezner, 'An Interview with Ishmael Reed', *Mississippi Review*, 20: 1 and 2 (1991): 115.
34. Ibid., p. 118.
35. Joe David Bellamy, *The New Fiction, Interviews with Innovative American Writers* (Urbana: University of Illinois Press, 1974), p. 133.
36. Bezner, op. cit., p. 118.
37. On this last point, Reed comments 'One trend I see now is that you are going to get other ethnic groups into the ball game. I'm interested in what the Asians out here in California are doing . . . . That engenders a hybrid that really fascinates and amazes me', in Bellamy, op. cit., p. 141.
38. E.L. Doctorow, *The Waterworks* (London: Macmillan, 1994), pp. 10, 11, and see p. 148. Further page references are given in the text. The novel uses frequent ellipses. Where this punctuation is not Doctorow's own it is written here as '[. . .]'.
39. This would seem to align Doctorow's work with a masculinist techno-rational tendency in modernism. Sartorius's theft of a baby from its mother and the dream of self-regeneration and reincarnation by men elsewhere in his fiction might suggest a double wish to usurp the mother and defy death. Marianne DeKoven sees the repressed feminine as characteristic of white, male high modernism – as existing in *Ulysses*, for example, in an 'impossible dialectic with the masculine mythmaking and father-searching' that has come in criticism almost exclusively to define Joyce's text, Marianne DeKoven, *Rich and Strange. Gender, History, Modernism* (Princeton: Princeton University Press, 1991), p. 195. Yet if Doctorow inherits this self-contradiction, his works do not seek the synthesis of myth or to mythologise the past (the father, tradition, etc.) in anything like the terms of the high modernists. On his treatment of the past, see Chapter 3 below.
40. See the discussion of rereading the decentred urban text in William Sharpe and Leonard Wallock, 'From "Great Town" to "Nonplace Urban Realm": Reading the Modern City' in Sharpe and Wallock (eds), *Visions of the Modern City* (New York: Proceedings of The Heyman Center for the Humanities, Columbia University, 1983), especially pp. 22–4.

41. This essay reads like a preface or autobiographical gloss on the novel, and shares many of its passages word for word. The death of Lincoln in 1865 is reported as a moment when 'the city is silent . . . unnaturally still, before some social resolve began to work itself out of his grave and rise again. And the city's new century began', *Poets and Presidents. Selected Essays, 1977–1992* (London: Macmillan, 1993), pp. 145, 147. The novel is set some half a dozen years after Lincoln's death, but provides an answer to the question the essay poses. 'Some regnant purpose was enshrouded in his death, but what was it?' Doctorow writes in 'The Nineteenth New York' (ibid., pp. 5, 6). The novel joins this and the above sentence ('some soulless, social resolve . . . and rise again') and McIlvaine goes on 'But I didn't anticipate . . . it would come through my young freelance' (*The Waterworks*, p. 5). The essay, it should be said too, expresses a stronger sense of continuity, perhaps of nostalgia, than the novel. Thus, on foggy nights in Manhattan, Doctorow writes, as the buildings disappear and 'modernity deconstructs' only 'the ghostly nineteenth' is left; 'still with us . . . the city that Melville saw' (p. 145). In the novel, McIlvaine feels rather that 'time estranges us', that the city becomes inexplicable over the years (p. 228).

42. David Harvey, op. cit., p. 21.

CHAPTER TWO

City of Modernity

They made New York a global city, the place to come from every
part of the world, the place to be.
                          E.L. Doctorow, 'The Nineteenth New York'

SIGNS OF DEMOCRACY: WHITMAN AND MELVILLE

Visiting the United States in 1796, Francis Baily wrote in fulsome
praise of the 'perfect regularity' and geometric order of the new
American cities of Philadelphia and Baltimore whose straight lines
happily expressed the straight dealing of the American character and
the destiny of the new nation.[1] The new American city was felt to
be an embodiment of scientific rationality, and a sign, therefore, in
one of its senses, of modernity.

How was it then that the social and literary critic Randolph Bourne
could complain in 1915 of the 'chaotic savagery' of 'our unplanned
cities', of passing from 'a vast incalculable metropolis' to 'the endless
chaos of straggling towns, which seemed not so much towns as
disgorged fragments of communities'?[2] Had modernity run aground
or somehow shown its true face at the very onset of modernism?
Evidently not, in philosophical terms at least, for Bourne appealed
much like Baily and other sons of the Enlightenment to the principles
of civic order and rationality. In the event, in the eighteenth as in
the twentieth century, it was a matter less of such ideas or ideals in
themselves than what they had been made to mean, what interests

they in practice served. Thomas Jefferson's own simple replicable design for the new cities of the new nation had been a case in point. Jefferson proposed a checkerboard model with alternate open spaces to prevent the spread of disease and to provide the pleasures of the country in the city. This was enthusiastically received, in principle at least, by Governors Harrison and Clairbourne of Indiana and Mississippi territories. In practice, where the plan was adopted, in Jeffersonville, Indiana, and Jackson, Mississippi, the open spaces intended for light, health and beauty proved too tempting a prospect to land speculators and business men. The idea of order, they discovered, was theirs to translate into the terms of practicality and profit, regardless of social good, civic health, aesthetic criteria or accidents of geography. The unqualified gridiron pattern of Philadelphia consequently served for a century as a model for the new Western towns, and in 1811 returned East to discover its apotheosis in the extended city grid approved for New York City, now the economic capital of the nation. The future pattern of the city was thus decided, as the commissioners made no attempt to hide, by the ruling criteria of cost, convenience, and plainness.[3]

Thus the growth of American cities between the 1790s and 1900s had been determined above all by commerce, to the point of an undisguised indifference to urban planning. The city grid suited the 'buying, selling and improving of real estate' in the bluff terms of the New York surveyor defending the city plan;[4] but then so did the disarray of pioneer settlements at the end of town where Bourne found 'attention to individualistic effort, to a competitive race'.[5] What had evidently emerged too, as Bourne's essay illustrates, was a tension between an aesthetic and civic sense of order and well-being and the requirements of economic convenience; between the idea of the town as 'a communal house', as Bourne put it, and the 'geographical expression of a business enterprise'.[6]

Such was the ambivalent, compound identity of the nation and its cities under capitalist democracy that both these ideas or initiatives could lay claim to the spirit of modernity. It was nevertheless 'business enterprise' that brought the most dramatic changes to the city, as the development of New York illustrates. Eighteenth-century New York had been no more than the commercial equal of Philadelphia and Boston. After the opening of the Erie Canal in 1825, however, it began to realise the potential of its waterways and central New England location to become by mid-century the major American city, the chief port of entry for European immigrants and for trade, offering unprecedented communication and access to the nation's interior. By 1890, as the population of Manhattan reached 1.4 million, New York was the largest metropolis in the world and the hub of American enterprise: a change that took it very rapidly from a predominantly mercantile to a predominantly industrial and administrative centre. Over the century as a whole and within the lifetime of some individuals, the form of the city changed from that of a 'walking city', which had been knowable on foot, to a city viewed from the omnibus, the horse-drawn street railway, the elevated railway (the harbinger of the 'El' transit system appeared in 1870) and, by the 1880s, the electric streetcar. Other signs of modernity accompanied these changes in transport and perspective. The first glass-fronted department store appeared in 1846, the Brooklyn Bridge was opened in 1883, the Statue of Liberty unveiled in 1886. And in 1898 the corporate limits of the city were extended by the addition of the four boroughs of Kings, Richmond, Queens and Brooklyn.

This expanded city area stimulated further modernisation and helped confirm already significantly altered social and labour relations. In mid-century New York the activities of work and leisure had taken place in close proximity: trades had clustered, noticeably in association with the counting houses, warehouses and shipping activities of the harbour; apprentices and clerks were often housed with masters, and residential separation by class or ethnicity was limited. The second half of the century saw the ending of the apprenticeship system for young artisans, the separation of master and workforce, of work-place and place of residence, and the growth of middle-class housing and of tenement buildings and slum areas. By 1880 half of the population was foreign-born and comprised the largest immigrant labour-force in the world. The overcrowded ghettos housing these new workers were just blocks away from the wealthiest mercantile and manufacturing firms the United States had ever seen, yet a world away from the riches of their owners (in 1892, 1,265 millionaires were reported to live in New York and Brooklyn).[7]

Thomas Bender suggests that the long-term effects of these changes, in forms of work, transport, architecture and social experience 'had become apparent by mid-century'; that the future of New York City could already be seen in the 1850s. 'To contemporaries', he says, 'the mid-nineteenth-century city most resembled chaos . . . a crowded jumble of small buildings' in which the already vast increases in population were restrained by building regulations and inadequate transport. From the 1850s the city became 'a multiplicity of environments that were not known' and could only be comprehended from some elevated observation point.[8] In this view the second half and last quarter of the century only compounded earlier developments.

There is good reason for thinking of the 1850s as a critical decade, but it would be a mistake to suggest that it predicted all that occurred later. New York in particular met the end of the century with a surge of development in which the dramatic leaps and bounds of new boroughs, buildings and bridges was soon to be joined by the most famous declaration of modernity: the transition from horizontal to upward vertical movement with all the aspiration and disparities this expressed. On this reckoning you hadn't seen the future until you had seen a skyscraper and the tenements of the Lower East Side. This was something like the New York Henry James saw in 1904, although he had less sense of the future than of present blight and the loss of the past. Others were moved by these developments to agitate for urban planning and for a new civic aesthetic which would belatedly introduce urbanity into increasing urban chaos. Such was the 'City Beautiful' movement associated first of all with the 'White City' built for the Chicago World's Fair of 1893, and with the writings and projects of C.M. Robinson, Daniel Burnham, the Frederick Law Olmsteads and others. Its *beaux-arts* heritage and civic sense was a lasting influence upon the idea of the modern in New York, and nationwide, and it is a fair guess that the ideas of the movement helped to form Bourne's views on urban chaos and the need for beneficent town planning in 1915.

Modernity in the city, we can conclude, evolved along a double axis, directed in part by ideas of the social good but overwhelmingly by commercial and business imperatives. Above all, this process produced a sense neither of simple continuity nor discontinuity but of continuous, accelerating change, giving rise to different perceptions of chaos and order and to different agendas for civic progress. And bound up with these ideas were conceptions of urban and national identity: what meanings, that is to say, a changing New York gave to being 'modern' and being 'American'. I want to return to some of the writings of the turn of the century and the 1910s and 1920s below with this in mind. First of all, however, I want to consider two earlier examples whose response to transformations in the city in the 1850s give us a sense both of that moment and of contrasting perceptual and cultural models available for the next century.

Walt Whitman, the first of these figures, worked, as befitted the new age of communications, as a printer, newspaper reporter and editor, notably for the *Brooklyn Daily Eagle* from an office overlooking the harbour. (In the year before the publication of *The Leaves of Grass* in 1855, for which he set the type, he had also worked as a building contractor, and speculated in real estate.) Whitman knew the city as a journalist and *flâneur* and reported on goods in the new Broadway shop windows with the same idle, loving fascination that he reported on its new people.[9] In the later 1850s he frequented Pfaff's bar in the bohemian quarter of Greenwich Village, and knew the proto-gay meeting places of taverns, city parks, public baths and swimming piers where others lounged and congregated. And of course he knew the harbour and the ferry. *Leaves of Grass* as a whole is in some senses a poem of the city, but it is 'Crossing Brooklyn Ferry' that is most often thought of as representing Whitman's New York, and I comment on this below.

We need first of all, however, to consider the more general association of Whitman and the American democratic ideal. Philip Fisher links Whitman's poetry with Jefferson's map of a model 640-acre farm and with Thoreau's experiment in solitary living at Walden Pond. All are examples, he says, of 'undifferentiated and democratic social space' produced by the replication without end of the same cellular unit. This uniformity of sameness (he might have added the gridiron city plan) Fisher associates with the logic of capitalism, which in the absence of common language, history, or customs became the driving force of American national unity. 'Mass production, exact replication and mass culture', Fisher concludes, 'made up a twentieth-century Jeffersonian ideal.'[10]

If Jefferson was the political philosopher of this mass democracy, Walt Whitman was its poet. 'I celebrate myself, and sing myself / And what I assume you shall assume', wrote Whitman in the opening to the 'Song of Myself', and later in the same poem: 'These are really the thoughts of all men in all ages and lands, they are not original with me, / If they are not yours as much as mine they are nothing, or next to nothing.'[11] In sentiments such as these Fisher finds a major precedent and prophecy of America's future bland democracy of unmarked difference; an arrangement in which Whitman's 'the word Democratic, the word En-Masse' came to prove synonymous, and American society put his aggregated 'single separate person' into mass production.[12]

In its more fully realised twentieth-century form the levelling equality of Whitman's 'democratic social space' has come to reside, Fisher believes, in the common possession of the material goods of consumer culture and common access to its nationwide information and entertainment networks: from Singer sewing machines and

Model T Fords, to Mack trucks, Levis, Coca-Cola; the same foods, the same films and TV programmes available at the same time of the same day, week by week and coast to coast. This scale of common possessions and media access has produced America's transparent 'democratic average', a national unity made up of reproducible units shaved of all marks of difference. This subtraction of differences, says Fisher, comprises an aesthetics which 'restates the central matter of American education: the subtraction of culture rather than its inculcation. Faced with the dozens of immigrant languages and culture, the first and perhaps only victory of American education has been to bleach out those differences in the act of producing 'typical' American children.'[13] We have come to recognise the bland uniformity of goods and services (and even people) Fisher describes as a mark of postmodern culture, and can hear something like it in Jean Baudrillard's view of America as a terminal utopia. What is extraordinary about Fisher's argument, however, is not so much that he should evoke this culture, nor that he should link American capitalism with Whitman and Jefferson, though this would surprise much received opinion, but that he should propose the triple identification of these founding fathers with mass society and with democracy.

As Whitman's lines above suggest, and as we shall see again below, it is all a matter of assumptions. Fisher assumes and endorses a conception of democracy as sameness, one which rests on the common denominator of possessions and access to the products of the dominant culture, but has nothing at all to do with equality of provision or access to society's decision-making processes. What I want chiefly to question in Fisher's argument, however, is the assumption of an 'undamaged' democratic social place and a contrasting 'damaged sphere' of actuality. In his account, the first is expressed by the model examples of Jefferson, Thoreau and Whitman, and is subsequently writ large in twentieth-century consumer and media culture. The prime example of the second, he says, is slavery, since this radically contradicts the idea of a uniform democratic social space. In fact, says Fisher, 'If any part of the society is a slave society, it must be so as a whole because the only form in which the Northern democratic identity would exist . . . would be one in which that identity were universal.'[14] But quite clearly this can only imply that 'damaged' space is internal to the original system and that there is consequently no undamaged pure expression of democracy. Or, to put it another way, Fisher unwittingly reveals how the idea of democracy in the United States is always already damaged.

In fact, this was the case as much with Jefferson's farm as with his idea of the nation. Though opposed to slavery, Jefferson was himself a slave-holder. Freed slaves he proposed, moreover, must be removed from society on the grounds of the likely animosities and divisions that would continue between themselves and their ex-masters. His ideal was a homogeneous, conflict-free republic. Yet this unity of identity could only be maintained by expelling the inner difference which contradicted it. It is this inner difference then, not something that comes after and outside it, that comprises the act of 'damage' to this idea of democracy.[15]

The same argument might be made in relation to Whitman. Though his poetry seems to work in the opposite direction, to embrace without discrimination rather than to expel, there can be no separation from his adhesive approach, no way within the terms of his social aesthetic of expressing difference or dissent. 'What is then between us?' he asks:[16] a question which allows only the answer 'nothing', since Whitman assumes a free transparent passage for his rhetorical love to ferry across from him to you. Where Jefferson excludes the challenge of the other to create a boxed-in unity, Whitman embraces allcomers in a burgeoning oneness, smothering difference in an essence of sameness.[17] In 'Crossing Brooklyn Ferry' he universalises this identity to its fullest extent, projecting this moment into an eternal future, out of contemporary history into a oneness that spans the ages. The 'democratic social space' Fisher identifies, in fact requires just such a strategy, for, as he writes, 'The more history the more broken the space.'[18] Yet Whitman's verse, for all its transcendent ambitions, was in the simplest sense historical: the Brooklyn ferry ceased to run, the Brooklyn Bridge was built, and the city, as described above, changed in its population, its forms of housing, transportation, work, commerce, and social and economic relations. Even Whitman's vocabulary of the 'great tides of humanity', the river, streams and currents of people and sympathies (though a familiar enough rhetoric) is a symptom of this temporality, nourished by the contemporary activity of the harbour. What he in fact sees, as in the poem 'Mannahatta' is not an eternal America but the 1850s; a harbourscape of masts, steamers, lighters, ferry-boats; 'the jobbers' houses of business, the / houses of business of the ship-merchants and money brokers, the river streets'; immigrants arriving, the carts, the drivers, the sailors: all in a 'City of hurried and sparkling waters! city of spires and / masts! City nested in bays! my city!'[19] Whitman's vision of the Republic, that is to say, was founded upon this location at this time, with its contemporary pace and movement, its new arrivals

33

and its predominantly artisanal labour: all of which were not simply multiplied 'en masse' but radically altered by events.[20] An important word here is 'vision'. The key verbs of the most quoted Section 3 of 'Crossing Brooklyn Ferry' are 'watched', 'saw' and 'look'd', and suggest a reporting observer – a figure who in marking difference, dangerously poised 'both in and out of the game and watching and wondering at it'[21] – troubles the unities required of 'democratic social space'. Whitman, the reporter, 'enumerates' places and people in random lists of items and individuals as if they are caught in a moment of discrete, unmolested integrity, as most noticeably in Section 15 of 'Song of Myself':

> The pure contralto sings in the organ loft,
> The carpenter dresses his plank, the tongue of his foreplane
> whistles its wild ascending lisp,
> The married and unmarried children ride home to their
> Thanksgiving dinner
> The pilot seizes the king-pin, he heaves down with a strong
> arm . . . .[22]

Whitman's method here appears to anticipate the imagists' 'direct treatment of the thing' or metonymic eye upon the world, but in the event does not. For in the end everything is absorbed 'all to myself, and for this song'.[23] Whitman's subjects are amassed in the cosmic net of his ego, his lists like snapshots of Manhattan assembled in a mighty photograph album with headlining caption and wrap-around voice-over. So, after some sixty lines, this section ends:

> And these tend inward to me, and I tend outward to them,
> And as such it is to be of these more or less I am,
> And of these one and all I weave the song of myself.[24]

There is a second aspect to Whitman's way of seeing, however. He spoke at one time of preferring to see the Hudson River from the vantage point of the pilot's house so as to take in the 'full sweep' of things.[25] In this manner too he surveys people and time, afoot with his vision, scanning the future from on high; from a ship's bridge, or we might just as easily imagine, from a Manhattan masthead or skyscraper (a term derived of course from the tallest masts of the New York clippers). In one of the first responses to the new tall architecture, Alfred Stieglitz saw the Flat Iron Building in 1903 as 'a monster ocean steamer – a picture of a new America still in the making'.[26] Whitman might well have applauded this view, though one suspects he would have preferred an alternating perspective, one which placed him as much at the prow of the building as at

Stieglitz's elbow. There is a further point of comparison, however. Stieglitz's photograph of the Flat Iron Building was an early example of the way photographers came to emphasise the height of skyscrapers, leading the eye upward.[27] The characteristic lists of Whitman's verse follow a similar movement; less, finally, like a set of Kodak prints than the upward movement of the camera eye or of an elevator. (First introduced in 1871 and an indispensable feature of the skyscraper, the elevator had the effect of equalising the rentable value of its upper floors — in perfect accordance with Fisher's idea of democracy.) Whitman's lists climb, as we have seen, to an all-embracing penthouse view, and it is this lofty, wide-angled vision which makes him in the end less a reporter or observer, whether inside or outside the game, than a (self-proclaiming) prophet and seer. In this respect, he versifies the perceptual shift associated with the breathtaking, celestial reach of the next century's skyscrapers. But this association then dubs him more poet of the commercial interests, corporations and assurance agencies, in whose name (Equitable Life, Western Union, Metropolitan Life, Radiator, Woolworth) these buildings were erected than poet of the common people, the mass who dwelt somewhere below.[28]

We therefore see in Whitman the germ of a naïve democratic formula (endorsed by Fisher), which assumes a simple arithmetic multiplication of one into '*en masse*'; which assumes the convertibility of 'America' and 'democracy'; and which aesthetically aspires to the totalising abstraction of a godlike proto-modernism which eternalised the contemporary fragment. The risk in looking off yonder for the future is that you will miss the present, or confuse the two. Whitman did of course look closely, and he looked downwards, but what he often saw, as off the side of the Brooklyn ferry was a haloed reflection of himself ('Look'd at the fine centrifugal spokes of light round the / shape of my head in the sunlit water').[29] At best 'Crossing Brooklyn Ferry' assumes that the transparent republicanism of water will reflect this crowned poet of liberty back to everyman and everywoman. What clearer image can there be of the narcissism and self-aggrandisement informing this idea of the nation? (For all its uncritical idealism the Statue of Liberty looks out to the Old World and offers to take in and enlighten the way of the lowly, not to show them back to themselves in its own classical garb.) If he looked into the watery mirror of the populace and environs ('Flood-tide below me! I see you face to face!'), Whitman did not look down into the murk of history to see the 'damage' done to 'democratic space' by the conflicting interests of commerce and the social good, nor, if he did see it, did he find reasons to deplore the resulting disparities between wealth and poverty, or the spacious living and extremes of overcrowding that accompanied the economic exploitation of new ethnic groups. (Another mid-century visitor, Charles Dickens, it might be said, saw the human effects of industrial capitalism plainly enough in the Five Points slum area, just east of the spectacle of Broadway, where 45,000 people were crammed into a quarter of a square mile.)[30]

Returning to New York in 1904 after twenty years in Europe, Henry James felt in the midst of his openly preoccupied bafflement the sense above all of impermanence and the loss of a personal past, rather than anything like Whitman's sentiments of loving oneness. Where Whitman eternalised the fragment, James saw a lack of taste, cultural tradition and authority, and a national identity unsettled by nothing but fragments of the new. His own undoubted social and historical sense showed him clearly enough, however, how commerce had dictated the growth of the city, how everything 'lately and currently *done*' in New York was done 'on the basis of inordinate gain' and how skyscrapers, 'impudently new and still more impudently "novel"', were, above all, the 'triumphant payers of dividends'.[31] But for James this scale and rate of things was bigger and went faster than words could describe its effects and his impressions. He reports how he cannot 'make a legible word' of the looming mass of facts confronting him, 'The *il*legible word, accordingly . . . hangs in the vast American sky, to his imagination, as something fantastic and *abracadabrant*, belonging to no known language.'[32] New York was beyond comprehension, even beyond literature (he has in mind Zola but also the impossibility of any poetic or dramatic representation of the city) since it 'was not going . . . to produce both the maximum of "business" spectacle and the maximum of ironic reflection of it'.[33]

If Whitman, refusing nothing, lacked one thing it was 'ironic reflection', and this we might see as the literary mode of an alternative view of the city than his own. We find it, perhaps even approaching its maximum, in Herman Melville.[34] Philip Fisher sees the riddling ambiguities of Melville's story 'Benito Cereno' as expressing the condition of American society in the aftermath of slavery. My point above is that this 'damage' necessarily intrudes upon the 'undamaged' purity of any original 'democratic social space', and in fact Melville's story confirms precisely this, since it works above all to expose the complacent innocence of the Yankee Captain Delano, a figure blinded to the reversals of a slave rebellion by the limits of a Republicanism which allows him to 'assume' everything but that such a thing can happen.

The full riddle of a modern New York existence, however, Melville presents in the story 'Bartleby'. The figure of Bartleby is in every important respect Whitman's opposite. Where Whitman's appetites are boundless ('Turbulent, fleshy, sensual, eating, drinking and breeding'),[35] Bartleby falls first to the task of copying 'as if long famishing', seeming 'to gorge himself on my documents' with 'no pause for digestion', only then to abstain.[36] Bartleby literally eats no more than ginger biscuits and some cheese; he 'prefers not' to take a lunch with the other clerks, nor to examine papers, to copy, to run errands, to walk abroad, to talk or to leave the narrator-lawyer's employ, nor even to quit his office. Where Whitman is all-embracing, Bartleby is without family or apparent social connection; where Whitman envisions the future, Bartleby stares in his 'dead-wall reveries'[37] at the wall three feet from his desk, itself secluded by a blind. Where Whitman spans continents, Bartleby prefers to be stationary.[38]

Could Whitman's 'Song' absorb such a figure: 'farmer, mechanic, artist, gentleman, sailor, quaker, / Prisoner, fancy-man, rowdy, lawyer . . . *scrivener*'?[39] Could Whitman's aesthetic embrace Melville, so full of discriminations and allegorical possibilities? For it is these, after all, which circulate in readings of the story. Is Bartleby the figure of the unpopular writer pressured to conform to custom and what is reasonable? As a 'copyist' does he lay bare the logic of Wall Street which imprisons all who enter? Does he represent the death-in-life of business; does he defy and refuse this world, a saint in its midst, and so go to his death? Is he the human become a fixture, a piece of office furniture, himself a brick wall to all enquiries and entreaties? Is the world of Wall Street one of blank mechanicals, worthy of notice only in so far as they function efficiently (like the other office clerks, Turkey and Nippers, in spite of all eccentricities) or cease to function?

The tale invites and confounds these interpretations; representing, to borrow James's image, the '*il*legible' written in the sky above New York. We can of course propose, on this very basis, that the story is 'about' unintelligibility, since the 'illegible' is what it writes, and say that it is 'about' the interpretative strategies employed by the lawyer-narrator to read intelligibility into the signs of the clerkly copyist's life. Bartleby at least that way remains an enigma, crucially in the present context, because his narrator-reader cannot *assume* that what he himself assumes – that a copyist will copy, that he will work for pay, leave when dismissed, and so on – are things that Bartleby also assumes. This radical difference between persons confounds Whitman's project and asks something more of a modern democracy and city life than 'the thoughtful merge' of simple separate persons into the word '*en masse*'.

Both Whitman and Melville offered perspectives and positions to the future. In so far as Whitman turns out to versify a basic common identity of consumption and property his 'sign of democracy' leads to the oldest cliché of all on twentieth-century American sameness: a low average decreed by the dominant culture. 'It avails not, time nor place – distance avails not', he assures us,[40] and true to his word he extrapolates (and is extrapolated upon) way beyond the historical moment which inspired his optimism. Melville's self-conscious, enigmatic narrative layerings perhaps seem more historically remote and introspective. Yet he has proved the more pertinent example for critics and thinkers of the late twentieth century who detect in Melville the irony and doubleness, the many-sidedness of identity and interpretation necessary to comprehend and contest an opaque and unequal, multiformed and homogenising world. Henry Louis Gates, for example, finds inspiration for a present multiculturalism in Melville's *Redburn*; Aldon Lynn Nielson speaks of the relevance of Melville's dramatic irony in *White Jacket* and 'Beneto Cereno' for a strategy of 'appropriation and alteration', of 'undoing within the reader, the knots of racist imagery produced by white discourse'; Irving Howe finds 'visions of anarchic bliss' and 'American fraternity' in Melville's early writings, and Ishmael Reed finds an early postmodernism in *Moby Dick*'s combination of fiction and non-fiction.[41]

These various attributions imply a literary and social model which combines as it respects modes and idioms, persons and races in a new cosmopolitanism and an alternative idea of democracy. However, we do not have to wait for the late twentieth century to rediscover this vein of thinking. Randolph Bourne spoke of a poetry of the city which would celebrate its industry and energy, its 'liberating forces of democratic camaraderie', beyond Whitman's moment of 'individualistic capitalism'.[42] The parochial nationalism and prejudice of the First World War provoked Bourne to think of an ideal America which would be a more complicated thing than Whitman's almighty oneness. It is time, he says, to ask 'what Americanism may rightly mean', time to look beyond the idea of 'the melting pot' at 'a new cosmopolitan ideal . . . a cosmopolitan federation of national colonies, of foreign cultures'; a new beginning for 'the great American democratic experiment'.[43] This transnational federation, what is more, attracted an appropriate mode to itself: the mode of irony. For irony, Bourne argued, was the mode of a democratic sensibility: 'the man with the ironical temperament is forced constantly to compare and contrast his experience with what was, or what might be, or with what ought to be . . . . That democratic, sympathetic outlook upon the feelings and thoughts and actions of men and women is the life of irony.'[44]

Melville's fiction and Bourne's arguments offer an alternative at once to Whitman's 'attested sympathy', to Henry James's lack of confidence and to Fisher's identical units of a production-line America. In this ironical, democratic frame of mind two things, the fragment and the whole, the self and the other, the singular and the plural, this time and place and social order and another, beyond its ken and better than itself could be held in dialogue: neither merged nor identical, but composed in a relation that made a new third thing possible.

MODERNISM, MONTAGE, MARXISM: FROM EZRA POUND TO JOHN DOS PASSOS

In 1910 Ezra Pound returned to America, visiting New York for the first time since his departure in 1907, and for the last time for twenty-eight years. In early 1912, back in London, he met Henry James. Pound knew James's *The American Scene* and the two writers discussed America. 'It is strange', said James, 'how all taint of art and letters seems to shun that continent';[45] a verdict Pound recalled in his essay 'The Renaissance' in 1914 and his long memorial essay on James in 1918. Pound was deciding on the colours in the 'Renaissance palette', a project that had the United States as its immediate object, and had settled accounts with Walt Whitman in the earlier 1909 essay referred to above. His visit to New York confirmed his view that Whitman was the thing itself, *echt* American. 'I see him America's poet . . . . He *is* America', he had written, and then in the record of his thoughts in 1910 collected as *Patria Mia*: Whitman is '"The Reflex" . . . our American keynote'.[46] Go where he would, the exiled American would stay American, Pound said, and would need the reassurance of the 'national *timbre*', the 'tonic' he found in Whitman.[47] 'The vital part of my message', he confirmed, 'is the same as his.'[48] But if this was the case, it was clearly a difficult message to swallow, for Whitman's 'crudity' made him 'an exceeding great stench'; he was 'an exceedingly nauseating pill'.[49] Even if he held his nose, Pound found Whitman difficult to take. (Pound 'can't take the democratic virus', commented William Carlos Williams.)[50] More to Pound's liking was 'the outstanding personality' (for the lack of whom 'Democracies have fallen').[51] In fact, Pound's message was closer to Henry James's who was to Pound's eyes in 1914, 'the greatest living American', an unflinching opponent of tyranny and 'the domination of modern life' who gave his labours to 'making America intelligible' (a 'labour of translation', as Pound interestingly put it).[52] Pound saw himself (like Whistler, like James and like Eliot) as an American abroad: one of those 'Who bear the brunt of our America / And try to wrench her impulse into art'.[53] America, that is to say, was 'impulse' and Europe was 'art' and civilisation, and like James, Pound strove 'to bring in America on the side of civilisation'.[54]

Pound's assumption, of course, was that the United States had no culture, and no capital (he was drawn to London, he said, because it was 'the capital of the US, so far as art and letters were concerned').[55] This is the force of Pound's comments on Whitman, as being 'so near the national colour that the nation hardly perceived him against that background'.[56] He was 'not an artist, but a reflex . . . for you cannot call a man an artist until he shows himself capable of reticence and restraint . . . in some degree master of the forces that beat upon him'.[57] For a 'renaissance' to succeed in America, for it to acquire art and be modern, it had need of models, the standards of a valued and revalued tradition, and it needed to support those artist-ambassadors who laboured as a curious back-to-front avant-garde at the door of established culture to make the new, the raw America intelligible. New York architecture, Pound thought, showed the first signs of this 'Renaissance' (or 'Risvegliamento' or 'Risorgimento') in the Pennsylvania Railroad Station and the Metropolitan Life Building. Typically, his terms and models are European: New York buildings are 'Egyptian', its crowd 'pagan', the Pennsylvania Station was like a copy of 'the baths of Diocletian', New York's urban night he compares with Venice and London.[58]

Much of Pound's thinking, and more than he intended, appears in the poem 'N.Y.'(1912):

N.Y,

My City, my beloved, my white! Ah, slender,
Listen! Listen to me, and I will breathe into thee a soul,
Delicately upon the reed, attend me!

Now do I know that I am mad,
For here are a million people surly with traffic;
This is no maid.
Neither could I play upon any reed if I had one.

My City, my beloved,
Thou art a maid with no breasts,
Thou art slender as a silver reed.
Listen to me, attend me!
And I will breathe into thee a soul,
And thou shalt live for ever.[59]

New York here is evidently the skyscraper who is a woman (a maid) in need of the fullness and soul of inspiration (Pound talked elsewhere more directly of the artist 'penetrating' the vortex of London). But just as interesting as these masculinist pretensions is Pound's momentary, italicised, unease about his assumed role and antique rhetoric in the crowded metropolis. Though he gathers the confidence to repeat his address to the city, his language neither approaches the American idiom his friend and contemporary William Carlos Williams was striving to develop (the volume *Ripostes* containing this poem was dedicated to Williams), nor does it have the directness and prose virtues he found in his English mentor of the time, Ford Madox (Hueffer) Ford.[60] On Pound's visit to Williams in Rutherford in 1910, Williams's father had berated him on the ornate superfluities of his style,[61] and Ford had famously rolled over with laughter at Pound's poor attempt at 'good English' in the volume *Canzone* (1911). Pound's self-consciousness in 'N.Y.' is a mark of his cultural displacement, of his being 'out of date' as he half admitted in *Hugh Selwyn Mauberley*, writing here at a point where his language is neither contemporary American nor English, but in some transatlantic passage from the old to the new. The poem is a sign, that is to say, as linguistic instability was in other writers, of his coming modernism.

The first real move in the direction of the 'exact rendering of things', of the simplicity and directness of utterance Pound talked of as necessary to this modern poetry, was the volume *Des Imagistes* (1914); and this again, in the double life of its publication in Chicago and Frenchified title, its English and American contributors, typically bridges two worlds. This was Pound's first real instalment in these years on an American 'renaissance', on his version of a Jamesean communication between cultures and on his understanding of a cosmopolitan modernism.

Pound's ideas of New York as 'pagan' and undeveloped, of Whitman its poet as the raw pigment barely distinguishable from the national, background, find an echo in the reaction to the city of another kind of 'imagist', the Russian poet Sergej Esenin. Esenin was a member of the 'Imaginist' group (a name derived from Marinetti's idea of a poem as an uninterrupted series of images), and in 1922 he sailed to New York in the company of Isadora Duncan. The immense size of the ocean liner itself convinced him that imaginism was exhausted, for here was 'an image with no likeness . . . the important thing', he decided, 'was not comparisons but the organic thing itself'. His first sight of New York only confirmed this self-sufficiency of the 'thing itself' and the poverty of art. Mayakovsky's poems about America (composed before Mayakovsky visited the United States) Esenin knew now to be inadequate, for 'How could you possibly express this iron and granite might in words? It is a poem without words.'[62]

Esenin's enthusiasm puts one in mind of Whitman's paean to the United States as 'themselves . . . the greatest poem'.[63] For both writers there was a sense, which Pound felt in reading Whitman, that America speaks for itself, without words, without art. For Pound this response to the modern world could only be a step backwards. If he and Esenin were both 'estranged' by the visual experience of the city, the context of their displacement and their reflections on it were quite different. Esenin was a rural poet (at one stage he appeared in stylised peasant garb) seeking a viable role at a moment of proletarian revolution and technological upheaval. The aesthetic models available to writers in this 'Risorgimento' were either naturalism or futurism. Mayakovsky was the principal literary example of the second, and I shall return to his account of New York below. The first mode, with its full assumptions of unmediated truth-telling, had been employed by Gorky in his visit to the United States in 1906. The result – which has its own context in contemporary attitudes towards the United States on the part of the Central Committee of the Bolshevik Party who sponsored his visit – is an example of genre writing, recalling Engels on Manchester, Dickens on Coketown and a generation of European naturalist writers of the 1880s and 1890s. The New York of Gorky's 'City of the Yellow Devil' is a murky, leaden chaos, a monster of iron and stone whose roaring and wailing silence its inhabitants, hypnotising them into the submission of hard labour and uncomplaining misery. It is the city, in short, of a rapacious and oppressive capitalism. Through it all runs the force of 'the yellow devil', the cruel drive to make money, which Gorky imagines as a spinning lump of gold located at the heart of the city.[64]

Esenin was therefore responding as much to Gorky, and to

Mayakovsky, as he was to New York City itself. If Mayakovsky's imaginings fell well below the reality, then Gorky's picture of monstrous greed simplified its mystery and grandeur. Esenin writes: 'Buildings block out the horizon and almost push against the sky. Over all this extend the most enormous arches of reinforced concrete. The sky is leaden from fusing factory smokestakes. The smoke evokes a feeling of mystery; beyond these buildings something so great and enormous is taking place it takes your breath away.'[65] Where Gorky's New York is 'leaden' and 'lifeless', Esenin's is 'leaden' and 'breathtaking'. At the same time both writers shared a basic affinity. Both visited New York, that is to say, as strangers (Esenin at least speaking no English), to some degree as celebrities, but in one sense much like thousands of immigrants seeing the city for the first time. As a consequence they both expressed a sense of the city as sublime: a sentiment they shared with Henry James (who returned like a highly-tuned Rip Van Winkle to the astonishments of his radically transformed native city) and, to some degree, with the self-exiled Ezra Pound.

We have become used, through the writings of J.F. Lyotard, to an association of the 'sublime' with the experience of postmodernity. To think of it in relation to this earlier modern moment may therefore give us some sense of the differences and continuities between these phases or movements. One of the features that made New York *the* city of modernity, as suggested earlier, was the unprecedented pace of change, the sheer rate of growth in its population and buildings, its expanding communications networks, its modes and systems of transport. The period from the late 1890s, and the addition of the Boroughs to the city's corporate identity through to the Second World War, was the 'golden age' of these developments, converting New York from the nation's major mercantile port to the emphatic centre of American industry and finance. The city's population climbed from 1.5 million to 7.5 million in fifty years; in the mid 1910s it was already over five million, one-sixth of whom resided in one eighty-second of the city land area in the Lower East Side. Mechanical and electrical power brought the full system of electric streetcars, the elevated and subterranean transit systems into operation (by 1937 the mass transit system covered 700 track miles). The Pennsylvania Station that impressed Pound was followed by the greater marvel of Grand Central Station, which in turn gathered a score of new office buildings and hotels to itself. This circulatory and intercity system helped make New York a networked colossus of monopoly capitalism. Wall Street became the home of investment banking, and by the 1920s New York was also the national centre of publishing, radio, and TV networks, of theatre, sport and fashion. In addition, from the mid 1920s Robert Moses was to embark on the decades-long building programme which brought the system of parkways, expressways, bridges and stadia by which contemporary New York is still known. The age of skyscrapers to which James draws such attention had barely begun in 1904. To those that he and Gorky in 1906 would have seen (the Flatiron, Equitable, Western Union, Radiator buildings) had been added the Metropolitan Life by the time of Pound's visit, the sixty-storey Woolworth (1913) by the time of Esenin's, and only after the 1920s the Chrysler (1930), and Empire State Buildings (1931) – the last three all for a time the world's tallest building.

The resulting sense of the city as perpetually unformed or in process of formation or re-formation made it possible to view it repeatedly as if for the first time. Pound's sense of Whitman as a document or reflex of the 1860s–1880s follows from this sense, as he put it, that 'The country is a different place each decade.'[66] Modernity did not mean that history disappeared so much as accelerated. The experience of the city's newness, so familiar that it became a truism, was consequently one of speed and mass, of growing size and mounting energy, the sight of new materials and the use of new technologies. Modernising New York was always extreme, and as such presented a reality (invariably very palpable and sensuous to its visitors and inhabitants) which was felt to be beyond or before language or comparison; to be inexpressible or 'illegible' in James's word once more. And since its extremes could not be comprehended in one scope or aspect, this inexpressible might be apprehended as a moment or object of horror (as Gorky and others have chosen to see it from the perspectives of naturalism or socialist realism) or of mystery and beauty (as described by Esenin, and Pound too, who thought New York at night almost 'the most beautiful city in the world').[67]

What in another way these examples reveal is a new self-consciousness about the means of representation available for this new sublimely 'unrepresentable' physical and social reality. The appearance of the investigative reporter, new communications technologies and organs of printed and visual record, from the mass newspaper to the still and movie camera, gave naturalist or documentary realist modes new authority in the period. Often too this was employed in reporting the city (in the work of Jack London, Stephen Crane, Upton Sinclair, Theodore Dreiser) and events of dramatic social and political import (as in the case of John Reed). Though these forms might claim a 'scientific' or transparent access to the real they were as much a sign of new subject matter and of attempts to render it in new ways as the more conspicuous means of selection, abstraction and formal transformation employed in the 'modernist' arts. The new journalistic realism of the turn of the century looked more to the disclosure of new social content than to matters of form. As always, however, its wonted authenticity depended upon particular methods of analysis, kinds of judgement and narrative mode. The 'truth' of realism, in short, is always motivated. Yet it cannot display this truth about itself, cannot adopt a self-consciousness which reveals the making as well as the unseen content of a new reality, without becoming a new form.

The appearance of these new forms of representation of modernity, and at points the conscious sense of a crisis of representation, stemmed in particular from the loss of an authoritative position from which to view or speak of the whole (for which in a literal sense one had to gain height, as Benton suggests above, even in mid-nineteenth-century New York). This is a question, as with Whitman, and Melville's 'Bartleby', of what can and cannot be assumed in an increasingly mass society. Pound spoke of this condition in his own terms in his complaint that the United States had no capital or cultural 'centre'.[68] And James's feeling of being 'haunted' after a visit to Ellis Island by a sense of dispossession, conscious that 'aliens' impinged upon an assumed '*whole* national consciousness' was a further symptom of this same decentring experience.[69]

We think of this sense of lack and of loss, and the accompanying search for stability in art, belief, and culture, as characteristically modernist. We should remember, however, that this response to fundamental change (for that is what it was) could take quite different forms. Randolph Bourne's belief that 'Americanness' might be re-composed along 'transnational' lines, for example, runs in the opposite direction to James's haunted shudder at the proximity of 'alienness'. And Mabel Dodge's conviction that in New York individuals were in revolt, 'because consciousness is expanding and is bursting through the molds that have held it up to now', is like a brash forward march to T.S. Eliot's plagued quest in Paris and London for deep, spiritual coherence.[70]

Examples such as these not only tell us that 'modernism' could take closed and open, conservative and progressive forms but that the affirmative response to decentred subjective and national identities associated with postmodernism also had its precedent in the earlier period. Also, if we are to get a fuller view of the different modernist interpretations of modernity, we cannot simply accept that America was without a capital (clearly in terms of economic power this was New York) or that New York was without a cultural centre fit for a 'Risorgimento'. Mabel Dodge's salon in Greenwich Village, Alfred Stieglitz's gatherings at 291 Fifth Avenue were very precisely meeting *places*, overlapping centres of assumption and difference, where, as Douglas Tallack puts it, 'intellectual collisions could occur in the midst of a city'.[71] Pound reckoned he was always on the look out for an American Renaissance, but he missed the 'renaissance' that was ready to break at the moment of his closest interest in it. His complaint about a lack of culture cites, for example, the stuffiness of magazines such as *The Atlantic* and *The Century*. But the 1910s was the decade of magazines of radical political, cultural and artistic opinion, often again associated with Greenwich Village and with what has been called the 'Lyrical Left'.[72] Those who met at Mabel Dodge's or Stieglitz's or joined Walter Arensberg's circle at 33 West 67 Street read and contributed to *The New Republic, The Seven Arts, Others, Camera Work, 291* and, above all perhaps, the *Masses*. The *Masses* (1911–18) was edited by Max Eastman and Floyd Dell, and included contributions on the new art, suffragism, birth control, free love, anarchism and bolshevism by John Reed, Emma Goldman, John Sloan, Art Young, Stuart Davis and Mike Gold, amongst others. It declared itself 'A Revolutionary and Not a Reform Magazine', was passionate in its support of the new Soviet Union and closely allied in the United States to the anarcho-syndicalism of the IWW (the International Workers of the World, or 'Wobblies', formed in 1912), whose leader 'Big Bill' Haywood was a frequent visitor to Mabel Dodge's gatherings.

It is plain then that there were venues in the city and an excited, evolving vocabulary of radical political, cultural and aesthetic forms to articulate just the decentred experience modernity presented; a language to express the inexpressibly faceted, fast-moving, dynamic modern world of opposite extremes. In art the names for this way of talking, writing and seeing were vorticism, simultaneism, precisionism, surrealism, dada, futurism and cubism. Francis Picabia, entering New York a year after Pound's departure (they were to meet in Paris in the early 1920s), employed this new vocabulary directly. New York, he said, was a cubist city.[73] Again America presented the thing itself; and New York was in its very being and presence an artist's city, or itself the work of art, awaiting no more in the way of representation than a naming of what it was. In short, New York was a 'found object' in keeping with the second sensation of the decade: Marcel Duchamp's signed urinal, titled 'Fountain', submitted to the Independents Exhibition in 1917. The first sensation had been the Armory Show where Picabia and Duchamp contributed to the 1,600 works exhibited in 1913. The show presented the work of Redon, Matisse, Picasso and many others to an American public. Here was a European avant-garde coming to New York rather than running ahead of and behind it in the manner of the school of Pound and Eliot. Duchamp showed 'Nude descending a staircase' at the Armory, and virtually inaugurated New York Dada. Virtually, because American painters, like American architects had already visited Paris or knew of the new movements. John Marin and Joseph Stella, for example, amongst others, exhibited works at the Armory Show depicting aspects of the city (its skyscrapers, the Brooklyn Bridge, the Port, Coney Island) in cubist, cubo-realist, or futurist terms, using geometric shapes, dynamic, diagonal lines and a rush of shape and colour. It was as if the abstract grid of the city had been turned vertically and then turned again; spun to produce 'a web of coloured geometric shapes' in Max Weber's description of his 'New York at Night' (1915), or viewed as in Stella's series 'New York Interpreted' in all the sublimity of its simultaneous menace and spirituality.[74]

Throughout this activity in New York radical cultural and political life in the prewar years we see an attempt to grasp and shape the altered conditions of modernity. At one point, in 1912, when Eugene Debs polled almost one million votes as the socialist presidential candidate it seemed indeed that cubism and socialism might come jointly to represent the new society. Beyond this temporary synchronicity the commingling of ideas and the openness to both artistic and social experiment inspired an early form of cultural politics and a cosmopolitan ideal (which, arguably, has continuing value for the Left in America and in Europe). Certainly, the exchange of ideas and the extent of travel not only between avant-garde Europe and the United States but New York and Bolshevik Russia was by any later perspective extraordinary (Max Eastman, Emma Goldman, John Reed, Isadora Duncan, Paul Robeson, Langston Hughes were only the most notable guests of the new Russia).

If we can identify a main concern in this new thinking it was with the relation of art and the new technology of mass production, and thus of the individual and the new mass society. I want here to look briefly at two 'modernist' responses to these aspects of modernity: Duchamp's 'Fountain' and Mayakovsky's poems and prose account of New York.

Duchamp's 'found object' was the thing itself once more: America in the shape of the new mass-produced article, accepted (in spite of its rejection by the Exhibition's organisers) as an 'art object' complete with individual signature ('R. Mutt', borrowed from a New York plumbing company). 'Fountain' posed Dada's one central question: 'Is it art?' Pound, Eliot and many not so high modernists would surely have answered 'no'. Yet Dada's own answer lies in its project to undermine the very assumptions and structures constituting art. 'Fountain' was either art because it could be construed as such, or it was not art because the distinction between art object and an anonymous, mass-produced, utilitarian object no longer applied. But this collapse of categories could mean two things: either that everything was art, or that all objects were simply utilitarian. The problem for this second interpretation was that exhibiting Duchamp's urinal as a single object meant removing it from the industrial series which otherwise defined it, thus severing it from its use-value. A urinal on display might seem like Ford's first airplane exhibited in a department store window (the example is Mayakovsky's), but aside from the matter of the airplane's price (anti-art objects have become notoriously 'priceless' collector's items, and Arensberg was already collecting Duchamp's in the 1910s) the airplane had a future as a working form of transport. 'Fountain' had no such future and could therefore only be understood according to the first option: as art, because everything was art. The only difference being that this word had now to be written as 'art'. Dada therefore challenged the artistic means of production and scandalised standard categories of perception, but it distracted attention from the industrial means of production. For in separating an object from its use-value and the labour process, 'found-objects', for all their transgressive intent, contributed to the commodity fetishism identified by Marx much in the way that an advertisement would.

Mayakovsky visited the United States in 1925. Well before his visit, the essay 'And Now to the Americas' (1914) had presented America as the future made manifest, and the poem '150,000,000' (1919–20) had rung with his admiration of the technological ideal the country represented. On seeing the real thing the champion of 'futurism' might have been expected to do no more than enthuse over the new technology, even to find in the United States the revolution in modern technology to complete the social and political revolution launched in the Soviet Union. Had not Lenin famously defined communism as 'electrification plus Soviet Power'? Mayakovsky was indeed thrilled by the sight of New York City, particularly by its unstinting use of electricity, and confirmed much that has been said above of its sublime impact. He was 'amazed . . . dumbfounded', it was 'scarcely possible to imagine this labyrinth as a whole', the city seemed 'always in the midst of construction . . . . Everything is the most, the most, the most.'[75] But what he came to see too were the underlying forces and divisions in this unimaginable whole: the key role of Wall Street, 'the primary capital . . . that actually rules the country'; the workings of American imperialism; the effects of class division between bourgeoisie and working class and within the working class itself; a history of industrial action; reports of poor working conditions at the Ford plant; ghettoisation; white prejudice and the exploitation of immigrants and black workers.[76]

Mayakovsky's poem 'A Skyscraper Dissected' follows the terms of this analysis. Contemporary visual art often showed the skyscraper as a distant and depopulated physical object. Mayakovsky's skyscraper, by contrast, is seen from within, as a living and working place, inhabited by rough American types ('film star policemen . . . an over-ripe miss . . . a honeymoon-couple . . . shareholders in conference jam . . . a sleuth . . . a freelance painter').[77] The poem ascends the numbered floors like an elevator to arrive at the top. This is reminiscent of Whitman's lists of American common people, but Mayakovsky does not arrive at a penthouse celebration of American oneness. What he discovers at the top is not the summation of democracy but 'a Negro cleaner' whose exploitation at 'the bottom' of society is a sign of this democracy's true backwardness.

> I look
> >in a blend
> >>of anger and boredom
> >at the inmates
> >>of the ninety-storey shack.
> I'd meant
> >to go 7,000 miles forward,
> >but it looks, ·
> >>I've been taken
> >>>seven years back.[78]

He concludes the essay 'My Discovery of America' by reflecting beyond the obvious fact of the US commitment to capitalism on the divisions this society has produced between workers, on their 'relative well-being' and low aspirations, on technology and the artist's role. The United States exhibits a 'primordial futurism' he says, 'the futurism of bare technology', which it is the task of 'the workers of art . . . to harness . . . in the name of the interests of humankind'.[79] There is no simple arithmetic sum such as Lenin's,

New York Fictions

therefore, which will produce the future from capitalist technology
and Soviet communism; nor any easy equation between artistic
and social values: 'Not the aesthetic admiration of iron fire escapes
on skyscrapers', is required, he says, 'but the simple organisation
of living quarters'.[80] Mayakovsky therefore perceives the kind of
irregularities and contradictions Randolph Bourne had associated with
a critical and democratic ironical attitude, here in the expression of a
revolutionary dialectical method: 'The goal of my sketches is to force
people', he says, 'to study the weak and the strong sides of America
in anticipation of the battle ahead in the distant future.'[81]
    This was in 1925, when some battles had already been fought and
lost. The *Masses* was closed in 1918 for its opposition to the war;
Debs was imprisoned in the same year for violating the Espionage
Act; hundreds of radicals and communists were arrested and some
deported; the IWW was decimated and the enthusiasms of the
'Lyrical Left' decisively quashed by the Palmer Raids instigated
by the Attorney General during 1919–22. For different reasons,
Emma Goldman, John Reed and Max Eastman grew disillusioned
with the Soviet example. In addition, Randolph Bourne died in
1918, John Reed in 1920 and Lenin in 1924. In terms of the history
of mainstream modernism, Pound's *Hugh Selwyn Mauberley* was
published in 1919, and *The Waste Land* in 1922 – a poem which in the
judgement of W.C. Williams set American letters back ten years.
    Malcolm Cowley remarked on how anonymous, philistine and
mechanical New York appeared in this postwar period, a time
when for the most part serious American writers withdrew from
the corruptions and complications of the modernised metropolis.[82]
To the many who saw Paris as the locale for twentieth-century
modernism, it may have seemed that Pound and Eliot had been right
about Europe if wrong about England, and wrong perhaps in their
political and religious convictions. The question of the relationship
between literary and social experiment, between a radical aesthetic
and a Left politics committed to unmaking and transforming both
art and society now seemed deeply problematic. For clearly these
were not in the postwar period the natural partners they had seemed
a decade before. Artistic innovation could evidently prove radically
conservative in its cultural and ideological intent, the analogy between
modern art and modernisation did not hold, and modernisation
of itself did not consort with any given social form. Form and
technology, to borrow Mayakovsky's conclusion above, needed to
be harnessed to a particular social content in the battle for the future;
a battle, as it turned out in the 1930s, when the opponents of Left

50

modernism might be themselves revolutionaries and reformists of a different kind who preferred a different conception of radical art and social change.

A writer who was much involved in these debates was John Dos Passos. The contemporary praise for his early work was extraordinarily high and has given way to relative neglect; perhaps because he now appears to be a 'reflex' of these decades, perhaps because his own career and changed opinions seemed to close the case on a radical Left modernism in American fiction.

Malcolm Cowley talked of Dos Passos as the most ambulatory of the lost generation.[83] Before the war, when he worked in Paris, he had gone in 1916 to Spain, returned there in 1919 and 1921 when he had also travelled to Turkey, the Soviet Caucasus, Iraq and Syria, and later in the 1920s travelled to Italy, Mexico and the Soviet Union. At the same time he was more closely involved in the 1920s in practical campaigns and Left political activity in the United States than any of his contemporaries. His writing and opinions in these years owed something to the travel journalism of John Reed and to the journals of the earlier generation of the 'Lyrical Left' such as the *Seven Arts* and the *Dial*, as well as the *Liberator*, the *Freeman* and the *New Masses* (begun in 1926), for which he wrote. He had read James Joyce's *Ulysses* in 1922, met Eisenstein, Pudovkin and the Tairovs in his visit to Leningrad and Moscow in 1928, knew of the work of Meyerhold, translated Blaise Cendrars and was a close friend of George Grosz.[84] The earliest signs of this avant-garde influence were an involvement in painting, in agit prop, and the New Playwrights Theatre project in the mid 1920s for a revolutionary workers' theatre. But Dos Passos began also to formulate a literary aesthetic which would use the techniques of film montage and of rapportage and apply these innovations of the machine age to American experience and materials. As he recalled later:

> My head stuffed with everything I could absorb in Europe and
> the Near East I came back to America. New York was the first
> thing that struck me. It was marvelous. It was hideous. It had
> to be described . . . . It was all an experiment . . . . Some of
> the poets who went along with the cubism of the painters of the
> School of Paris had talked about simultaneity. There was something
> about Rimbaud's poetry that tended to stand off the page. Direct
> snapshots of life. Rapportage was a great slogan. The artist must
> record the fleeting world the way the motion picture recorded it.
> By contrast, juxtaposition, montage, he could build drama into

his narrative. Somewhere along the way I had been impressed by
Eisenstein's motion picture, by his version of old D. W. Griffith's
technique. Montage was his key word.[85]

Manhattan Transfer (1925) was the first striking result of this
thinking. For observers and commentators New York City had
meant the vertical, soaring movement of its skyscrapers. At one
point in the novel the character Jeff Herf comes upon a skyscraper
that has obsessed him in his night-time wanderings. Muttering the
promises of the Declaration of Independence he sees the face at
every window of a Ziegfeld Follies girl and then of his estranged
wife Ellen. But search as he might he can find no entrance to the
building.[86]

The skyscraper is a sign of the city's beckoning charms and
frustrations. Already, at the heart of this most modern city, at the
point of modernism's heyday, its city-dwellers are disorientated, flung
up and down upon the wheel of capitalist fortune or in and out of
its revolving doors (sections of the novel are called 'Metropolis',
'Rollercoaster', 'Revolving Doors' and 'Skyscraper'). As one time
Wall Street big noise Joe Harland hits bottom, so another, the lawyer,
George Baldwin or the scheming political boss Gus McNeil rises in
the system. Bud Korpening asks when he first arrives in the city
for directions to 'the center of things' (p. 16), but there is no centre,
only the way people are made to think there is and they themselves
are 'Johnny on the spot in the center of things' as Ellen Herf plans
for the readers of a new magazine (p. 330). But Ellen herself is also
Ellen, Elaine and Helen and plans to be Mrs Baldwin. She feels she
is a 'hypothetical dollself', who can be wound up and put in different
positions and once she has decided on a role is set 'in her own place,
forever frozen into a single gesture . . . rigid as a porcelain figure'
(pp. 334–5). Where Jimmy is giddy and adrift and she is ice-cold,
another young woman, the Jewish seamstress Anna Cohen, is lost in
dreams of revolution and Hollywood romance.

Alienation in the city is therefore accented by gender, class and
ethnicity, and derives less from the sickening ups and downs of
the capitalist rollercoaster than from the second, lateral, movement,
expressed in the book's title, of the criss-crossing, intersecting but
never-for-long touching lines of downtown life. The echo here is
of the transit system, the new railway termini, the commuter and
automobile life of new middle-class New Yorkers as well as the less-
noticed horizontal emphasis in New York's civic buildings rather than
its skyscrapers.[87] In Dos Passos this association of horizontal low-
level buildings and the horizons of its average citizens corresponds

to a band of middle-range characters and a direct colloquial prose style (free of the allusions of high modernist discourse). The result had the 'quality of cliché', said Lionel Trilling. It required, said other commentators, not much more reading ability than was needed for the daily press; his characters' lives read like the stories on back page of a local newspaper.[88]

Here was Dos Passos's rapportage, a fictional news-sheet of social types, full of the circumstantial physical detail of New York City, threaded with the language of advertisements, headlines and newspaper reports. But this was flanked too by anonymous, sharply imagistic prose poems which comprise the chapter heads. A block of deterministic, naturalist narrative therefore runs in the novel beneath an accelerated, yearning impressionism. Thus the dual perspectives and discourses on the city – the horizontal and vertical, the descriptive and lyrical – were brought together in what looked like the makings of an experimental popular fiction, working upon the sensational, the tawdry and everyday materials of the modernised city; seeing them afresh, if the characters themselves could not, in the prose poems which, as it were, editorialised the stories.

But for all this, the popular modernism of the novel could show little or no social connection between its people. Whereas Eliot, Joyce and Virginia Woolf had sought and found some stabilising structure or motif amidst the fragments of urban life, the characters of *Manhattan Transfer* are atomised units in transit who no more connect in a sustained relationship or unifying perspective than the fleeting groups, diagonal lines and patches of colour of a John Marin painting. That Ellen the actress and Anna, caught in a fire in the back of the fashion shop the day Ellen visits, do not meet is a telling example of this missed human and social contact. The main linkage between individuals and groups is provided by Jimmy Herf, a reporter and aspiring writer. But he ends up jobless, on the point of a divorce and departure. Words, crucially, fail him. His meandering 'The pursuit of happiness . . . unalienable pursuit . . . unalienable right to life liberty and . . .' (p. 327) becomes in a judge's portentous address on behalf of middle America, 'The unalienable rights of human life and property' (p. 349). The average is mediocre and acquisitive, but the artist too 'is a fardel' (p. 323). Through Jimmy the novel exposes the corruptions of power, the cheat of mechanical lives, but neither he nor the novel can propose a social alternative. He leaves the city, become now 'Ninevah', the city of destruction, in archetypal fashion: a non-conformist who would wear a straw hat out of season. Down to his last two cents, he takes pleasure in a new dawn and a chance lift at a new crossroads which will take him nowhere in particular, only 'pretty far' (p. 360).

Manhattan Transfer was an instalment on the 'collective novel' developed as the trilogy *USA*. Here Dos Passos attempted a more politically engaged, more explicit and more ambitious montage of the personal, public and historical. The novel interleaves four narrative discourses: the impressionistic autobiography of its 'Camera Eye' sections, the collaged daily record in pages of 'Newsreel' of headlines, adverts and snatches of song, the historical biographies of contemporary individuals, and the fictional narratives of a world of characters, involved in public relations, entertainment, labour unions, political and business life between the turn of the century and the late 1920s. The titled sections link the composition with European avant-garde experiment in Soviet cinema, German *Neue Sachlichkeit* ('new objectivity') as well as documentary movements in art and photography (and the technologies of modernisation) in the United States. The whole was designed to capture the idiom ('mostly *USA* is the speech of the people', said Dos Passos) and the shaping forces of recent history in a multiformed national epic.[89]

Contemporary Left opinion tended to judge *USA* by the bench marks of proletarian realism and the communist cause urged especially by Michael Gold and *The New Masses*. By the end of the 1930s Dos Passos was found to have failed this test. But neither he nor the American Left ended this period as they had begun it, and it would be a mistake to think that the issue of political and artistic commitment explicitly raised by the 1930s meant taking sides in a simple way for or against Marx or modernism or socialist realism. The longer period of the interwar years, as suggested above, saw the consolidation of capitalist modernity in New York as in the nation. The Left was transformed in these years from the sometime Marxist, libertarian anarchism of Reed, Eastman, Goldman, Bourne, the *Masses* and the IWW to the more narrowly ideological in-fighting provoked by the hegemony of the Communist Party and the Soviet Union under Stalin. Dos Passos's political education, as is well known, bridged these two generations. He campaigned actively on behalf of Sacco and Vanzetti and the Scotsboro Boys, he went as a reporter to the strike of Passaic textile workers and to the Harlan County miners' strike in 1931, and in 1932 declared his readiness to vote for William Z. Foster, the Communist Party candidate for President. Just as important, however, had been his earlier visits to Spain and the Soviet Union after the First World War and in the 1920s. In Spain he was impressed by the promise of a pre-industrial co-operative commonwealth, founded on local anarchist traditions, which he saw as an example to the United States, but in danger of losing its original liberties in the modern era of militarist capitalism.[90] In the new Russia he was appalled by the suppression of the seamen's revolt by the Cheka at Kronstadt, and feared that the 'terror machine' had 'eaten up everything good in the revolution'.[91] The undemocratic tactics of the Communist Party in the Harlan County miners' strike, the communist attack upon a Socialist Party meeting in 1934, news of the Soviet purges, and events once again in Spain in 1937 (the execution, in particular, of his friend José Robles as a spy, which sparked a serious quarrel with Hemingway) decided him against communism.

From this point on, Dos Passos turned away from European ideologies to the 'story book' Anglo-Saxon democracy of the United States. His subsequent fiction, some still of epic proportions, and the textbooks – on Tom Paine, the founding fathers and Thomas Jefferson – which followed, took him further to the Right, to a tolerance of McCarthyism, to the support of Barry Goldwater and the denunciation of anti-Vietnam War protesters.

Two moments remain instructive in this career with its sometimes startlingly symptomatic reversals. In *1919*, written in the early 1930s as the second volume of the *USA* trilogy, Dos Passos chose to reconstruct the events of a critical year for the American Left at what was the high point of his own left-wing commitment. The year 1919 was one of high tension: of pro-Bolshevik militancy, Mayday riots, the Seattle general strike, factionalism on the Left and anti-radical hysteria. It ended with the battle between Wobblies and Legionnaires in Centralia, Washington, the deportations of anarchists and members of the Union of Russian Workers and the infamous Palmer Raids on the homes and organisations of suspected dissidents.

As Barbara Foley shows, the four-tiered sections of *1919* are arranged so to present the contradictory forces shaping this moment of crisis. Thus Debs's imprisonment is set against proclamations of wartime prosperity; the biographies of Randolph Bourne and John Reed and Paxton Hibbin – similarly opposed to the war and sympathetic to socialism – are arranged so that they 'coincide with the Newsreels depicting the slaughter on the battlefield and the cant on the home front'; the biographies of the villains of the period, Woodrow Wilson and the House of Morgan, are set against 'the betrayal of democratic idealism at Versailles'; and the subjective life of the 'Camera Eye' persona (modelled on the author) is flanked by the career of Richard Ellsworth Savage, who gives up writing for a cynical involvement in public relations.[92]

Foley suggests that the form Dos Passos chose for this indictment of capitalism in *1919* was the satire, which she describes as 'characteristically non-teleological' and 'disjunctive and non-progressive' in its plot structure.[93] At this same time, she points out, Dos Passos expressed a knowledge and liking for Marx's *The Eighteenth Brumaire*. In their layered analysis and cross-sectional 'narrative approach as well as their *ironic* vision, *1919* and *The Eighteenth Brumaire*', she says, 'stand forth as curious twins of historical discourse'.[94] At a later date, Dos Passos liked to think of his work as 'chronicles', of the novelist as 'second-rate historian', but in this volume the relation of autobiographical and fictional narratives with documentary materials is more conjunctural than chronological or hierarchical. *1919* therefore appears as Dos Passos's most Marxist modernist satire.[95] It is worth pursuing his particular conception of Marxism further, however, both to appreciate this work and the subsequent change in his writing and political beliefs.

In 1932 Dos Passos talked of the need to 'Marxianise the American tradition' or to 'Americanise Marx', and Foley is surely right to see *1919*'s 'historical satire' as consistent with this thinking.[96] At this time, and into the mid 1930s, he was also careful to distinguish Marxism from Party dogma. Stalin's excesses, he wrote in 1935, did not have 'anything to do with Marx's work' and this 'enormously valuable body of ideas, aspirations, humane rebellions, etc.' had to be distinguished from the Marxian 'political groups'.[97] Already there is an important distinction here. Marxism impressed Dos Passos as a form of undogmatic economic and social critique, 'an important basis for the . . . sociological sciences', as he put it,[98] but not as a basis for political action. The terms of his own *political* analysis are suggested more by the conclusion he draws in *USA* from the Sacco and Vanzetti case: 'all right we are two nations' (p. 1105). These 'two nations' Dos Passos characteristically thought of less in terms of social class than in terms of the divided interests of the individual or 'the people' and the businessmen, industrial magnates, judiciary, political and union bosses who had trampled on American civil liberties. His sympathies, that is to say, as his attachment to Spain, his response to the repression of the anarchist sailors at Kronstadt, his admiration of the Wobblies and his defence of Saccho and Vanzetti all showed, were with forms of anarchism and, in the United States, an ideal of democratic self-government associated with the pioneer ethic and the Nation's beginnings. In terms of any direct philosophical debt Dos Passos owed more, as became clear, to Thorstein Veblen than to Marx. Veblen's work was 'a sort of anthropological footnote to

Marx', he said in 1934 in recommending him to Edmund Wilson.[99] Of the works he mentions, Veblen's *The Vested Interests and The Common Man* (published in 1919) perfectly summarised Dos Passos's concerns with the abuse of power and the plight of the working stiff and the little man.

In the late 1930s and 1940s, as he became more adamant in his opposition to communism, so he became less watchful of distinctions between Stalinism and socialism and more dubious about the usefulness of Marx. To Edmund Wilson he could write in 1934, for example, that the only interest of Russia was 'as a terrible example – for world socialism – if you take socialism to mean the educative or constructive tendency rather than the politics'.[100] But by the mid 1940s, clear in his 'unreasoned belief in individual liberty' and turning more directly to the example of Walt Whitman, he had concluded that 'socialism is a new system of exploitation of man by man very much more total and without any of the loop holes that capitalism allows – through which the individual can escape'.[101] Effectively, at this point, he had accepted the identification the Stalinist Left itself forced upon American political life of communism with socialism. To reject one, as Dos Passos did on the evidence of Communist Party sectarianism, intimidation and anti-democratic procedures was to reject the other. This meant the rejection too of course of any association touted in the early 1930s of communism with twentieth-century Americanism. Marxism for its part he saw as at best splintered into Stalinist, Leninist, or Trotskyite groupings.

Dos Passos's politics did not so much undergo a volte-face, therefore, as discover an inherent emphasis as events at home and in the Soviet Union and Europe closed down options and drew out the nostalgic conservatism latent in his libertarian populism. We can see this position emerging in his reflections on Sacco and Vanzetti. Their trial and execution had been a decisive radicalising event of the 1920s, for Dos Passos and many others. In his treatment of this ten years later in *The Big Money* the 'Camera Eye' sections (49, 50), the 'Newsreel' (66) and the fictional narrative of Mary French who goes to Boston to work for the Sacco and Vanzetti defence committee have, quite exceptionally in this novel, the kind of focus and conjunctural treatment of materials present in *1919*. The implications are different, however. The theme of the betrayal of language, glimpsed through Jimmy Herf in *Manhattan Transfer* surfaces here once more as a major concern.

> the ruined words worn slimy in the mouths of lawyers
> districtattorneys collegepresidents judges without the old

words the immigrants haters of oppression brought to Plymouth
how can you know who are your betrayers America . . . .

(p. 1084)

'We have only words against / POWER SUPERPOWER' the 'Camera
Eye' sections of *USA* end (p. 1155). Dos Passos's answer to the
'ruined words worn slimy' is to speak and write the clean 'old
words', to assert the survival of 'the old American speech of the
haters of oppression . . . in the mouth of an old woman from
Pittsburgh of a husky boilermaker from Frisco . . . in the mouth
of a Back Bay socialworker in the mouth of an Italian printer of a
hobo from Arkansas' (p. 1106). He does not draw the implication,
that is to say (as Marxist theory might) from this corruption of the
'old words' that the meanings of the words of political discourse are
not self-evident but the product of coded systems of representation
and the site of ideological struggle. Instead the episode confirmed
him in a positivistic defence of true facts against false representations,
a belief in the original meanings of words like 'freedom', 'happiness',
'unalienable [*sic*] rights' and a defence of the cause of the common
man and woman in whom these meanings might survive in the face
of corrupt corporations. The writer, Dos Passos said in 1935, found
himself on the side of people not doctrine and 'on the side . . . really
and truly, of liberty, fraternity, and humanity. The words are old and
dusty and hung with the dirty bunting of a thousand crooked orations,
but underneath they are still sound.'[102] Hence his polemics on behalf
of a 'passionate unmarxian revival of AngloSaxon democracy'; a
return to the pure Jeffersonian source prior to its pollution in mass
life and the course of US history.[103]

The anti-communism that Dos Passos found necessary to a defence
of true Americanism turned out to be the first position of the postwar,
postmodern Right. There is in one way therefore something very
contemporary about Dos Passos's (very early) rejection of Stalinism,
his distrust of 'totalising' corporations and big business, his seeking
some new ground in a non-, even post-Marxist, democratic tradition.
In another way, his appeal to the liberties of Jeffersonian democracy
looks like an example of the naïve self-deceptions of Enlightenment
thought, an object lesson in the obsolescence of modernism in a
postmodern age. His career demonstrates in fact how we would do
better to think of a range of 'postmodern' positions, encompassing
not only the familiar anti-Enlightenment versions of postmodernism, but the anti-communist conservative populism of Dos Passos
and the 'New Right' (which came to include other former radicals
such as Sidney Hook and Max Eastman), as well as the liberal-Left

positions taken by other contemporaries, amongst them Edmund Wilson. It is the ambiguous potential of Dos Passos's individualism which is in the end most striking, making him both a curious exception and a deeply symptomatic figure. His modernist technique produced on balance an uneasy combination in *USA* of uncoordinated materials and deterministic social narrative. In his subsequent writings this attempted collage was overtaken by the idea of the 'contemporary chronicle' which narrowed both history and fiction to the common content of the individual biography and a no-nonsense belief in facts, 'straight writing' and plain speaking.[104] Naturalism, as it were, got the better of modernism.[105] Yet in this complex changing history, the novel had at moments suggested the form of a dialogic modern epic, a multi-voiced narrative of the personal, public and historical to challenge both the uniformities of conventional socialist realism and the totalitarian epics of high modernism. The rhizomic structure and dialectical montage of *1919*, in particular, presents an alternative to the random juxtaposition of materials elsewhere in the trilogy and to the assembly-line montage of his increasingly pessimistic determinism. Dos Passos's libertarianism found its progressive side in a controlled satire which could accept the social critique but not the contemporary political forms of Marxism. These were the revealing terms of his 'Americanised Marxism' and Americanised modernism. The fact that this was a temporary affinity is as instructive as that it occurred in the terms it did, determined on both counts by the political and historical conjuncture Dos Passos sought to report upon.

PARTISANS, PARANOIDS, PARADOXES: FROM BRECHT TO BARTHELME

Like Mayakovsky, Bertolt Brecht had imagined America before he saw it. The early plays of the late 1920s and 1930s, *In the Jungle of the Cities, Mahagonny*, and *Saint Joan of the Stockyards*, recycled and pastiched the evocative stereotypes of an America of lumberjacks, cowboys and gangsters, boxing matches, jazz, fast cars and giant cities. In 1926 Brecht had drawn up a list for a proposed *Revue* on Americanism: 'Record Girl, Smiling, Advertising, Boxing match, Revue, Tarzan, Sixday races, Slow Motion Film, Business,

Radio'.[106] The list captures above all the newness represented by American modernity, a land of new technologies, mass entertainment, consumption and business. Brecht's box of images was derived from cinema (Chaplin remained a model for the epic theatre's external treatment of character), from his reading of Jack London, the Chicago novels of the Danish writer J.V. Jensen, and Upton Sinclair, particularly his picture of the workings of US capital and labour relations in *The Jungle* (1910).

Brecht's enthusiasms were shared by his contemporaries in the German avant-garde (amongst them George Grosz, Otto Dix, Hannah Hoch and John Heartfield). Grosz in particular (a close friend and influence upon Dos Passos) did dozens of drawings and illustrations depicting the iconography of American popular culture, the mythology of the West, the impact of the cities, its slovenly sexuality, and the predatory attitudes of American business. In 1916 he accompanied his Whitmanesque chant 'America!!, The Future!!' with a ragtime dance in American patent leather shoes.[107] Four years later, after the war and the defeat of socialism in Germany, however, attitudes changed. America and modernity were synonymous but now ambivalent. As the United States boosted the postwar reconstruction of German markets and German industry, the cultural and technical inspiration of the New World which had formed an exhilarating counter-image to the reactionary bourgeois culture of Europe was seen more as the modern face of capitalism. The German business class was now impressed in its own terms by the rationalised working methods represented by Fordism; a changed mood that Grosz expressed in his drawing, 'Soon Europe will be a Suburb of New York' (1924). The techniques of collage and montage (a term applied in German to assembly-line production, and which seemed at first to express the synchronicity of Dadaist technique and industrial technology) became a means of analysis of the object itself. This was especially true of the photomontages of John Heartfield who sought to expose the contradictions of US capitalist democracy in a radical popular art of posters, magazine art and dust-jackets (in book-covers for Sinclair's *100%* and *Mountain City*, and Dos Passos's *Three Soldiers*, for example).[108]

The 'Great Crash' of 1929 confirmed the developing scepticism of the Berlin Dadaists. In Brecht's 'Late Lamented Fame of the Giant City of New York' (1930), the city which had seemed so outsized and indestructible is diminished; the Americans' 'broad-gauged overcoats' are now empty with hunger, the city's skyscrapers cannot house its unemployed and destitute. The future which New

York had represented has here come to a premature end, proving the United States to be just like other capitalist nations, only more so.

> Truly their whole system of communal life was beyond compare
> What fame! What a century!

> Admittedly that century lasted
> A bare eight years.[109]

The actual New York when Brecht visited it in 1935 for the Theatre Union production of *The Mother* presented him with the obstructive methods of naturalist theatre. Later in the 1940s, after he had been forced out of Nazi Germany and from his European exile, he discovered what it meant to live by the commercial methods of Hollywood, 'the market where lies are bought'.[110] Brecht was frustrated and largely unsuccessful, whether in Los Angeles or New York, at odds not only with American attitudes and culture but with his fellow German expatriates: Marcuse, Leonhard Frank and notably Thomas Mann.[111] He planned a 'Tui novel' to satirise the delusions, compromises and nostalgia that characterised their lives, and began another work which would set *The Communist Manifesto* in verse, so as 'to renew its propaganda effect . . . supporting it with recent authority'.[112] In an essay in 'Art and Culture' in 1941, reviewing Brecht's poetry, Clement Greenberg suggested that the infusion of popular attitudes in Brecht's modernism made his position less embattled and defensive than that of his American contemporaries.[113] In fact, 'embattled and defensive' exactly described his position in the United States, where, oddly enough, his political aesthetic proved untranslatable into the language of American popular art and politics in the 1940s. In 1947, one day before his departure for Europe and the new East Berlin, Brecht appeared before the House UnAmerican Activities Committee to answer charges on his affiliation with communism. He answered with his usual guile, but the exchange symbolically ended any possible dialogue across radical cultures. In a poem from this period on fellow exiles who found a home and livelihood in the United States, Brecht wrote:

> I praise those who can change
> And yet in changing remain the same.[114]

In Brecht's own case this 'changing same' was expressed by his unequivocal commitment to Marx and Engels and to proletarian revolution, and his wish to renew this message, as for example in the planned *Das Manifest*. To embark on such a work at this time also expressed a belief in the strength of democratic forces in the new

Germany and indirectly a commitment to the new GDR. Through all the manoeuvrings of the subsequent period, the 'Marxist classics' (Marx, Lenin, Mao) remained an inspiration to Brecht's conception of socialist realism, one which in the famous exchange with Lukács in the 1930s had enlisted the use of a variety of means of artistic representation to achieve its ends. This was the 'changing same' of Brecht's 'Marxist modernism', a combination of political conviction and technical experiment. As such, his political art was a reply not only to Lukács's 'formalism' but to the anti-modernist notions of socialist or proletarian realism on the orthodox American Left.

Brecht appeared truly exiled in the United States: an illustration of what was impossible in that country in that period. His criterion of the 'changing same' is one we can bring, nevertheless, to American writing and culture. What remained the same and what changed in American conceptions of Marxism and modernism? Dos Passos, as we have seen, rejected communism, and found Marxism less and less relevant to his series of plain tales of America's 'story-book democracy' and the villainous power-brokers who had betrayed it. As he and others who followed the rightward trend of American intellectual and political life in the 1940s and 1950s show, communism and Stalinism became virtually synonymous. Those on the Left had themselves to contend with this equation after the Moscow purges, but once the ball had started rolling, Marxism and, at an extreme, any radical position was likely to be damned by association as Un-American. Where an anti-Stalinist Marxism was upheld it was in defiance of this trend: in the thought and writings of Edmund Wilson, for example; in a maverick figure such as Dwight Macdonald, and in the pages of the *Partisan Review*, a magazine which contested the field of political literature with the *New Masses* in the 1930s and became subsequently the intellectual home of the so-called New York Intellectuals.

According to *Partisan Review*'s editors, William Phillips and Phillip Rahv, the writer's task was to use Marxism as a philosophical framework rather than a political guide (not unlike Dos Passos's understanding of Marxism above),[115] and in this respect the magazine looked above all to Trotsky as an exemplary revolutionary Marxist, the enemy of Stalin, and a supporter of artistic freedom.[116] The literary modernism associated with this position, however, was the European modernism of Dostoevsky, Proust, Kafka, Thomas Mann and Yeats, the work of the expatriates James and Eliot, and at home figures such as Wallace Stevens and Faulkner at the expense of a more indigenous 'Redskin' tradition. It did not include Eisenstein or Mayakovsky or the Russian art movements, nor Brecht, nor the Berlin Dadaists – of those whose political affiliations were obviously on the Left; nor did it promote American modernists such as William Carlos Williams, Gertrude Stein, Mina Loy or Langston Hughes. 'Marxist modernism' in this milieu therefore meant the defence, endorsed by Trotsky's support of artistic autonomy, of works of formal innovation by conservative artists, often accompanied by the denigration of what Phillips and Rahv described as 'popular' or 'commercial' writing.

If we substitute the names of Adorno, Horkheimer or Marcuse for Trotsky in this statement, we approach the position Brecht's fellow expatriates were developing in the New York School of Social Research in the 1940s and early 1950s, and which was to become so influential later. And if, secondly, we extract any explicit philosophical or political endorsement from this position we discover the 'modernism' of the equally influential New Critics. From their different perspectives, both *Partisan Review* and the New Critics sought to reconcile the conservative with the radical aspects of this literature, coupled in the case of *Partisan Review* with an affirmation of contemporary American society. For its part the transplanted Frankfurt School did not assume any such reconciliation, but on the contrary, in a third modernist position, valued the uncompromising obscurity and experimentation of modern art as the sign of its refusal of the conditions of present mass society.

If 'Marxism' and 'modernism' could change in these ways in the altered conditions of postwar intellectual and political life, so too could the conception of 'class' which had been a defining aspect of the *New Masses* leftism and an important assumption in Brecht's already quite different political aesthetic. To many observers the concept was irrelevant because postwar American society was no longer a class society. This at least was the reasoning of a generation of 'modernist' sociologists and historians, some of whom were again associated with *Partisan Review* or the circle of New York Intellectuals, amongst them David Riesman, Daniel Bell, Seymour Martin Lipset, and Arthur Schlesinger Jr. The chief tenet of their writings, says Douglas Tallack, was 'that power has been dispersed from a ruling class or party into a plurality of veto groups'.[117] Bell's sense, in particular, of the 'end of ideology' and of the postwar or post-industrial period as introducing a political culture of negotiated compromise amongst interest groups under a generally beneficent welfare capitalism has emerged as an important reference point in debates on postmodernism (both Fredric Jameson and Jürgen Habermas take issue with Bell). Just as interesting is the invocation in these writings, as Howard Brick and Tallack have pointed out, of modernist sources and idioms: Schlesinger's epigraph from Yeats, for example, in *The Vital Center* (1949) and Bell's announcement in *The End of Ideology* (1960) that the key terms of contemporary discourse are 'irony, paradox, ambiguity, and complexity'.[118] This is the 'modernism' once more of the New Critics, at the twilight of their own influence in literary studies, transferred to an analysis of the social and political texts of modernity.

Both these groups interpreted the literary and social texts before them in terms of an eventual reconciliation of their inner tensions, whether of word and image or ideology and social class. At the same time, the erosion of class identity and of a revolutionary Marxist perspective in postwar society was being theorised by the exiled members of the Frankfurt School, based in New York. Herbert Marcuse, for instance, came in *One-Dimensional Man* (1966) to view late capitalist society as a totalising universe: 'an omnipresent system which swallows up or repulses all alternatives'.[119] The feelings this experience could evoke had been anticipated in another way by David Riesman in *The Lonely Crowd* (1950), reflecting on the nature of American power: 'people are afraid', he writes, 'of this indeterminacy and amorphousness in the cosmology of power. They preferred to see a frightening system in which others have power over them in spite of the truth that these structures have evaporated.'[120] The choice these thinkers set before the American people was therefore either assimilation or paranoia.

Thomas Pynchon's *Gravity's Rainbow* offers to define paranoia as 'the discovery that *everything is connected*'.[121] Perhaps this is to say that paranoia is always imaginary. It was a condition that had nonetheless invaded the anti-communist thinking of Dos Passos and others to real effect in the 1940s and 1950s, and grew subsequently to become a dominant if more shapeless mood in American cinema and literature as the scare word 'communism' was thoroughly mixed in with a pervasive sense of the 'indeterminacy and amorphousness' of power.[122]

We enter here the more recognisable vocabulary and themes of postmodernism. I shall return to some of the questions of its meaning and provenance below. In the present context we can say already how in one way the many tendencies this term seeks to encompass can be thought of as related to matters of power and authority, both in its increase and ubiquity and in its indeterminacy and loss. In the

United States, one of postmodernism's first effects, for example, was the de-categorisation of high and low culture. It posed a challenge, in other words, to the cultural authority invested in canonic texts, the academy, museums and establishment ideas of art.[123]

The first signs of this postmodernism were a re-evaluation of kitsch, and formulaic genre fiction, a defiant enthusiasm for 'trash' and the new electronic media of TV and rock music. The major novelists of this first postwar avant-garde were Kerouac and Burroughs. Kerouac embodied the idea of the artist as footloose bohemian rebel, swinging between New York and California, and the idea of art as spontaneous free expression: a double protest against the conformities of literary and social life in the name of American individualism which took him, as it took others in the 1940s and 1950s – if along a less dissolute and incoherent course, to a position of conservative reaction. To say what is obvious about Kerouac: that he was not connected to any formal Left political movement, nor drew upon the formal innovations of earlier avant-garde or modernist writers, confirms how threadbare, discredited or simply forgotten these traditions had become. Burroughs was a more avid experimentalist, whose fold-in and cut-up techniques and scurrilous content owed something to Dada and surrealism. His unstinting opposition to bureaucracy and systems of control (of which drug addiction was his prime metaphor, but including the control of his own public image) has given his work a tougher political content than Kerouac's. Its wild satirical edge has also helped make him a hero of at least three generations of the 'underground', where as a cult figure he has inspired 'postmodern' connections across the arts and media, including science fiction, film and punk music. In these two guises, as militant avantgardist and anarchistic die-hard, he has combined the issues of power in American postmodernism, presenting a linked protest to the dispersed powers of the state and the cultural establishment.

Burroughs returns us to the broader parameters of postmodernism. As a period concept, rather than the term for an artistic or cultural style, postmodernism has come to name the expansion and increased anonymity of state and business bureaucracies in the postwar period of late capitalism. Allied to changes in the modes and periods of employment, patterns of consumption, the use and effects of global information and media networks, this new phase of technological and capitalist development has induced a crisis of representation and subjectivity (for which paranoia is one name). A would-be dissenting or oppositional art is thought in these circumstances to have neither the stability of an alternative political analysis, nor the assumption of artistic or subjective autonomy to call upon. It is as if this universalising, all-assimilative society can buy up any protest and put it out as disposable produce on vinyl, or TV or in book form for its own purposes. The postmodern subject is therefore strung out (or 'floats', like the mere signifier the person has become) across former cultural divides, lost in the playground of media systems and consumer markets controlled by who knows what multinational corporations. The goal and booty of this society becomes information; its criteria effective management and increased profit.

That at least is one postmodern scenario. The mention of Thomas Pynchon, of Burroughs and the echoes some will hear in the above of cyberpunk narratives (of which Pynchon and Burroughs are deemed father-figures) suggest how the psychic, social and technological features of postmodernism are as much the stuff of fiction as social and economic fact (and perhaps indeed are 'always already' fiction, such is the crisis of representation entailed in a world where discourse is power). In his study of Pynchon, Donald Barthelme and Robert Coover, Paul Maltby remarks that in one way paranoia is an appropriate response to living in the total system of late capitalism.[124] In these 'dissident postmodernists', as he terms them, however, he finds, as he says of Pynchon, a 'critique of the system's control of the process of signification'.[125] Given the times and terms of the battle – the hegemony of technological rationality, a public sphere evacuated of critical thinking, the continued rule of binary thinking – the dissent this fiction voices will be provisional and textual, and in all ways marginal. Thus it seeks in a variety of discursive and narrative strategies to generate a range of new meanings *within* but yet against the ruling system of representation. To this end, Maltby suggests, it plumbs pre-verbal, intuitive states of consciousness (at an extreme invoking the absolute non-compromise of silence, since in Burroughs' phrase 'To speak is to lie'), undermining the pretensions of power through hyperbole and parody, mimicking the prevailing banalities of political and media discourse, or recycling the supplementary detritus of its rejected abundance (the W.A.S.T.E. of Pynchon's *Crying of Lot 49*).

Maltby's argument counters the more familiar view that the generation of 'literary' postmodernists of the 1960s and 1970s turned inwards to a fictive world of self-reflexive technical play and display: a final nay-saying to the illusions of realism and the delusions of committed writing. I want to take this up in relation to the New York-based example of Donald Barthelme. Almost immediately, however, one has to say that this description 'New York-based' has little to do with the city locations of his stories which, as if in sympathy with the groundlessness of postmodernism, are minimal and fleeting. Pynchon's San Narcisco or William Gibson's Chiba are the more obvious first-order postmodernist urban locales of the late twentieth century. The experience of New York, meanwhile, is overlaid and transitional, offering a simultaneity of places and times, or the jolt of counterpoint and disruption. And, oddly enough, this means that, even more than in the modernist period proper, the city has come to present the experience of spatial and historical montage. Barthelme responds to this in the themes and in the method of his stories which assemble characters and narratives from the waste or 'dreck' of urban life (the languages of tests, questionnaires, TV quiz shows, movie magazines, political campaigns, stories of having a baby, having an affair, having a divorce). Some of this daily debris comes back in new arrangements with new symbolic mystery; the banal pasted together to produce the out-of-the-ordinary. At such moments his art becomes less a fiction of report, or pastiche or mimicry than of estrangement. It is from this, in turn, that it gains a critical function.

In postmodern New York textual dissent 'offered the possibility, in its randomness, of mislocation of the self, in contradistinction to the grid of precise, rectangular pathways under our feet'.[126] So at least we might say of Barthelme's story 'The Balloon', whose possible effect these words describe. The balloon has the capacity to change shape, which 'was very pleasing, especially to people whose lives were rather rigidly patterned, persons to whom change, although desired, was not available'. The balloon appears one morning and covers forty-five blocks from 14th Street to Central Park, and most frequently has been taken to emblematise the playful autonomy of Barthelme's postmodernist art. There is much in the story, however, which suggests what (temporary) social meaning this fabulous addition might have for city-dwellers as well as the function it performs in expressing the unease and sexual deprivation of the narrator who constructs it. Not only does it signify a change of environment and attitude; it might also serve, so it is said, as 'a prototype, or "rough draft"', to which people may turn in lives of 'bewildered inadequacy' (p. 58), occasioned by the demands of contemporary city life ('specialised training . . . long-term commitments . . . complex machinery': p. 57).

In the essay 'After Joyce' (1964), Barthelme aligns himself with the modernists Joyce and Gertrude Stein, with artists who 'modify the world by adding to its store of objects the literary object'.[127] His art, it seems fair to say, picks out and works up the superficialities, non-sequiturs, clichés, slogans of this world store before it adds to it. The question we might ask then is what it means to think of this kind of additional literary object as 'modifying' the world. Does it restore use and value to its degraded objects or merely polish them for the pleasures of display?

A story like 'The Glass Mountain' shows how Barthelme appears to entertain the adventure of newness, even the promise of romance and revelation, only to undercut all meaning and worldly purpose. The 'glass mountain' is a skyscraper at the corner of 13th Street and 8th Avenue which the narrator climbs through a numbered series of observations. Below he sees his 'acquaintances'. They curse his foolishness, anticipate his fall, and think only of acquiring his apartment. The narrator aspires to a magical scene at the top, where there awaits a princess in a room in a tower of a castle of pure gold. He reports that in 'the conventional means of attaining the castle' an eagle takes a boy above the mountain top and drops him into the presence of the princess (p. 181). The skyscraper, we might say, is in this way transfigured by means of the conventional plot of the standard fable (from *The Yellow Fairy Book*), transporting the narrator and reader by analogy and association above the ignoble feelings of the urban populace below.

We have met skyscraper stories and analogies before, and it is worth comparing this example with them. Unlike Walt Whitman, Barthelme's figure does not climb to the heights of a democratic vision, nor like Mayakovsky ascend to the insight of this democracy's underlying hypocrisy. Nor is he like Dos Passos's Jimmy Herf, bedazzled and frustrated by its impenetrable eroticism and illusive security. What fabulous symbolic promise the 'glass mountain' skyscraper holds is entirely textual: a composite of national and conventional mythology. And this finally evaporates like a puff of magic. The narrator is deposited on a balcony at the top of the 'castle tower', he sees 'the beautiful enchanted symbol', and the story ends:

> 97. I approached the symbol, with its layers of meaning, but when I touched it, it changed into only a beautiful princess.
> 98. I threw the beautiful princess headfirst down the mountain to my acquaintances.
> 99. Who could be relied on to deal with her.
> 100. Nor are eagles plausible, not at all, not for a moment.
> Barthelme, 'The Glass Mountain', (p. 182)

The enchanted is disenchanted and meaning falls to the ground. But not in the restoration of a 'realistic perspective' since 'layers of meaning' have been preferred to the real thing, which, as part of the story's fantasy, was itself hardly 'plausible'. If the story is about the need for complex symbols, and this is unsatisfied since the world's store of symbols is so tawdry, then all that is left is this empty need.

In Barthelme's fiction there is no 'straight writing' of the kind Dos Passos appealed to, no sense that the 'old words' any more than the new words retain their first meaning. Words are not 'sound'; though they do 'sound' through literary, philosophical and other language networks. Dos Passos's positivism and Barthelme's intertextuality might be taken as representing opposite reactions to the crisis of representation marking the postmodern period (their careers briefly overlapped in the early 1960s). The second in its association with post-structuralism is thought to offer the pleasure and play of unchained signifiers after the naïveties of an assumed one-to-one relation between signifier and signified. (Barthelme's story 'Falling Dog' provides the new image for a sculptor in the puns and associations that fall from the word dog: 'dog tags . . . dog-ear . . . dogfight/doggerel/dogmatic', pp. 173–4). What in all its fun and sophistication this conscious intertextuality cannot conjure into existence, seemingly, is the conviction and commitment of an earlier generation. However, Barthelme's stories, as I have wanted to indicate, are not without social reference or a 'social message': the balloon presents a possible 'prototype' for jaded city-dwellers and the glass mountain reveals an insatiable yearning in their cruel lives for something better.

The reason these stories are open to such 'social' readings is because they are referential (however minimally) and always relational. That is to say, the balloon, the princess, the eagle, the falling dog image echo other fables and fantasies, just as they contrast with other more consequential, naturalistic narratives. The story 'City Lives' presents a narrative which, unlike these others, neither repeats nor unwinds a standard code of daily life or fable, but offers a positive 'rewriting' of codes. The character Ramona in this story is always on the outside. Her friend Elsa has two lovers while Ramona has none. Together they enter Law School, but Ramona engages in 'extralegal' sexual practices (or fantasies), in bouts of 'hilarity', 'jokes' and 'gibes' (pp. 148–9). Elsa marries and becomes pregnant, and Ramona finally has a baby by virgin birth. The father could be any one of three men, or all three – 'the engendering force was, perhaps, the fused glance of all of them' and she responds to their invitation because it 'leads one down many roads' (p. 159). The city in its ordinary 'muck' is transfigured, 'it is multidirectional and has a mayor'; it has 'a touch of sublimity' (p. 158). Ramona is neither unmarried nor an ordinary mother, but chosen by more than one suitor; this making her 'more me' and headed down many directions. Thus the story finds the route of diversity and plurality between the position of the outsider and the norm.

The mode or tone Barthelme's stories develop so as to negotiate this kind of betweenness is irony. In the story 'Kierkegaard Unfair to Schlegel' Kierkegaard is said to argue that irony makes the subject 'negatively free', that it is destructive of the old and has 'nothing to put in the place of what it has destroyed' (p. 164). Directed at the whole of existence (what one might call the 'life of irony') it becomes 'infinite absolute negativity'. In being unfair to Schlegel, Kierkegaard is being unfair to the ironist of the story who wishes therefore to 'annihilate' him. In answer to the question whether his own irony 'could be helpful in changing the government', he argues that the government is put into a 'helpful' position of self-irony by the 'clown army' of young people dressed in a parody of all manner of army uniforms, since this ironic relation of parody to real 'constitutes a very serious attack on all the ideas which support the real army including the basic notion of having an army at all' (p. 162).

We might compare these ironies with those we have encountered above. Kierkegaard argues in the story that what is wanted is 'reconciliation with actuality and the true reconciliation . . . is religion'. This resembles the 'irony, paradox, ambiguity, complexity' of the 'modernist' New Critics and sociologists, or at least how they would wish to resolve the tensions and irresolution these rhetorical figures set in motion. The irony of Barthelme's character is closer to the type celebrated by Randolph Bourne. Bourne writes of irony as a 'pleasant challenging of the world, this sense of vivid contrasts and incongruities, of comic juxtapositions, of flaring brilliances, and no less heartbreaking impossibilities'.[128] His 'life of irony', we remember, was a life of democratic sympathies, neither 'a method', nor 'a pose or an amusement'. It neither seeks 'the quiescence of resignation', nor to defend a 'citadel of truth',[129] but is questioning and constructive: 'If irony destroys some ideals it builds up others', he writes. 'It tests ideals by their social validity . . . if it leaves the foundations of many in a shaky condition and renders more simply provisional, those that it leaves standing are imperishably founded in the common democratic experience of all men.'[130] Much of this comes close to the more sober aspect of Barthelme's stories, if not quite to their jokes and gibes: up to the point, at least, of the close of Bourne's last-quoted statement. One cannot imagine talk from

Barthelme of 'ideals . . . imperishably founded, etc.', unless in an abbreviated mode of this very kind, within the distancing self-irony of quotation marks.

This is not to imply that a 'first person' should step out from behind the quotation marks and in front of the parentheses of Barthelme's work and speak straight: firstly, because this difference between Bourne and Barthelme is a measure of what has become impossible in what we might think of as a tradition of principled, comic irony; secondly, because these quotation marks are the marks of language in use, in its intertextual relations, and most importantly in dialogue. (Barthelme often employs the direct form of a dialogue between speakers A and B.) His stories do not engage in 'pure' aesthetic play. They do not suggest 'everything is connected' in the paranoid's vision, nor that the connecting structures of meaning and power have evaporated; rather, they set the objects of the world and their languages in the ironic play of dialogue. Maltby suggests that a mark of the postmodern lies in the winding down of the centrifugal forces that in Bakhtin's dialogics run counter to its univocal centripetal tendencies. In Barthelme, at the onset of this period, the voices in dialogue are few, but they are sometimes 'multidirectional' and enough to spin the universe comically out of its old orbit. This is one way of coming after Joyce and of modifying the modern.

NOTES

1. John W. Reps, *The Making of Urban America. A History of City Planning in the United States* (New Jersey: Princeton University Press, 1965), p. 294.
2. 'Our Unplanned Cities' in Olaf Hansen (ed.), *The Radical Will: Randolph Bourne. Selected Writings 1911–1918* (New York: Urizen Books, 1977), pp. 275, 277. The essay first appeared in *The New Republic*, June 1915.
3. The city plan for New York was designed to regulate its expansion on Manhattan Island above Houston Street to 155 Street, well beyond the point of its early nineteenth-century population. The street system thus established, comments Reps, 'is totally unrelated to the contours of the land', Reps, op. cit., p. 298. Even Baily had earlier come to feel there was a dullness and prejudice in the American habit of persevering with "'right angles *without any regard to the situation of the ground*'",

preferring the mixed radial and grid pattern of Washington (quoted, ibid., p. 294).

4. Ibid., p. 299.
5. Bourne, op. cit., p. 277.
6. Ibid., p. 278.
7. I have relied for the account of these developments chiefly on Kenneth Jackson, 'The Culture of Capitalism' in Anthony Sutcliffe (ed.), *Metropolis 1890–1940* (New York: Alexandrine Press Book, 1984), pp. 319–53. See also Edward Spann, *The New Metropolis: New York City, 1840–1857* (New York: Columbia University Press, 1981) and David C. Hannack, *Power and Society. Great New York at the Turn of the Century* (New York: Russell Sage Foundation, 1982).
8. Thomas Bender, 'The American City. What Shapes its Development' in Liza Taylor (ed.), *Cities: the Forces That Shape Them* (New York: Cooper-Hewitt Museum, Smithsonian Institution, National Museum of Design, Rizzoli, 1982), p. 51.
9. 'A man can edify himself for hours', Whitman wrote in an editorial for the *Brooklyn Eagle*, 'by looking in the shop windows of Broadway . . . . How active and inspiring the spectacle of so much passage and life', quoted in Malcolm Andrews 'Walt Whitman and the American city' in *The American City. Literary and Cultural Perspectives*, ed. Graham Clarke (London: Vision Press; New York: St Martin's Press, 1988), p. 186.
10. Philip Fisher, 'Democratic Social Space: Whitman, Melville, and the Promise of American Transparency' in *The New American Studies. Essays from 'Representations'*, ed. Philip Fisher (Berkeley: University of California Press, 1991), p. 76.
11. Walt Whitman, *The Complete Poems*, ed. Francis Murphy (Harmondsworth: Penguin, 1975), pp. 63, 80.
12. 'One's-self I sing', ibid., p. 37.
13. Fisher, op. cit., p. 81. This astonishing version of the idea of the 'melting pot' allows Fisher to account also for the failure of Marxism in the United States, since as a critical philosophy Marxism depends precisely on the perception of difference and division, and thus on the social critic who will voice an alternative from outside the accepted public space; a position inimical to the unities of 'democratic social space'.
14. Ibid., p. 89.
15. See the discussion of Jefferson's ideas along these lines in Thomas Bender, 'New York as a centre of "Difference"' in *In Search of New York*, ed. Jim Sleeper (New Jersey: Transaction Publishers, 1989), pp. 23–9. Bender concludes, 'The great defender of democracy based on sameness, Jefferson could find no way to accommodate difference' p. 25.
16. *The Complete Poems*, op. cit., p. 192.
17. D.H. Lawrence famously objected to Whitman's 'merging', based on his confusion of 'sympathy' with 'love'; of 'feeling with', for 'feeling for' in 'Whitman', *Studies In Classic American Literature* (1924; London: Mercury Books, 1965), pp. 154–68. Ezra Pound also had difficulty with Whitman's influence; he was 'America's poet . . . His crudity

is an exceeding great stench, but it *is* America . . . . The vital part of my message taken from the sap and fibre of America, is the same as his', *Selected Prose 1909–1965* (London: Faber, 1973), p. 115. Clearly both responses register a sense of unwanted proximity and physical contact. My own view is that Whitman's comradely adhesion no more represents a model for democracy than the impersonal comradeship of traditional Left politics.

18. Fisher, op. cit., p. 108.
19. *The Complete Poems*, op. cit., pp. 485–6.
20. Paul Zweig writes that 'the world he celebrated was fading'. The artisan, Whitman's chief point of reference in the world of labour 'was being replaced by the factory worker' and repetitive labour practices, long known and deplored by English social critics, *Walt Whitman. The Making of the Poet* (Harmondsworth: Penguin, 1986), p. 138.
21. *The Complete Poems*, op. cit., p. 67.
22. Ibid., p. 76.
23. Ibid., p. 74.
24. Ibid., p. 79.
25. *Specimen Days*, quoted Andrews, op. cit., p. 185.
26. Dorothy Norman, *Alfred Stieglitz: An American Seer* (New York: Aperture, 1990), p. 45.
27. See on Stieglitz and the photography of skyscrapers the discussion in Thomas Bender and William R. Taylor, 'Culture and Architecture: Some Aesthetic Tensions in the Shaping of Modern New York City' in *Visions of the Modern City*, ed. William Sharpe and Leonard Wallock (New York: Proceedings of the Heyman Center for the Humanities, Columbia University, 1983), pp. 200–3, 211. Alan Trachtenberg and Sam Bass Warner have pointed out how the photography of skyscrapers aesthetised the buildings, introducing distance and order where there was perceived disruption. Trachtenberg examines an essay by the journalist Alfred Corbin on Stieglitz's work in these terms, 'Image and Ideology: New York in the Photographers Eye', *Journal of Urban History*, 10 (1984): 453–64. The 'skyline photographers', says Warner, turned the 'corporate towers' of capitalism, into 'art objects', thus solving the 'conflict between the democratic and capitalistic elements of contemporary ideology' – 'The management of Multiple Urban Images' in *The Pursuit of Urban History*, ed. Derek Fraser and Anthony Sutcliffe (London: Edward Arnold, 1983), p. 393.
28. If this is thought to be unduly harsh on Whitman, he was pleased to see himself 'in all people', *Complete Poems*, op. cit., p. 82, and was as enthralled by the 'complicated business genius . . . all this mighty, many-threaded wealth and industry' of Wall Street as by any of the other sights of the city – *Democratic Vistas* in *Walt Whitman. Leaves of Grass and Selected Prose*, ed. and introduced by John Kouwenhoven (New York: Random House, 1950), p. 469.
29. *The Complete Poems*, op. cit., p. 191.
30. Charles Dickens, *American Notes* (1842; Oxford: Oxford University Press, 1987), p. 90.
31. Henry James, *The American Scene*, Introduction and Notes by Leon Edel (1907; London: Rupert Hart-Davis, 1968), pp. 73, 76.

32. Ibid., pp. 121–2.
33. Ibid., pp. 82–3.
34. The opening of *Moby Dick* (1851) shows how alive Melville was to the mid-century transformation of New York from a mercantile into an administrative centre summarised above:

> There is now your insular city of the Manhattoes, belted around by wharves . . . commerce surrounds it with her surf . . . . Look at the crowds of water-gazers there . . . . What do you see? – Posted like silent sentinels all around the town, stand thousands upon thousands of mortal men fixed in ocean reveries . . . . But these are all landsmen; of week days pent up in lath and plaster – tied to counters, nailed to benches, cliched to desks . . . .
> (*Moby Dick*, Harmondsworth: Penguin, 1993, pp. 21–2)

35. *The Complete Poems*, op. cit., p. 86.
36. Herman Melville, *Billy Budd, Sailor and Other Stories*, ed. Harold Beaver (Harmondsworth: Penguin, 1967), p. 67.
37. Ibid., p. 78.
38. In his longest verbal exchange with his employer Bartleby responds to ideas of alternative employment with the words, 'I like to be stationary . . . I would prefer not to make any change at all' (p. 94). For some readers this suggests his absolute identification with Wall Street. However, we should remember that the narrator himself feels this most of all when he discovers Bartleby occupying his office on a Sunday. Bartleby abstains from Wall Street's weekday hurry and business.
39. *The Complete Poems*, op. cit., p. 80.
40. Ibid., p. 191.
41. Henry Louis Gates Jr writes, 'So, it's only when we're free to explore the complexities of our hyphenated American culture that we can discover what a genuinely common American culture might actually look like. Is multiculturalism un-American? Herman Melville – canonical author and great white male – didn't think so. As he wrote in *Redburn*, "We are not a narrow tribe, no . . .: We are not a nation, so much as a world"', 'Good-bye, Columbus? Notes on the Culture of Criticism', *American Literary History*, 4 (Winter 1991): 713. See, for the other references here, Aldon Lynn Nielson, *Reading Race. White American Poets and the Racial Discourse in the Twentieth Century* (Athens and London: University of Georgia Press, 1988), pp. 2, 134; Irving Howe, *Selected Writings* (New York: Harcourt, Brace, Jovanovitch, 1990), pp. 115, 334; Ishmael Reed, 'An Interview with Ishmael Reed', *Over Here*, 9: 2 (Winter, 1989): 79.
42. Bourne's example is Jules Romains and the Unanimistes. Romains, he suggests, is Whitman 'industrialised, and . . . sociologised', *The Radical Will*, op. cit., pp. 520, 522, 523.
43. 'Trans-National America', ibid., pp. 248, 250, 258.
44. 'The Life of Irony', ibid., pp. 135, 136–7.
45. Henry James, quoted in Noel Stock *The Life of Ezra Pound* (London: Penguin, 1974), p. 142.
46. 'What I feel about Walt Whitman' in *Selected Prose, 1909–1965*, ed.

William Cookson (London: Faber, 1973), p. 115, and *Patria Mia and The Treatise on Harmony* (London: Peter Owen, 1962), pp. 31, 45.

47. Ibid., p. 47.
48. *Selected Prose*, op. cit., p. 115.
49. Ibid.
50. Quoted in Charles Norman, *Ezra Pound A Biography* (London: MacDonald, rev. edn, 1969), p. 69.
51. *Literary Essays of Ezra Pound*, ed. and introduced by T.S. Eliot (London: Faber, 1960), p. 224.
52. Ibid., pp. 218, 296.
53. 'To Whistler, American', *Collected Shorter Poems* (London: Faber, 1968), p. 251.
54. *Literary Essays*, op. cit., p. 295.
55. Quoted in Hutchins, *Ezra Pound's Kensington* (London: Faber, 1965), p. 47.
56. *Patria Mia*, op. cit., p. 46.
57. Ibid., pp. 24, 31.
58. Ibid., pp. 14, 18, 19.
59. *Collected Shorter Poems*, op. cit., p. 74.
60. See my *A Student's Guide to the Selected Poems of Ezra Pound* (London: Faber, 1979), pp. 61–7.
61. See Stock, op. cit., p. 118.
62. Sergej Esenin, *An Iron Mirgorod*, in O.P. Hasty and S. Fusso (eds, *America Through Russian Eyes* (New Haven: Yale University Press, 1988), pp. 148, 149.
63. Kouwenhoven (ed.), op. cit., p. 441.
64. Maxim Gorky, *City of the Yellow Devil*, in Hasty and Fusso, op. cit., pp. 128–43.
65. Ibid., p. 149.
66. *Patria Mia*, op. cit., p. 20.
67. Ibid., p. 19. The *locus classicus* of this response occurs a decade and a world later in Nick Carraway's remark in the famous passage from *The Great Gatsby* – to which I return below – that 'The city seen from Queensboro Bridge is always the city seen for the first time, in its first wild promise of all the mystery and the beauty in the world' – Scott Fitzgerald, *The Great Gatsby* (1926; Harmondsworth: Penguin, 1990), p. 67.
68. *Patria Mia*, op. cit., p. 42.
69. *The American Scene*, op. cit., p. 86.
70. Mabel Dodge's remarks appeared in *Camera Work* (June 1913) 7; quoted Bram Dijkstra, *Cubism, Stieglitz and the Early Poetry of William Carlos Williams* (Princeton: Princeton University Press, 1969), p. 25. On T.S. Eliot's lonely wanderings and anguished night-time vigils in Paris around 1911, see Lyndall Gordon, *Eliot's Early Years* (Oxford: Oxford University Press, 1977), Chapter 3.
71. Douglas Tallack, *Twentieth-Century America. The Intellectual and Cultural Context* (Harlow: Longman, 1991), p. 156.
72. On the 'Lyrical Left' see John Patrick Diggins, *The Rise and Fall of the American Left* (New York and London: Norton and Co., 1992), pp. 93–144, and Tallack, op. cit., pp. 147–65.

73. Reported in Tallack, ibid., p. 83.
74. For some discussion of the Armory Show and the context of American painting see Tallack, ibid., pp. 78–113; and Paul Oliver 'Visual America' in *Modern American Culture: An Introduction*, ed. Mick Gidley (Harlow: Longman, 1993), pp. 287–311.
75. Vladimir Mayakovsky, 'My Discovery of America' in Hasty and Fusso (eds), op. cit., pp. 169, 191, 197.
76. Comments to this effect run through the essay, but see ibid., pp. 186, 187, 192–3, 199, 204.
77. Vladimir Mayakovsky, *Poems* (Moscow: Progress Publishers, 1972), pp. 57–9.
78. Ibid., p. 59.
79. 'My Discovery', op. cit., p. 206.
80. Ibid., p. 207.
81. Ibid., p. 208.
82. Malcolm Cowley, *Exile's Return* (New York and London: Viking Penguin, 1951), especially Chapters 6 and 7. He had learned in Europe under the influence of the avant-garde and Soviet writers, he says, to be 'enthusiastic over America', but returned to a city 'where Dada was hardly a name' and where writers had only three justifications for their work: 'to make money, or to get their name in the papers, or because they were drunk' (p. 170).
83. Ibid., p. 292.
84. Melvyn Landsberg, *Dos Passos's Path to 'USA'. A Political Biography 1912–36* (Boulder: Colorado University Press, 1971), pp. 117, 156, 184.
85. 'What Makes a Novelist' in Donald Pizer (ed.), *John Dos Passos. The Major Non-Fictional Prose* (Detroit: Wayne State University Press, 1988), pp. 271–2. See also 'Translator's Foreword to *Panama* (by Blaise Cendrars)', where Dos Passos links the modernist and avant-garde explosion in the arts with the October revolution and Einstein's physics (ibid., pp. 134–5).
86. John Dos Passos, *Manhattan Transfer* (1925; Harmondsworth: Penguin, 1986), p. 327. Further page references are given in the text.
87. Thomas Bender and William R. Taylor discuss this distinction between skyscrapers as symbols of corporate wealth and the monumental style of public buildings, or the lower storeys of buildings, which they associate with a sense of civic responsibility, 'Culture and Architecture: Some Aesthetic Tensions in the Shaping of Modern New York City', in *Visions of the Modern City*, ed. William Sharpe and Leonard Wallock (New York: The Heyman Society, The University of Columbia, 1983), pp. 185–215.
88. See Lionel Trilling, 'The America of John Dos Passos' in Allen Belkind (ed.), *Dos Passos: The Critics and the Writer's Intention* (Carbondale: Southern Illinois University Press, 1971), p. 35. See also in the same volume, essays by Marshall McLuhan and J.P. Sartre, and the discussion by Diana McCormick, *The City as Catalyst. A Study of Ten Novels* (New York: Associated University Press Inc., 1979), pp. 141–57.
89. John Dos Passos, *USA* (1938; Harmondsworth: Penguin, 1973),

Preface, p. 7. The three volumes, *The 42nd Parallel, Nineteen Nineteen* and *The Big Money* were separately published in 1930, 1932, 1936. Further page references are given in the text.

90. See the essay 'Young Spain' in Pizer (ed.), op. cit., pp. 39–47.
91. Quoted Landsberg, op. cit. See his account, pp. 154–60.
92. Barbara Foley, 'History, Fiction, and Satirical form: the Example of Dos Passos's *1919*', *Genre*, XII (Fall, 1979): 364–5, 367–8.
93. Ibid., p. 369. See Dos Passos's essay welcoming the 'satirist and moralist' George Grosz to the United States in 1936, in Pizer (ed.), op. cit., p. 177.
94. Foley, op. cit., p. 372, my italics. See comments above on Randolph Bourne's association of the ironic attitude – alive to contrasts, incongruities and values (things 'as they are' and 'ought to be') – with the democratic ideal. Significantly too, Walter Benjamin at one point characterises Marx's writings as satirical: 'Marx who was the first to illuminate the debased and mystified relations between men in capitalist society, thereby became a teacher of satire and he was not far from becoming a master of it', *Understanding Brecht* (London: New Left Books, 1973), p. 84.
95. Foley – I think mistakenly – associates this 'Marxist' approach with the synchronic analysis of structuralism – which is not to say that Dos Passos is not sometimes more 'structuralist' than 'Marxist'. Pizer suggests Dos Passos's technique is 'cubist'; '*USA* as a whole', he concludes, 'is like a cubist painting at the height of the movement' – Donald Pizer, *Dos Passos's USA, A Critical Study* (Charlottesville: University of Virginia Press, 1988), p. 54. Again, for the most part, the flat juxtapositions or centrifugal display of material in *USA* do not deserve this description.
96. 'Whither the American Writer?' 1932, in Pizer (ed.), op. cit., p. 150.
97. Townsend Ludington (ed.), *The Fourteenth Chronicle. Letters and Diaries of John Dos Passos* (Boston: Gambit Incorporated, 1973), p. 465.
98. Ibid., p. 514.
99. Ibid., p. 443. See also the biography of Veblen in *USA*, 'The Bitter Drink', op. cit., pp. 806–15.
100. Ibid., p. 459.
101. Ibid., pp. 533, 579.
102. 'The Writer as Technician' (1935) in Pizer (ed.), op. cit., p. 172.
103. Ludington, op. cit., p. 436.
104. Dos Passos commented, 'I think there is such a thing as straight writing . . . . A writer who writes straight is the architect of history', Pizer (ed.), op. cit., p. 147.
105. Of the later work, *Midcentury* (1961) returned to the methods of *USA* but contained no 'Camera Eye' sections, thus omitting their imagistic, indirectly autobiographical and, some have said, 'feminine' aspect.
106. Quoted in *Envisioning America. Prints, Drawings and Photographs by George Grosz and his Contemporaries, 1915–1933* (Harvard: Catalogue of the Busch-Reisinger Museum, Harvard University, 1990), p. 14.
107. Ibid., p. 10. The poem 'Song of the Golddiggers' is quoted, p. 63.
108. Heartfield remained a member of the Communist Party and never went to the United States. In this respect, and in his politicised use

of mass-produced materials, his work contrasts with the unique '*objets trouvés*' of Duchamp. In visual art the closest comparison to Heartfield in the United States might be Stuart Davis. Tallack suggests Davis's position on art and politics was close to Brecht's, *Twentieth-Century America*, op. cit., p. 96.

109. Bertolt Brecht, *Poems, 1913–1956*, ed. John Willett and Ralph Manheim (London: Eyre Methuen, 1981), p. 171.

110. Ibid., p. 382.

111. Frederic Ewen, *Bertolt Brecht: His Life, his Art, and his Times* (New York: The Citadel Press, 1969), p. 385.

112. Ibid., p. 392. Ewen gives sections of the unfinished poem on p. 294.

113. Cited Tallack, op. cit., p. 190.

114. 'Hounded out by seven nations', *Poems*, op. cit., p. 383. This translation is by Frederic Ewen, op. cit., p. 385.

115. See Terry A. Cooney, *The Rise of the New York Intellectuals. 'Partisan Review' and its Circle* (Madison: University of Wisconsin Press, 1986), pp. 53 and 287, n. 50.

116. See Tallack, op. cit., pp. 186–8 and the major assessment of *Partisan Review* and the New York Intellectuals' Trotskyite affiliations in Alan M. Wald, *The New York Intellectuals. The Rise and Decline of the Anti-Stalinist Left from the 1930s to the 1980s* (Chapel Hill and London: University of North Carolina Press, 1987).

117. Tallack, op. cit., p. 224. I am indebted in these paragraphs to his discussion. See pp. 193–8 and 243–50. Many of these figures, as Tallack points out, were members of the American Committee for Cultural Freedom in the early 1950s, as were William Phillips and John Dos Passos.

118. Bell, *The End of Ideology. On the Exhaustion of Ideas in the Fifties* (1962), quoted Tallack, ibid., p. 228. See Howard Brick, *Daniel Bell and the Decline of Intellectual Radicalism* (Madison: University of Wisconsin Press, 1986).

119. Herbert Marcuse, *One-Dimensional Man* (Boston: Beacon Press, 1966), p. xvi.

120. Quoted Tallack, op. cit., p. 227.

121. Thomas Pynchon, *Gravity's Rainbow* (London: Pan, 1978), p. 703.

122. See Fredric Jameson's discussion of the 'conspiracy' films of the 1970s and 1980s in 'Part One; Totality as Conspiracy' of *The Geopolitical Aesthetic. Cinema and Space in the World System* (Bloomington, Indiana: Indiana University Press and London: BFI, 1992). In a film such as *The Parallax View* (1974) the manipulating power-seeking enemy is the unseen but, one suspects, American face of corporate business.

123. Interestingly, this moment gave rise to a double act of definition, not only amongst those who welcomed the new popular or counterculture (Leslie Fiedler and Susan Sontag, for example – both renegades from the New York Intellectuals) and thus anticipated the fuller accounts of postmodernism, but from liberal-Left critics (Harry Levin, Irving Howe and others) who were provoked to define modernism at the very moment when its associated set of literary and cultural values seemed at greatest risk. In this climate the radicalism of *Partisan Review* could begin very rapidly to look stuffy and academic.

See 'Introduction' to Peter Brooker (ed.), *Modernism/Postmodernism* (Harlow: Longman, 1992), pp. 9–11.

124. Paul Maltby, *Dissident Postmodernists. Barthelme, Coover, Pynchon* (Philadelphia: University of Pennsylvania Press, 1991), pp. 150–1.
125. Ibid., pp. 152–3.
126. Donald Barthelme, *Sixty Stories* (New York: Dutton, 1981), p. 57. Further references to this story and to others in the same volume are given in the text.
127. 'After Joyce', *Location*, 1 (1964): 13–14.
128. Randolph Bourne, op. cit., p. 135.
129. Ibid., p. 136.
130. Ibid., p. 138.

CHAPTER THREE

Fellow Modernists in Postmodern Times

In this fiction of truth, 'America' would be the title of a new novel
on the history of deconstruction and the deconstruction of history.
(Jacques Derrida, *Memoires for Paul de Man*)

WHAT'S LEFT? OLD, NEW AND POSTMODERNIST

The Left under capitalism seems destined to shift between moods of
hope and despair. Some moods, however, last longer than others. In
the 1960s, after the cold war had induced a long bout of paranoia,
retreat and reaction into large sections of the Old Left, the New
Left discovered a remarkably sustained optimism of both will and
intellect. Its new constituencies of students, blacks and women were
mobilised around an unfolding and unheard of agenda of civil rights
agitation, anti-war protest, democracy in education and equality for
women. The political excitement of the decade persuaded many,
Paul Buhle amongst them, that this was 'the best moment of our
lives'.[1] Unprecedented numbers of protestors joined in campus and
street demonstrations (some 400,000 in 1967 and around 50 per
cent of US students on 80 per cent of campuses in 1970 following
President Nixon's announcement of the invasion of Cambodia in
April and the killing of four Kent State University students in May).[2]

By common consent, the shock of all of this had fizzled out by
the early years of the next decade, and weakened further over the
next twenty years. For in the usual history the tale of the newness
of the New Left is a story also of its defeat. Internal factionalism and

the shapelessness of mass support meant that by the early 1970s the student and black protest movements, especially, had lost coherence and direction; their energies – already sapped by the assassinations of Malcolm X, Martin Luther King and the Kennedys – slowed to a halt by the withdrawal of US troops from Vietnam in 1972. Tom Hayden, one-time leader of Students for a Democratic Society, and main author of the famous 'Port Huron Statement' in 1962, became State representative for Santa Monica. Jerry Rubin, one-time street-fighter and supporter of Castro turned to money-making on Wall Street. Susan Sontag, the author in 1968 of 'Trip to Hanoi', an essay sympathetic to the North Vietnamese, spoke in New York in 1982 against communism and in favour of the Polish 'Solidarity' movement. John Diggins adduces changes of heart and mind such as these as evidence of a general process of compromise and co-option through the 1970s and 1980s, as former radicals fell like dominoes into the arms of the institutions they had excoriated.[3] Campuses that were once the site of sit-ins, ferment and freedom became the haven of the academic Left, whose readings of Gramsci, Critical Theory and French post-structuralism conducted them, Diggins believes, to the impasse of a sceptical textualism or, at best, on to the shaky bridge spanning 'the American idea' and deconstructionism:

> The American Left stands with one foot planted firmly on the
> Declaration and the other caught in the quicksand of deconstruction.
> . . . One half of the Left relies upon self-evident truths from
> which freedom derives, the other half denies the existence of an
> autonomous self and posits instead history as the story of precisely
> the opposite vision of the Enlightenment – the self's relentless
> subjection to domination by structures of power.[4]

Diggins sees the solution to these divided loyalties in a return to American pragmatism, in the traditions of William James, John Dewy and in the present period, Richard Rorty. Behind such figures, in an important distinction, he discovers the scepticism of the Scottish and American Enlightenments; representing a turn of mind quite different from the predominantly French tradition critiqued by the Frankfurt School and by post-structuralism. The academic Left, meanwhile, Diggins sees as a homogenous bloc, safely tenured in the ivory tower of theory and uniformly out of touch. Leaving aside the general issue this raises of the role of ideas or of theory in academic and social life, it is quite possible to take a different view of the New Left. It is quite clear, for example, that there have been changes within academic institutions themselves in the last twenty years, in matters of recruitment and curriculum innovation (the growth of women's studies, of black and African-American studies, for example, and the advent of cultural studies) which would have been impossible but for the inspiration of the 1960s. At the same time, we might see readings in Gramsci or Foucault or Derrida or Cixous, or indeed Rorty, as having generated debate and difference rather than sameness. Where Diggins sees compromise we might see continuity and effective change; where he sees obscurantism we might see the politicisation of intellectual life.

Or we might see both. For in a fuller picture, by the moment of the New Left's official disappearance, the cultural and political world, indeed the understanding of culture and politics, had changed radically and irretrievably, largely as a result of its actions. Whatever the fortunes and career choices of former individual activists, that is to say, the widespread perception in the 1960s themselves of entering upon a new era had been a true one. For Jerry Rubin this had felt like the difference between Stalin and supermarkets.[5] Paul Buhle, recalling the experience of 'We New Left Marxists', puts it as follows:

> the Old Left intellectuals' loss of realistic hope had been at least accompanied, perhaps (they always thought) even caused by the spread of mass culture. They were the last generation to revere, above all things, European high culture and the printed word. We were the first generation of American radicals born into the television era and the all-embracing mass culture. We thought in terms dictated by our surroundings. . . . The media invasion of the mind, worse to Old Left intellectuals than the nuclear arms race, had become part of our assumed reality and one of the rare sources for subversive signals.[6]

While the Old Left adhered, in other words, to a (European) modernist practice which typically assumed a transcendent set of cultural and political criteria, the New Left found itself, existentially and politically, within the new networks of mass culture. As the media invasion advanced, so, in a now familiar account of this episode, modernism surrendered to an institutionalised orthodoxy, the avant-garde fell prone to instant reproduction and commodification, and the modern political project sank slowly and then once and for all with the failure of communism in the late 1980s. Buhl greets the fall of high into low culture as analogous to the end of divisions between mental and manual labour and as necessary to an understanding of history 'for the *first* time'.[7] Even if we do not share this view, we realise that the 1960s were a transitional period in a broader and more long-term sense than the particular events of those years might suggest. If the detail of incidents and issues receded the massification of culture advanced, accompanied by a new political style and orientation. As notions of the 'political' were redefined, so issues of race, sexuality and gender became matters of consistent principle, tied in with the forms and effects of everyday life in an advanced consumer and media society.

The growth of mass society, plus, in the post-1960s era, the new intellectual and theoretical interests in power and ideology which Diggins points us to, invited a move away from the traditional concerns of political economy, labour markets and the mode of production to an analysis of modes of representation, consumption and communication. 'In modern society', writes Diggins, 'in a predominantly service economy run by computers and supported by data banks, men and women no longer work upon things to produce products. Access to knowledge and its transmission renders the "mode of information" the crucial institution of postindustrial society.'[8] What Diggins calls modern and postindustrial society others were already describing in the 1960s in the language of postmodernism. The 'Age of Eliot' was over, Leslie Fiedler announced in 1969, replaced by the popular culture of American youth with its science fiction, westerns and pornography.[9]

It was in the face of this emergent counterculture that what had overnight become a now traditional liberal–left intelligentsia was moved to define and defend 'modernism' – most revealingly as in the plangent title of Harry Levin's classic essay 'What was modernism?' (1960) – as a cultural mode that was slipping away at the very moment of its belated definition.[10] In his essay on 'The New York Intellectuals' (1967), published in the again significantly titled *Decline of the New* in 1970, Irving Howe concludes his case for a renewed 'liberalism' or 'democratic radicalism' with the sobering admonition that the 'usual condition' of the intellectual who chooses to defend 'the norms of rationality and intelligence . . . the standards of literary seriousness . . . the life of the mind as a humane dedication' will be that of 'a minority, even a beleaguered minority'.[11] This embattled defence of modernist literary and ethical values was of a piece with Howe's double disapproval of New Left hedonism and majority culture.[12] The New Left, that is to say, was identified with the new culture, and these together comprised, as we can now see, the first postmodern political movement: a new in the ascendant rather than in decline.

If this association spelled a disastrous surrender to vulgarising market values and 'parodic mimesis', in Howe's words,[13] in its own terms, the New Left was of course critical of US materialism and warmongering. As the name of the SDS implied, and the Port Huron statement made clear, the radical student body campaigned for the genuine democracy America still promised, in the face of the 'the Military–Industrial complex' it had become. We catch sight here of the fraught commitments shaping the hope and despair of future generations on the Left, bound within the freedoms of postmodern society. On the one hand the New Left's enthusiasm for the new media and popular culture, its sympathies for minorities, its involvement in Third World and ecological issues, its 'dispersed . . . multi-centred' narrative, as Tallack describes it,[14] anticipated much that has become characteristic of the Left agenda of the 1980s and 1990s (addressed by both the academic Left and by Left publications such as *Nation*, and *Dissent*, with which Howe continued a long and forceful association as editor). On the other hand, life within the all-embracing, ever-expanding walls of mass culture and American military and economic hegemony in this late capitalist phase has posed increasingly taxing problems of intellectual autonomy and political and artistic strategy. This was the problem raised in his own terms by Irving Howe, and, more awkwardly for the New Left, by a figure such as Adorno and the School of Social Research whose critique of the Enlightenment and of mass society was being popularised on American campuses at precisely the moment this society was effecting a contrary erosion of distinctions between high and low culture. How could a hatred for US capitalism and a love of American culture coexist? Gramsci, counter-hegemonic cultural politics and the transformation of the popular was one answer. Another, and in the United States this has appeared to have a stronger appeal, was supplied by versions of post-structuralism, since this offered a simultaneous critique of false totalities (as of capitalism) and of violent hierarchies (as of high and low culture). Hence, latterly, we might think, the attraction of the vocabulary of deconstruction, whose metaphors of decentring and hybridity, of the borderline and margin, so aptly describe the Left's attempt to sustain a critical position within and without late capitalism.

Paul Buhle suggests that the epicentre of the new theoretical activities of the academic Left was English, and that the work of Fredric Jameson seems best to personify this.[15] In effect, this is to say that Jameson is known principally as a leading commentator on postmodernism. Increasingly, we know postmodernism less as an ontological or cultural entity than a set of debates and positions; as a description of the postwar period, or phases within it, as a condition, a structure of feeling, an ideology and an aesthetic which has (inconveniently) progressed at different paces across the arts, various academic disciplines and world culture. In addition 'postmodernism' is of course a relational term, used to suggest a radical break or some degree of continuity with modernism or social modernity. There are consequently all kinds of reasons for being for or against it. Jameson, somewhat uniquely, is often both, and this makes him a symptomatic and instructive example of precisely the dilemmas of the American Left described above: an American Marxist receptive to trends in European post-structuralist theory whose findings challenge some of Marxism's fundamental assumptions. Amongst several direct descriptions of postmodernism in his work the following occurs in his account of the 1960s:

> Postmodernism is one significant framework in which to describe what happened to culture in the 60s, but a full discussion of this hotly contested concept is not possible here. Such a discussion would want to cover, among other things, the following features: that well-known poststructuralist theme, the 'death' of the subject (including the creative subject, the *auteur* or the 'genius'); the nature and function of a *culture of the simulacrum* (an idea developed out of Plato by Deleuze and Baudrillard to convey some specificity of a reproducible object world, not of copies or reproductions marked as such, but of a proliferation of trompe-l'oeil copies *without originals*); the relation of this last to media culture of the 'society of the spectacle' (Debord), under two heads: (1) the peculiar new status of the image, the 'material' or what might better be called the 'literal', signifier: a materiality or literality from which the older sensory richness of the medium has been abstracted (just as on the other side of the dialectical relationship, the old individuality of the subject and his/her 'brushstrokes' have equally been effaced); and (2) the emergence, in the work's temporality, of an aesthetic of *textuality* or what is often described as schizophrenic time; the eclipse, finally, of all depth, especially *historicity* itself, with the subsequent appearance of pastiche and nostalgia art (what the French call *la mode rétro*), and including the supersession of the accompanying models of depth-interpretation in philosophy (the various forms of hermeneutics, as well as the Freudian conception of 'repression', of manifest and latent levels).[16]

Many of the standard features of postmodernism appear here as they do in parallel and later accounts: principally the loss of the real, the loss of affect and the loss of historicity in a world of all-pervading pastiche and hyper-reality. Clearly this poses problems. If in a Baudrillardian scenario media society has undermined any common sense of a stable reality, if subjectivity and social identity are simply the latest products of a market economy, if the 'grand narratives' of the Enlightenment have lost credibility, as J.F. Lyotard contends, and if, above all, a predominantly service and information society has decimated the traditional working class then classical Marxism finds the broad planks on which it has stood sagging and slipping from under its feet.

For Jameson, this new disorientation is expressed metonymically by our experience of the new postmodern built environment (his prime example is the Bonaventure Hotel in Los Angeles) which stands in for our inability to comprehend this expanding all-encompassing totality of late capitalism. Finding ourselves lost in postmodern hyperspace is 'the symbol and analog of that even sharper dilemma which is the incapacity of our minds, at least at present, to map the great global multinational and decentred communicational network in which we find ourselves caught as individual subjects'.[17] His solution – to anticipate – is two-fold, and lies firstly in theorising postmodernism as the 'cultural dominant' of late capitalism, and in therefore attempting a dialectical reading which will identify its alternative and transgressive features, and secondly, in insisting on the totalising understanding conveyed by the activity of 'cognitive mapping' (however seemingly unmappable the object), which will make capitalism's newly invasive effects known and open to transformation.

Above all, Jameson's work raises the question of the possibility, or impossibility, of postmodern critique, or a critique of the postmodern ('cognitive mapping' he describes as a 'modernist strategy').[18] The older modernism assumed an antagonistic relation with society, its methods were 'critical, negative, contestatory, subversive, oppositional. . . . Can anything of the sort', asks Jameson, 'be affirmed about postmodernism and its social moment?'[19] These are important questions for many contemporary writers as well as for Left radicals within the academy and professions, and much of what I have to say in following chapters will relate to them. In this chapter I am more concerned to track Jameson's own thinking as a road taken on the American Left from the postmodern political moment of the 1960s. The theme of the loss of history and of the prospect of a postmodern political art I want to take up here in a discussion of the fiction of the New York novelist E.L. Doctorow, a writer Jameson refers to many times in relation precisely to these questions. Doctorow, I believe, provides in the event less a confirmation of Jameson's thinking than a comparison, a confirmation of difference.

Jameson considers the 'radical left-wing novelist' E.L. Doctorow, as he describes him, in both the key essay 'Postmodernism, or the cultural logic of late capitalism' and other surrounding statements.

Doctorow, he argues, presents a form of 'homeopathic' postmodernism: an attempt 'to undo postmodernism . . . by the methods of postmodernism' – a strategy, he says, which helps reconquer 'some genuine historical sense'.[20] Yet it is not clear what Jameson means to claim for Doctorow by this. For in the same interview he suggests that by turning the past into 'a black simulacrum', Doctorow shows us 'that this is the only image of the past we have'.[21] The extended discussion of Doctorow in the most recent version of the essay on 'the cultural logic of late capitalism' reinforces this second view, for here Jameson concludes that the historical novel 'can no longer set out to represent the historical past; it can only "represent" our ideas and stereotypes about that past (which thereby at once becomes "pop history")'.[22] On this reckoning, a 'genuine historical sense' becomes no more than an awareness that 'real history' is a mirage, 'forever out of reach' behind the degraded pop images and simulacra by which we know it.

Most of Jameson's discussion here is given over to the novel *Ragtime*, which in his view exemplifies this consequence of the loss of historicity. I want to consider this and other novels below. Meanwhile, Doctorow's more evidently political and fully 'historical' work from the earlier period is not *Ragtime* but the previous novel, *The Book of Daniel* (1971). Here, in fictionalising the case of the 'atom bomb spies', Julius and Ethel Rosenberg, Doctorow employs legal and other documentary material so as to provoke a sense of its fictionality alongside the more conventionally obvious fictional narrative. 'There is no history', he comments, 'except as it is composed . . . there is no fiction or non-fiction as we commonly understand the distinction: there is only narrative.'[23] Doctorow therefore quite consciously attempts – to adopt another vocabulary – to deconstruct the 'violent hierarchy' of historical fact and fiction. And indeed the novel's textualising effects might be appropriately glossed by reference to Jacques Derrida, or to Hayden White. Derrida's epigraph to the seminal essay 'Structure, Sign and Play in the Discourse of the Human Sciences' – the statement from Montaigne that 'we need to interpret interpretations more than to interpret things'[24] – is particularly apt, moreover, to the character Daniel, who follows his biblical namesake in assuming the office of interpreter of dreams and visions.

This affinity with deconstruction brings us already to the borders at least of the *politics* of representation, or of interpretation, engaging both fictional character and novelist in a critical hermeneutic which comes to question the more pessimistic view that a screen of pop images and stereotypes frustrates our access to history. At the same time Doctorow hangs a comparative exploration of the Old and New Left, and by implication of modernity and postmodernity, upon his interleaved deconstructive text. Daniel, what is more, as the interpreter now in Doctorow's novel of modern political and cultural myths (of which his parents are both source and object) brings a political concern and edge to the realm of textual narratives lacking in the arguments of Hayden White, and more often latent than pronounced in deconstruction. The key episode in this respect in *The Book of Daniel*, occurs, appropriately enough, in Disneyland, the final proof for Jean Baudrillard of the unabashed simulation of American life. Daniel's analysis proves, on the contrary, that Disneyland does not compute into a whole, undifferentiated society of autonomous simulacra. He sees Disney's 'relentless program of adaptation of literature, myth and legend as an attempt to escape [the] dark and rowdy conclusions of the genre';[25] its sanitised reductions of popular stories such as *Alice in Wonderland* and Mark Twain's *Huckleberry Finn* and *Life on the Mississippi* as producing a 'sentimental compression of something that is already a lie' (p. 294). These set the Disneyland customer (amongst whom there are noticeably small numbers of black people and Mexicans, and a total absence of 'long-haired youth, heads, hippies, girls in miniskirts, gypsies, motorcyclists'; p. 296) at a remove of 'two ontological degrees' from the original cultural artifacts and history (p. 294). 'What Disneyland proposes', Daniel concludes, 'is a technique of abbreviated shorthand culture for the masses . . . that insists at the same time on the recipient's rich psychic relation to his country's history and language and literature' (p. 295). Disneyland is seen, in short – in a judgement that plainly in no way submits to its effects – as a form of social control which reinforces a selective, ruling-class version of cultural history, sponsored by the multinational corporations Daniel notices offering shows and exhibits.

Through Daniel, Doctorow therefore offers a mode of supposedly impossible cultural critique which exposes surface to depth, the imitation to the original, and the false to the true. And this, as it turns out, is near neighbour to the 'ideological analysis' Jameson had proposed in *The Political Unconscious* as 'the appropriate designation for the critical "method" specific to Marxism',[26] Jameson's own Marxism is not without its tensions here, for while he is prepared to put the essentially post-structuralist case that, in his words, 'history is inaccessible to us except in textual form', he insists nevertheless that 'history . . . is *not* a text, for it is fundamentally non-narrative and non-representational'.[27] This is where Doctorow firstly, and profoundly, differs. In some way, for Jameson, there does appear to be a 'real history'; a level of 'Necessity' whose effects can make themselves truly felt. In this sense 'History', in his ringing axiom, 'is what hurts.'[28]

At first sight *The Book of Daniel* might seem to agree with this too. At the end of the novel the university where Daniel is working is closed by a student revolutionary committee, and he is forced to quit the library and thus enter a world beyond his 'book', and Doctorow's own: a world of non-textual experience where the interpreter and writer becomes a witness and possible actor. In fact, this ending retains the self-conscious textuality the novel has exhibited throughout, since what happens at 'the end', the literal close of the novel, is one of three endings and overtakes, we are asked to accept, an intended third ending which would have taken up the issues posed by the previous narrative. This 'final' ending implies neither a fall into the 'metaphysics of presence', nor that the undiluted 'real' of Jameson's capitalised 'History' will be met with the Marxist conviction he brings to it in *The Political Unconscious*. But nor does it concede that this world is composed of stereotypical images of the past substituting for its lost reality. Doctorow's novel shows rather that the world, and very acutely in the historical case study it fictionalises, is constructed out of different competing histories; that is to say, of interpretations and analyses of myths and ideologies, which bring with them different images or ideas of national identity and destiny. To re-enter the non-textual world at a point of confrontation between students and the authorities, as in the plot of the novel Daniel is about to do, confirms that this is to enter a world of power relations, of contestation, and therefore of different possible outcomes. It is to enter a world, in short, neither of continued pure textuality, nor of a starkly ultimate Reality, nor of simulacra, but of possible histories – possible further narratives – in the making. Daniel exits from the library accordingly to 'see what's going down' (p. 309).

The Book of Daniel can therefore be read as a postmodern novel, displaying the decentred subjectivity, hybrid discourse and open endings said to characterise this fiction, but as retaining a critical aspect and the assumption of a material yet textualised history, or better, of histories, which much post-structuralist and postmodern commentary would dispute. We might stop there in a reply to Jameson. Yet it is clear that this single novel, however instructive, cannot stand in for Doctorow's *oeuvre*, nor in itself be used to confirm or contradict scenarios of postmodernism. Firstly, because these are so broad and inconsistent, and secondly because, as is often pointed out, the periodisation of postmodernism remains problematic. Aside, on this issue, from the question of postmodernism's grounding in late capitalism (a proposition itself open to refinement and dispute), postmodernism is called upon to stretch across a period which runs from postwar affluence to yuppie boom, recession and wide unemployment; from the Cold War to the fall of communism; from CND to ANC; from flower-power and the Bomb to post-punk and global warming. No single literary text could possibly focus or represent these changes, nor illuminate in any really decisive way the most pressing but still general issues raised in Jameson's account: the possibility under postmodernism, that is to say, of retaining some critical distance; of gaining a narrative grasp upon the past, or in the political aspect of Jameson's 'cognitive mapping', of discovering an orientation and ways of acting in the world so as to counter the hegemony of late capitalism.

We should not be surprised if Doctorow's earlier and later fiction over a period of some thirty years discovers a different response to these issues. I want in what follows to comment on this fiction, with Jameson's readings still in mind, and to draw attention to a work, *Lives of the Poets*, which he ignores. Yet what is true of Doctorow is true also of Jameson. Postmodern positions, Jameson's included, have their own histories and conditions of possibility, as much as do fictional texts. I want therefore to track both writers' ideas and positions, not so much to set critic against novelist (or one critical reading against another, however inevitable this is) but to treat them alike, as figures on the American Left who have responded in the respective terms of their work to the challenges raised by this period. This approach might help us assess the postmodern period not only as a period of change, but in terms of the philosophical, political and narrative options this has presented to the American cultural Left, as Jameson has made us aware. Since, with one exception, Doctorow's fiction is set in New York, his writing offers a way too of thinking what form Jameson's guiding concept of 'cognitive mapping' might take in this emblematic metropolitan space.

FREDRIC JAMESON'S TORN HALVES

Jameson's ever-impressive cognitive adventure has taken him in the 1980s and 1990s into cultural debates on the Third World or postcolonialism, and the role of film rather than literature. At the same time, on another front, he greeted the new decade with a study of Theodore Adorno, announcing him as the new-found late Marxist for the period of late capitalism; the philosopher most 'consistent with and appropriate for the current postmodern age'.[29] With some weariness, *Late Marxism* turns away from a conventional biographical account and from the debate on Adorno's Marxist credentials and political opinions to stress the 'genuine praxis' of his restoration of sociology in the postwar Federal Democratic Republic and the contribution especially of his philosophy and aesthetics to an understanding of the mode of production. His originality in this respect, says Jameson, 'lies in his unique emphasis on the presence of late capitalism as a totality within the very forms of our concepts or of the works of art themselves'. His 'life's work', he adds, 'stands or falls with the concept of "totality"'.[30] Most strikingly, Jameson discovers in Adorno a social and cultural antidote, a 'counter-poison' to the plight of living under postmodernism. For in the 1980s, 'Adorno's prophecies of the "total system" came true'; the moment of his Marxism had belatedly arrived, bringing a resilient dialectical finesse and 'sense of doom and crisis' which 'may turn out to be just what we need today' to map ourselves differently across the flashy postmodern scene.[31]

This is at first sight an unexpected move. And indeed, writing in *Late Marxism* of changes in his own thinking in 'the stream of time', Jameson says that this has involved some change in his view of Adorno. This personal narrative is worth re-examining, however. Jameson calculates that his earlier 'increasing distance' from Adorno made itself felt in *Marxism and Form*, published in 1971. This study (which includes Jameson's most sustained earlier discussion of Adorno) predicts a fresh relevance for the newer 'relatively Hegelian kind of Marxism' appearing in American intellectual life. This 'postindustrial Marxism', as Jameson terms it, aims to theorise the questions raised particularly by monopoly capitalism. And here, Jameson argues 'the great themes of Hegel's philosophy – the relationship of part to whole, the opposition between concrete and abstract, the conception of totality, the dialectic of appearance and essence – are once again the order of the day'.[32]

There is a family resemblance, obviously enough, between the terms making Adorno appropriate in 1990 and Hegel 'the order of the day' close to twenty years earlier. (In *Late Marxism* Jameson also sees 'an impending Hegel revival, of a new kind'.)[33] More striking still is the fact that the socio-economic and political reality for which he finds an appropriate philsopher is, in both cases, by any other description, postmodernism. Thus in *Marxism and Form*, a good ten years before his most remarked upon commentaries on postmodernism, Jameson writes how in 'postindustrial monopoly capitalism' and in the United States particularly, 'we inhabit a dream world of artificial stimuli and televised experience . . . entangled in the sticky cobwebs of the false and unreal culture itself with its ideological mystification on every level' (p. xviii). We were, it seems, as politically and spatially disorientated in the early 1970s as in the 1980s and 1990s. Thus, 'our experience is no longer whole; we are no longer able to make any felt connection between the concerns of private life, as it follows its own course within the walls and confines of the affluent society, and the structural projections of the system in the outside world' (pp. xvii–xviii). The political activist was similarly at a loss. Thus, the heroic 'street-fighter or urban guerrilla' of the 1960s had become uncertain 'precisely where the street *is* in the superstate, and indeed, whether the old-fashioned street as such still exists in the first place in the seamless web of marketing and automated production which makes up the new state' (p. xviii). Meanwhile, the mystifications perpetuated by the media and advertising had, in Frankfurt School style, brought an 'increasing occultation of the class structure' (p. xvii). The consequence of this enforced suspension of direct political action was, so Jameson reasoned, a period of theoretical advance and refinement.

Marxism and Form does not sound very far off in all this from Adorno's obsession, as Jameson recalls it later, 'with the doom and baleful enchantment of the "total system"'.[34] His description of Adorno in the earlier text as 'perhaps the finest dialectical intelligence, the finest stylist, of them all' (p. xiii) would also fit quite comfortably into the arguments of *Late Marxism*. Above all, he sees the present moment as once more a theorising interregnum; as a time when what were once 'powerful and oppositional political currents . . . are themselves quiescent'.[35]

There is some reason, therefore, for thinking of Jameson's 'return' rather than of his 'turn' to Adorno in 1990; though not to suggest an undeviating continuity in his work. A sign of the 'increasing distance' from Adorno he later associates with *Marxism and Form* appeared, if not at that time, then, in one example, in his views on the Brecht–Lukács debate some half a dozen years after this study. In this essay he describes Adorno's proposals for the political virtues of an autonomous modernist art as an 'aesthetics, under the spell of a political and historical despair that plagues both houses and finds praxis henceforth unimaginable'.[36] He turns here instead – unfashionably in the Brechtian hey-day of the 1970s – to Lukács who, suitably revised, 'may be . . . has some provisional last word for us today'.[37]

Yet, given Jameson's abiding concern, as he puts it here, with 'our cognitive relationship with the social totality', this more Lukàcsian and less Adornian moment amounts to little more than a swerve in the stream of his Hegelian Marxism. The more significant change, and one Jameson does not draw attention to in *Late Marxism*, appears later still, at the end of the decade and into the early 1980s, in *The Political Unconscious* (1981). For here Jameson shifted quite dramatically from a commitment to the concept of expressive totality to the anti-Hegelianism of Althusser's theory of structural causality, a move which in *Fables of Aggression* (1979) received its accompanying Macheryan literary analysis.[38] *The Political Unconscious* strengthens and extends Althusser's interpretative method, drawing upon Freud, Northrop Frye, Kenneth Burke, Greimas and Lévi-Strauss at the same time as it parries and adopts positions in post-structuralism. The result is a remarkable event in the development of American Marxist criticism. Yet this produces its own problems. As J.A. Bertoud points out, Jameson does not resolve the difficulty of applying Althusser's notion of history as 'a process without a subject' to the reading of subjectively motivated authorial projects; namely the novels the book examines.[39] Nor does he succeed in reconciling the Althusserian conception of history as 'absent cause' with the more traditional sense he wishes to retain of 'History' as master text and point of ultimate material necessity (the idea of History as 'what hurts').[40]

Effectively, Jameson's answer to these dilemmas was simply to steer away from the Althusserian model. (By *Late Marxism* he says that Adorno not Althusser had influenced the proposal of 'levels' of the political, social and economic in *The Political Unconscious*).[41] And, in fact, as Dowling's commentary on *The Political Unconscious* suggests, Jameson's use of the concept of 'mediation' had already re-introduced a more Lukácsian concept of the social totality in that text.[42] He turns, that is to say, to the true pole-star of an older Marxism. In whatever guise – as 'the mode of production', 'late capitalism', 'postmodernism', or simply 'society' or 'the economic system' – the concept of the social totality appears as the most profoundly consistent aspect of Jameson's thinking: both its driving impulse and the source of major frustrations. It is this of course which he seeks to map throughout his work, adopting in turn the methods of 'metacommentary', 'transcoding', 'allegory' or 'stereoscopy', so as to navigate the dialectical relations within the totality of particular to general, non-identity and identity, contingency and necessity, text

93

and history. In this way he hopes, he says, to avoid the charge of 'synthesizing and "Hegelian" . . . all inclusionary system building'.[43] Yet even as he does so, he is pulled increasingly in another direction, towards the blankness of the postmodern sublime, as late capitalism further engorges the world, rendering the totality 'unimaginable', and so dumbfounding the map-maker.[44]

The effects of this were becoming particularly acute in this same period of the late 1970s and early 1980s. For a figure such as Lukács, as Neil Larson points out, adopting the 'stand-point of the proletariat' in the logic of a fully partisan traditional Marxism supplied the epistemological ground from which the social and historical totality would become knowable.[45] Without a confident grounding of this kind the totality will remain unmappable, since the 'dialectical and historical self-consciousness' which would conceive it has neither home nor agency. The consequence is a disembodied (Larson says Hegelian) form of dialectical thinking as self-conscious reflection and the conception of 'History' as absolute and hypostatised limit, the bottom line of 'Necessity'. This is the position Jameson takes in *The Political Unconscious*, but it is fraught with philosophical and political problems. As Larson puts it, this is a 'History' that 'in its very fateful and transcendent agency, seems to have severed itself from the real forces, agents, and events to which the concept is simultaneously held to refer'.[46]

Jameson might reply that he is invoking new agencies of social transformation in *The Political Unconscious*, in response both to critics of the concept of totality and the intense social fragmentation in the United States which has made united political action on the Left so difficult:

> Ethnic groups, neighbourhood movements, feminism, various 'countercultural' or alternative life-style groups, rank-and-file labour dissidence, students' movements, single-issue movements – all have in the United States seemed to project demands and strategies which were theoretically incompatible with each other and impossible to coordinate on any practical political basis. The privileged form in which the American left can develop today must therefore necessarily be that of alliance politics; and such a politics is the strict practical equivalent of the concept of 'totality' in the American framework means the undermining and the repudiation of the only realistic perspective in which a genuine Left could come into being in this country.[47]

Jameson's insistence ('must therefore necessarily be', 'strict' equivalence, 'only realistic perspective', and so on), plus the fact that this important argument is crammed into a (longer) footnote, reveal more frustration than conviction. Where he finds an equivalence between alliance politics and the totality, others will find precisely the opposite: the confirmation of difference and an ever-receding social whole. In fact, it is exactly here, in this lack of obvious fit between a totalising model and the social forms he describes, between a 'Hegelian' theoretical commitment and a 'postmodern' social perception, that the source for much of Jameson's subsequent theoretical manoeuvring and political anxiety lies.

The social movements Jameson refers to had in many ways inherited the styles and tactics of the countercultural and protest movements of the 1960s. Larson suggests that the essay 'Periodising the 60s' is a key expression of Jameson's debt to this decade: his 'own testament to both a generation and a conjuncture, preconditioning his own somewhat later discursive moment'.[48] Elsewhere, Douglas Kellner argues that in his work as a whole Jameson remains 'true to the revolutionary spirit of the 1960s'.[49] It is surprising, therefore, to find that 'Periodising the 60s' (published in 1984, three years after *The Political Unconscious*, and at the same time as the keynote essays on postmodernism) more than anything admonishes the decade for its utopian delusions. Though the period is presented in a way that is consistent with an Althusserian concept of a decentred structural causality, Jameson's political judgments come from a quite different source. Thus he calls at the end of the essay for an effort in the 1980s 'on a world scale, to proletarianise all those unbound social forces' released by the 1960s, foreseeing 'the new vocation of a henceforth global capitalism' – very significantly in relation to the comments on alliance politics above – as being 'to unify the unequal, fragmented, or local resistances to the process'. This extension of unified class struggle will, what is more, solve the 'so-called crisis of Marxism', Jameson assures us, since '"traditional" Marxism, if "untrue" during this period of a proliferation of new subjects of history, must necessarily become true again'.[50]

There is nothing, really, in Jameson's previous studies or in his contemporary essays on postmodernism to prepare us for this visionary surge of class politics, whose Old Left 'revolutionary spirit' plainly runs counter, what is more, to the perceived spirit of the 1960s themselves. It is as if, indeed, a 'political unconscious' had risen to the surface, ready to take up the newly massed proletarian struggle, supplemented now by the unequal fragments and proliferating new subjects of history.

Jameson returns here then, with a vengeance, not to Hegel or Adorno, but to a 'traditional Marxism' associated with a proletarian standpoint and a negative conception of ideology as 'inverted consciousness' amenable to correction. As it turns out his writings do not adopt this conception of ideology, nor resume the noticeably mechanical, homologising, view of the unifying force of capitalism upon its opponents the essays expresses. Nor does he commit himself to the revolutionary rhetoric of this piece in his studies of postmodernism, or in *Late Marxism*. What follows in his writing, in the different logic of 'untraditional' Western Marxism described by Perry Anderson and in the felt absence of working-class solidarity and political activity, are the insights of 'class struggle at the level of theory', ideological intervention, and the self-conscious dialectical thinking of a critical and philosophical Marxism. It is at a very contemporary moment in this tradition and socio-political tendency that, for Jameson, Adorno becomes appropriate, or appropriate once more.

Two connected issues here – the legacies of Western Marxism and the 1960s in America – help further situate Jameson's thinking. Firstly, in drawing upon Adorno, at different points in his career, Jameson is aligning himself not simply with developments in Hegelian Marxism, but more selectively with the tradition of 'Critical Theory' associated with the Institute of Social Research or Frankfurt School. The School had transferred to New York in the 1930s but its effective life as a 'School' there had ended in the 1950s. At which point, though certain members of the School remained in the United States, it returned to Frankfurt under Adorno and Horkheimer. Douglas Kellner views Jameson's Hegelian–Lukácsian Marxism and his contemporary project of 'cognitive mapping' as paralleling that of the Frankfurt School in the earlier phase of the 1930s.[51]

Initially, as Kellner shows, the Institute had adopted a materialist social theory and mode of ideology critique, marked by an explicit concern with class society and oppression. By the 1930s this had been moderated into a less orthodox Marxism and was, in subsequent years, to undergo a further shift towards a post- or unMarxist accent and vocabulary, in reaction to the impact of European fascism and the growth of the 'administered society' in the United States.[52] In this history, Adorno, in particular, Kellner suggests, wavered in the 1950s and 1960s between concrete Marxist social analysis and philosophy and cultural criticism. Arguably, he discovers a more suggestive parallel with Jameson here than in the work of the 1930s. In *Late Marxism* at least (Kellner's comments were written prior to its appearance) Jameson suggests the value of Adorno's contribution to Marxism 'is not . . . to be sought in the area of social class' but in the contribution of his philosophy and aesthetics to an understanding of the economy, or mode of production.[53] Accordingly, he draws on later rather than earlier texts (*The Dialectic of Enlightenment*, 1947: translated 1972, *Negative Dialectics*, 1966. translated 1973; and *Aesthetic Theory*, 1984).

In general terms, too, Jameson's studies on postmodernism share the tones and themes of postwar social theory (the manipulative role of the mass media, transformations in postwar capitalism, the crisis in Marxism, and a loss of faith in the working class), even if it is right to see these themes as initiated by earlier work in Critical Theory. The whole burden of Adorno's negative dialectics is of course to resist the alienated and thoroughly administered society of the present, to refuse the blandishments of mass culture and wholesale commodification, and to defend an autonomous, authentic art whose virtues depend on subversive non-conformity or incomprehensibility, even silence. The rise of the New Right would seem to many to confirm the gloomier prognosis of the Frankfurt School theorists, and to further countenance the 'inviolable opposition' thought to reside in the avant-garde and the radical discourse of the academic Left. The result is a Marxism whose social criticism, once again, is transcoded into the realms of aesthetics and philosophy (the tendency Kellner sees in the Adorno of the 1950s and 1960s) and a politics of isolated pessimism and negativity, alleviated only by the fragile assurance of an indefinitely postponed 'reconciliation', when the false totality of the present will be abolished. Jameson's belief that there is little to no hope of concerted, direct political action in the present tempts him too in this direction.

Critical Theory does not produce an Adornian pessimism as its only and necessary outcome, however. There are marked differences between Jameson, for example, and other second- and third-generation 'Critical Theorists' such as Jürgen Habermas, Albrecht Wellmer, or Oscar Negt. In the United States, too, it is Kellner himself, interestingly enough, rather than Jameson, who has sought to revitalise the radicalism of this tradition in relation to contemporary cultural and political realities. His purpose, he says, in *Critical Theory, Marxism and Modernity*, is to 'present a case for the need to re-politicise Critical Theory today, while attempting to link it once again to socialist politics and the most advanced new social movements'.[54] In Adorno, Kellner detects a retreat from social theory and activism, a failure to analyse the developments of the 1960s, or to extend his concepts beyond this point:[55] more the Adorno, in short, of Jameson's comments in the earlier 1977 essay than of his *Late Marxism*. The rights and wrongs of such readings (though they are not a matter of indifference) are less significant, however, than the simple fact of their coexistence. We see, in other words, that it is possible to think differently on the American Left in the 1990s, even within the traditions of Critical Theory.

Theoretical divergencies of this kind have themselves been shaped by the events of social and political history; and of these the 1960s remain a key moment and touchstone. The important Frankfurt School philosopher in this context is less Adorno than Herbert Marcuse, whom Jameson indeed names as the representative thinker of the period.[56] His comments on Marcuse in 'Periodising the 60s' are therefore all the more bewildering. These occur in a section titled 'The adventures of the sign' and directly follow his description of the serial features of postmodernism quoted above. After praising Marcuse's introduction of the notion of the cultural 'sphere' in 'the great essay, "The Affirmative Character of Culture"' Jameson connects this with 'the possibility that in our own time this very autonomy of the cultural sphere (or level or instance) may be in the process of modification'.[57] This modification entails the separation of the sign from its referent:

> the inner convulsion of the sign is a useful initial figure of the process of transformation of culture generally, which must in some first moment (that described by Marcuse) separate itself from the 'referent' the existing social and historical world itself, only in a subsequent stage in the 60s, in what is here termed 'postmodernism', to develop further into some new and heightened, free-floating, self-referential 'autonomy'.[58]

Marcuse's views on the autonomy of art are in this way placed in a cultural narrative which ends with the Baudrillardian scenario of the floating postmodern signifier, when the usual history would read this back through structuralism rather than through any member of the Frankfurt School.[59] In fact, it would be more appropriate in periodising the 1960s to associate Marcuse less with a doctrine of autonomous art or culture than with a programme for the aesthetic affirmation of experience and the emancipation of the imagination from instrumental reason. It was this belief, after all, which most inspired the happenings, free love and flower-power of the counterculture. At the same time, Marcuse's critique of technological rationality and of the repression endemic to advanced industrial society was an influence on the more militantly active politics of the New Left. In this connection, both Kellner and Perry Anderson see Marcuse as a more consistently radical figure than any other contemporary member of the Frankfurt School: a thinker committed from the 1940s and 'for next three decades', in Kellner's view, to Marxist categories, while seeking a new vocabulary appropriate to the emerging social movements in the United States.[60]

Coupled with this radicalism, Marcuse had reconciled himself to American intellectual life and culture to a degree that the other main members of the Frankfurt School never did. Whereas he helped found and, with some reservations, endorsed the optimistic, liberationist rhetoric and cultural politics of the period, Adorno held aloof, relatively unconvinced by both Marxist class analysis and student radicalism. (Horkheimer meanwhile moved ever further to the Right in the postwar period). It is difficult, with this in mind, to resist setting the image of Marcuse addressing students in California on the limits of flower-power against the notorious episode of Adorno, now returned to Frankfurt, calling in the police to prevent what he mistakenly saw as a student sit-in there. Jameson describes this as a moment of 'deathless shame',[61] but prefers to pass on to the philosophical case for a postmodern negative dialectics. He therefore protects Adorno from any Brechtian-style 'crude thinking' on the proper relation between theory and political action just as, effectively and more perversely, his skewed, aestheticising presentation of Marcuse, sets him up as a target for exactly this in the essay 'Periodising the 60s'. The effect of this reading, along with Jameson's conclusions to the essay, is to administer in the end a double blow, both to the 1960s and (given the continuity Jameson contrives between them) the more hedonistic, Baudrillardian version of postmodernism. Herbert Marcuse, the 1960s pied-piping philosopher, is charged with having misled his children on to the paths of postmodern play, thus aiding and abetting a general distraction from class politics. From this perspective it becomes the task of those who have come later, in the here and now of the essay in the early 1980s, to proletarianise the United States as if from scratch, as capitalism calls in its bets and exacts its revenge.

The question of course is why Jameson should take this view of the 1960s at this time. The obvious explanation would be the movement's 'failure': the rapid splintering of what unity it possessed, and the subsequent retreat, incorporation and 'normalisation' of ex-hippies, student and black radicals mentioned above. One form of 'retreat' of course, in Diggins view, took former political radicals into the academy and the realms of radical theory. The fact that Althusser was to a marked degree associated through the notion of 'theoretical practice' with the style and agenda of this new academic Left, yet was rounded on with some vehemence by more orthodox Marxists, might also account for the change of tone and heart in Jameson's own work over the short space of three years since *The Political Unconscious*. But this would then have to count as a moment of curiously unannounced self-critique. Jameson's own account (that US radical culture was made to pay for the 1960s 'superstructural' advance by the encroaching infrastructural transition to global capitalism) is a noticeably external and of course retrospective one.[62] There can be little doubt that, in the terms he employs, the decade went on to prove the gloomy infrastructural projection rather than the essay's revolutionary vision; installing global capitalism, full postmodernism, and a Radical Right rather than a united class opposition. Approaching the 1990s from this angle it might well seem that the 'total system' had triumphed and one was living a script written by Adorno.

To step from Adorno to Marcuse, however, or a different reading of Marcuse than Jameson's own, is to see a differently scripted history and possible future. For the moment of Jameson's appeal to class unity in 'Periodising the 60s' is the moment in which he simultaneously depresses the potential of an alternative New Left, associated not with an all-or-nothing class politics and 'total system', but with the social movements glimpsed in the more Althusserian *Political Unconscious* and associated historically with a neo-Marxist cultural politics derived in part from a figure such as Marcuse. Jameson indicates this connection of culture with ideology in Marcuse's thought in the final paragraph of his section the 'The adventures of the sign'; and earlier in the same essay, connects it, though parenthetically, with Wilhelm Reich and Antonio Gramsci. A major initiative in this and the following decade, one which was to inspire the revision of Adorno and Horkheimer's unrelenting rejection of mass culture, therefore receives scant attention.

This is linked perhaps with the distinction Jameson eventually makes between two kinds of strategies within cultural politics. One is the 'homeopathic' method, which seeks to undermine the image of society from within. This is associated with a postmodern political aesthetic (Doctorow and Hans Hacke are his examples) and, fleetingly, with Gramsci. The second strategy is that of 'cognitive mapping', a method which retains the 'impossible concept of totality' in seeking to represent the space of capital. This, quite evidently, is Jameson's own preferred strategy.[63]

Perhaps a last note is permitted on these issues via the question of periodisation. *Late Marxism* would seem to present its own moment as the moment equally of postmodernism and the renewed relevance of

Adorno. But this, once again, gives a twist to the personal intellectual and general cultural narrative Jameson is relating which his own writings will not quite bear. 'Periodising the 60s', as the discussion above shows, presents *this* decade, the 1960s, as the decade of both late capitalism and postmodernism – which would make sense of the descriptions of post-industrial capitalism in postmodern terms in *Marxism and Form* in 1972. We can only conclude that though its explicit naming might wait upon later essays and its proposed periodisation might alter, postmodernism is, by implication, in Jameson's writings, a continuing and deepening set of psychic, ideological and cultural features to which he responds in different ways. The result is more than one Jameson (just as there is more than one Adorno or Marcuse) engaged in a dialogue with changing social forms which extend or revise the theory produced to meet them.

What, in particular, controls such changes, as we can see, is the perception in this period of the working class or social movements as effective political agencies: which is to say, in Jameson's terms, the degree to which they can be thought of as the practical equivalent of the theoretical concept of the social totality. Jameson is consequently more Hegelian, more Lukácsian, more Althusserian and more Adornian; but not, shall we say, more Derridean or Foucauldian, or Gramscian. The models or examples are those of a tradition first of all, or such that that tradition attempts to adapt to or absorb. But none of these are 'the order of the day' in any stronger sense than the imperatives of theory declare them to be so. Jameson himself, as this discussion has implied, is not necessarily *the* order of the postmodern day. What, compared with other positions, is most telling and inspiring about his present thinking in the 'stream of time' is what, in fact, is least comfortable and confident in it: less the equivalence between theory and culture than their lack of fit, and the anxiety this gives his writing; less its achieved totalities, or totalising grasp, than its self-conscious ambition and anticipated falling short. For it is this which shapes Jameson's project, as if his map-making took him on some Odyssean voyage beyond known boundaries, into the space, in Tennyson's 'Ulysses', of the 'untravelled world whose margin fades'. Jameson often seems indeed to talk himself through just such a venture, calling on all his fluency to talk down another voice which knows in its chattering, paranoid wisdom that there is no way out, no maps, no totality; or to talk over the threat of immobility and silence. Beneath his richly-laden, exploratory and supremely assured text we hear, that is to say, the grim messages of a Kafka or a Beckett, even of Adorno's Kafka and Beckett.

In his essay on Jameson, Terry Eagleton dares to suggest that the liberal panacea 'only connect' could stand as a description of the 'immense *combinatoire* of his texts'.[64] This will to connect applies to more than Jameson's stylistic verve and intellectual eclecticism, however, and should not imply that he is in the end 'only' a liberal. For in truth his cognitive mapping, the unyielding ambition 'to seek, if *not* to find' the totality, in the style of a latter-day Tennyson, takes his work beyond the late Romantic irony of such a poet, and beyond the self-deceiving unities of liberalism, to bring it alongside, in his words, the 'failures of variously monumental kinds', characterising classic and 'survivor's modernism'.[65] Jameson shares with Joyce, Pound, Proust, and a figure such as Jean-Luc Godard, 'the modernist ideal of formal totality by way of the impossibility of achieving it'; a 'longing' for closure 'about which the postmodern text could care less [*sic*]'.[66] Like the modernist he writes in the knowledge of failed connection (one thinks of Pound's self-reflexive 'I cannot make it cohere . . . it coheres all right' of the *Cantos*).[67] Perhaps Adorno's defeatist modernism belongs in this same category, though Jameson's 'longing' would seem a more popular candidate for 'what we need today'. The idea, in any case, I suggest, of Jameson as a 'surviving modernist' not only helps explain this renewed affinity with Adorno, but gives us a proper sense of his struggle with both late capitalism and postmodernism.

DOCTOROW'S DIFFERENCE

We see from the above how formative readings of the 1960s and of the American New Left can be for political and cultural positions taken in the following decades, including revisions or reappropriations of critical theory, and encounters with post-structuralism. Jameson's *Marxism and Form* and Doctorow's *The Book of Daniel*, to return to this example, were published alike in 1971, and both can be seen as reflections, amongst other things, upon that fleetingly utopian moment, when, as Jameson recalls, 'everything was possible'. *Marxism and Form* represents a narrowly philosophical advance, one might think, compared with Doctorow's investigation of a national trauma and the shadow American communism and anti-communism cast upon the postmodern cold world. If Hegelian Marxism did in its own way help radicalise the new intellectual culture, Doctorow's character has to negotiate the transition from one radical generation to another; to develop a practical cultural politics out of the available 'failures of analysis' spanning the naïveties of his father's communist conviction and the situationist histrionics of the hippy image-maker Artie Sternlicht. This he does, as Doctorow points out, by staying open to the conflicts in himself and his life in an era of state paranoia, the Vietnam War and anti-war protests, the novelty of TV and the world of Disney. In short, he is exposed to a level and range of postmodern entanglements, and of pain, quite simply, beyond the theoretical purview of *Marxism and Form*. And this experience Daniel shares, in Doctorow's view, with the writer of fiction, burdened and emboldened by the 'limitless possibility of knowing the truth'.[68] As readers we are asked, moreover, to accept that Daniel discovers and the book delivers some such knowledge.

When Jameson comes, in 'Periodising the 60s', more fully to document and reflect upon the decade, he concludes, as we have seen, that any 'truth' came later, that the earlier 'sense of freedom and possibility' could be seen now as 'a historical illusion'.[69] By contrast, Doctorow's statements in talks and interviews in the comparable period after *The Book of Daniel* show how he continued to draw more fully and with less reserve on sixties and New Left radicalism. Speaking in the late 1970s, for example, in the context of a perceived retreat from political and social awareness, he sees the 'right direction' as lying in 'an effort to find some mediation between individual psychology and large social movements'.[70] His remarks recall the attempts by figures such as Marcuse and Norman O. Brown in the 1960s and 1970s to marry Marx and Freud, and indeed Doctorow acknowledges these. His more explicit reference, however, is Wilhelm Reich, associated with the sixties 'sexual revolution', and – in some proximity to the work of the Frankfurt School – with a psychological rather than purely economic and class analysis of fascism.

Doctorow hesitates to call himself a 'Reichian' but he remains attracted, all the same, to the early project and to the transgressive openness of Reich's work. Two further references in the later *Lives of the Poets* (1985) confirm this. There Reich appears as a source for the imagined 'primal scene' in the story 'Willi', and explicitly in the title story as a 'classic case' of the ostracism and disintegration awaiting those who go 'marching on, in logic and in faith' beyond accepted protocol.[71] In 'going on' Reich echoes Daniel who is also 'trying to go on', open to 'however cold and frightening an embrace with the truth' just as he in turn echoes the novelist, braving the world of fiction which 'has no borders [where] everything is open.'[72] As a writer Doctorow does his best work, he says too, 'out of a spirit of transgression' which defies the commissar's rule-book. Politically, such thoughts bring him, in their own logic, to the prospect of anarchism:

> Reich himself was excommunicated by both the Marxists and Freudians as a result of his insights. He was driven right out of Europe because of that direction in his work. But surely the sense we have to have now of twentieth-century political alternatives is the kind of exhaustion of them all. The only one to my mind which stands out clean and shining – because it has never really been tested in any serious way – is a philosophical position of anarchism, which at this point seems to be so totally utopian in character as not to be seriously attainable. But certainly everything else has been totally discredited: capitalism, communism, socialism. None of it seems to work.[73]

Doctorow therefore arrives at a sense of political direction Jameson would appreciate but not share; inspired in part at least by an earlier sixties radicalism and consistent with a post-structuralist scepticism on the totalising, repressive grand narratives of the Enlightenment. Or so it seems. Behind his reservations on the late Reich and his caveat on the utopianism of the anarchist ideal there lies a commitment to a radical liberalism in which social change will be 'pragmatic and honest and plain spoken'.[74] This he derives from the US constitution; 'a precipitate', he says, 'of all the best Enlightenment thinking of Europe'.[75] In a seemingly impossible U-turn, transgressive non-conformity marches Doctorow not forward but suddenly back into the arms of a common heritage and founding document, which bear no apparent relation to their discredited offspring. The solution can only be to understand this 'best Enlightenment thinking' as itself representing an unachieved ideal, to see American liberal or radical democracy as a corrupted or never seriously tested option. 'Going on' in this light becomes an evolutionary struggle, attempting in the face of a history of contrary evidence, to sustain 'our best illusions about ourselves' in the living self-contradiction driving American life.[73]

'Going on' comes therefore to imply more endurance and surviving hope than the 'going beyond' of social experiment or liberated psychic flows. And it also implies looking back: to restate ideals, to narrate a best and worst history in an act of attempted continuity and community. For Doctorow, this is to recall a personal family history whose sensibility was 'Humanist, radical Jewish', and informed, importantly, by 'The sense of possibility'.[77] Doctorow speaks in this connection of 'a lower-middle class environment of generally enlightened, socialist sensibility', of a Russian-born grandfather – 'a printer, an intellectual, a chess player, an atheist, and a socialist' – who gave him Tom Paine's *The Age of Reason,* and of his father, a New York-born store-owner, salesman, romantic dreamer and socialist. This personal history then joins the broader intellectual inheritance of modern Jewish history, marked by persecution and prophecy, critique, political scepticism and a desire to change society. In this tradition Doctorow numbers Freud, Kafka, Schoenberg, Walter Benjamin, and in the history of American radicalism, Emma Goldman and Allen Ginsberg.[78]

Doctorow's views are plainly not without their inner tensions or problems: not least because the terms he uses (leftist, humanist, radical, liberal, socialist, anarchist) cast such a wide political net – partly in an aversion to ideological pieties which in another way defines his position. We might see parallels with Jameson here (the 'postmodern Marxist' to Doctorow's 'post-structuralist democrat'); yet even where their citations and cautions run quite close, Doctorow's thinking is more socially anchored in traditions of American and specifically Jewish radicalism. The result is a stronger 'sense of possibility'; the belief, keyed to a newly mediated relation between 'individual psychology and large social movements' that the best dissident opinion (the ideas of a Eugene Debs or an Emma Goldman, for example) will prevail as common wisdom.

'Going back', as here, to draw upon the resources of an American radicalism, is also what Doctorow's novels do. Firstly, and most obviously, in their recovery and reconstruction of past eras – the 1910s (*Ragtime*), the 1930s (*Billy Bathgate, Loonlake, World's Fair*), and the 1950s and 1960s (*The Book of Daniel*), and most recently the 1880s (*The Waterworks*) – always in some way, in a double function mirroring their own postmodern times in the decades of modernity. Doctorow 'turns back' also in a second regular strategy in the novels to probe the mediations between psychology and society at the critical point of their formation in the individual's life. Without exception his novels at some point follow a young boy's initiation, tracking the options of conformity and dissent, denial and continuity in the son's relation to his father (or substitute father), and beyond this in a widening series of embodying contexts, to parents, families, community, class, and the generations and moments of American history these sons are brought to negotiate. The result is a series of mediations on how to be American: versions of the Horatio Alger stories for an infinitely more complicated postmodern age. *The Book of Daniel*, once more, is quite evidently one such *Bildungsroman*: the narrative of Daniel's education, of his coming to know and accept his biological parents and his name as their son. Through his investigations of their role in the national mythology of Left and Right, he discovers a personal and political continuity which prepares him for history. After the schizophrenic voices of the novel he can speak in the first person, having produced in the 'book' of his life something like a 'cognitive map' or the narrative of 'real individualism' Doctorow speaks of elsewhere.[79]

It is from this material that Doctorow seeks to forge an aesthetic, a 'poetics of engagement', as he terms it, in a phrase at pains to respect fiction's distinctive rhetorics and the terms of a 'leftist, humanist critique' wary of the fixities and fervour of history's discredited ideologies.[80] He writes, he says, as an 'independent witness', deploying the self-consciously 'false documents' of fiction to expose the lies of expert opinion and specialised discourses. The writer hopes to jolt society from its impacted amnesia, to provide a memory and wise counsel and thus regain the authority Walter Benjamin had ascribed to the story-teller. 'Only connect' might seem once more an appropriate motto for all this. Yet Doctorow does not imagine a reconciled unity. As US history reforms its 'polyglot mixture' through successive waves of immigration, so literature, mixing 'the real and possibly real' with breadth and variety will seek to match and serve 'the absolute multiplicity of us all'.[81]

All the same, Doctorow sees this ideal as having to contend with manifestly opposed tendencies: the failing connection in a 'post-humanist society' between the individual and the collective fate, the retreat from social and political life in the 1970s and, most acutely in the 1980s, the bland one-dimensionality of the Reagan era. Under Reagan, Doctorow sees a final public abandonment of liberal rhetoric, and thus of the vital 'conflict between our democratic ideals and real political self-interest', between 'our constitutional obligations and the expediencies of economic capitalist reality'.[82]

Like Jameson, Doctorow has sight here in the early 1980s of a new phase in the totalising ambitions of capital. Yet where Jameson urges global proletarianisation and late Marxist dialectics, Doctorow turns to a now-dissenting defence of the pragmatic, democratic Left and the occluded dialectical pressure this had exerted upon American power. The task of writing therefore becomes less to connect, than to recover the materials for connection; to illuminate 'the best' in the energising contradictions of American life, perhaps, but to rescue this conflict first from beneath the flattened, postmodern, surface spreading from the eighties alliance of religious fundamentalism and the New Right. In this light the 'indwelling of the art in the real life . . . the 'mixing up of the historic and the aesthetic' Doctorow speaks of is less a description of a homeopathic practice which would seek to cure late capital by administering some of its own poison, than the therapy which will return its repressed other.

If Doctorow's fiction works within something like these general terms, it has done so in a changing history and increasingly assimilative political climate which everywhere exerts its heavily magnetic influence. The Reagan–Bush era all but deprived the writer of his public role as conscience and counsel; 'the sense of possibility' was obscured, and Doctorow found the odds lengthening against his search for the individual story which would imply the social whole. His fictional strategies (the use of parable and historical reconstruction) have nevertheless remained strikingly persistent: less, whatever the air of nostalgia, in a desire to 'escape' the constricting uniformities of the present than to restage contemporary dilemmas; either at an earlier, historically rhyming moment, or closer to their starting point, so they can, as it were, be run through again. This is not to say these recreated eras are without the estranging effect of historical distance, nor to suggest that they follow a systematic chronology. The latest novel, *The Waterworks*, for example, 'goes back' furthest, to the late nineteenth century, after three novels on the 1930s, none of which employ public or social historical materials with the fullness of *The Book of Daniel* or *Ragtime*. To compare *Loon Lake* with the earlier 'historical fiction' of John Dos Passos (which Jameson suggests Doctorow here reinvents), is in fact to see how this novel skirts the historical personages and common tale of the Depression, and to realise at the same time how the society it 'implies', behind this ostensible period, is that of its own moment of composition, the onset of the Reagan era, when Doctorow feels a narrowing of social reference taking effect.

In Jameson's view Doctorow's fiction, and *Ragtime* in particular, confirms the historical novel's inability under postmodernism to do more than 'represent' the stereotypes and blank simulacra of the past. In fact, the stereotype of the prewar period, that here was a summer-time, tennis-playing, trouble-free and patriotic America without negroes and immigrants, is immediately checked in this novel by 'the revolutionary' Emma Goldman, who reprimands the 'celebrated beauty' Evelyn Nesbit whose naïve view of the age – if it is anybody's – this is. 'Apparently there *were* Negroes. There *were* immigrants.'[83] As Goldman's name suggests Doctorow here tries out in fiction the anarchism yet to be seriously tested in American history, returning to the moment of vibrant libertarian radicalism associated with the 'Lyrical Left' of the 1910s, behind the Old and New Left of the previous *Book of Daniel*, and behind the writing career of John Dos Passos. At the same time Emma Goldman's reprimand and later wise counsel to Evelyn Nesbit on sexual inequality and the bondage of marriage tell us that this is a novel of the mid-1970s, when questions of race and ethnicity, of sexuality and gender raised within the black power and women's movements vied with the older ideologies of class and party. The time of *Ragtime* therefore brings with it the oxymoron of promise and failure, a past sense, typical of Doctorow, which combines innocent memory and knowing retrospect, whether of epochs or of parents.

In the novel, the impersonally-named members of the middle-class 'American Family' of New Rochelle, New York are defined in terms of their exposure to these issues, to the real inequalities beneath the bland and borrowed surface that leads the visiting Freud to declare America a 'gigantic mistake' (p. 31). Just as the explorer Father's liberalism peels back to reveal his actual conservatism and prejudice, so the Mother and Younger Brother develop in sexual and social awareness and expand their sympathies for the oppressed (negroes and immigrants). Emma Goldman is an influence on both figures, but their transformations are inspired principally by the black pianist Coalhouse Walker Jr and the Latvian socialist immigrant Tateh.

I shall return to Coalhouse Walker in a later chapter, in a discussion of the 'jazz novel'. For the moment, the more interesting figure is Tateh who enters the novel and the United States with his daughter aboard a 'rag ship – packed to the railings with immigrants' (p. 15) – the second group ignored in the America of nostalgic stereotype. Tateh is the President of the Socialist Artists' Alliance; he finds meagre work in the streets of the Lower East Side cutting silhouette portraits, and soon departs for the mill town of Lowell, Massachusetts. Here his socialism is tested, and abandoned. Delirious from a police beating during the last days of a strike led by the Wobblies, he decides to leave with his daughter for Philadelphia and there finds a new resolve: he 'began to conceive of his life as separate from the fate of the working class. . . . The I.W.W. has won. But what has it won? A few more pennies in wages. Will it now own the mills? No' (p. 109). He sells a book of moving drawings, called a 'movie book', to the Franklin Novelty Company and his career is set. 'Thus did the artist point his life along the lines of flow of American energy' in a world where the entrepreneur not the worker succeeds, and where 'The value of the duplicable event was everywhere perceived' (p. 111).

Tateh reappears in the life of the Family as the movie director Baron Ashenazy; his name changed, his hair dyed, and with a pronounced Yiddish accent. On Father's death he marries Mother and they move to Hollywood to make money and movies, including preparedness films. It is a tale of compromise. Yet Tateh is inspired by his new family of children (his daughter, Mother's son, and Coalhouse and Sarah's son) to make a film of a gang of children ('white black, fat thin, rich poor, all kinds . . . a society of ragamuffins like all of us', pp. 269–70).

Several films, we are told, were made of this vision, and we are left to ponder. Is this a vision of equality and a multi-racial society, popularised and disseminated via the new media of mass production? Is it that vision infantilised and commodified?[84] Certainly the novel provides no other position of ideological or philosophical principle, unless it is in the perspective of the young boy who is the vehicle of the tale. He too is fascinated by replication and the duplicable event, which he tests on the victrola, and is interested in photography and moving pictures. What is more, he accepts stories as images of truth, proof of the instability of both things and people. In Ovid he finds confirmation that forms of life, including language, 'were volatile and that everything in the world could as easily be something else . . . it was evident to him that the world composed and re-composed itself constantly in an endless process of dissatisfaction' (pp. 97, 98). The boy's perception of endless difference and transformation mocks the quest that so occupies the others for reincarnation, sameness and unity. It would seem to align him more with his new self-made father than his natural father, and with the deconstructive (one might say Ovidian) wisdom of his author. But if so, the boy's sense of perpetual instability and fragmentation undercuts any assumption of a recoverable 'history' (for there are only 'traces quickly erased of moments past, journeys taken'), or social objective of the kind to which Doctorow is committed in contemporary statements. Who is father, boy or man? What kind of text has the greater authority – the personal opinions and public statements, or 'the illuminated way of thinking' which is fiction? *Ragtime* provokes this question of teller and tale, but one does not have to step outside the text of the novel to appreciate it. In Jameson's view it deliberately stages this contradiction, holding out while it simultaneously withdraws 'an older type of social and historical interpretation'.[85] Yet what happens to the knowledge that 'there *were* negroes. There *were* immigrants', the appreciation in the novel that there are inequalities and not only variables in things? Are we to understand this as no more than a quotation, the 'represented' remarks of the deported Emma Goldman? Are they reposed in no other consciousness? Do they have no historical referent and veracity?

The later novels, *Loon Lake* and *Billy Bathgate*, published at either end of the 1980s underline a disillusionment with Left political ideologies already evident in *Ragtime*. Both are pessimistic narratives, surely, of distorted individualism: parables of the contemporary triumph of neoconservatism, in which, in the thirties of the stories, the lure of the capitalist magnate and his shadow, the gangland boss, is only matched by the frailty of family, community, group or class identity. In *Loon Lake*, a complexly layered, discontinuous narrative of textual echoes, parallels or 'repeats' in plot and motive is drawn, almost in spite of itself, to confirm the inescapable, unswerveable power of capital. At Loon Lake, the retreat of the industrialist F.W. Bennett, Joe 'Paterson' joins the figure Warren Penfield, who first came to Loon Lake to kill Bennett in an abortive act of class revenge (which it is assumed also motivates Joe). Penfield is now the compound's pet resident poet, a destiny which says everything about the neutered role of the would-be radical and artist. Penfield's verdict that the 1919 General Strike in Seattle ('the first of its kind in the whole history of the United States of America'), which at first so thrills him, will become a dictatorship led by men insensitive to the affairs of personal life[86] is the novel's final word on any alternative social organisation, aside from the circus Joe joins before Loon Lake. Penfield becomes Joe's first 'second father' having in a sense lived and decided the issues of his life before him, and Joe dutifully 'infolds' Penfield's verse chronicle 'Loon Lake', with annotations, in his own record which is the book *Loon Lake*, a text which further alternates between first- and third-person in an authorial mode sometimes given the high impersonality of a computer print-out. Joe escapes with Bennett's mistress, Clara, to Jacksontown only to find work in one of Bennett's auto factories, and returns, inevitably, to Loon Lake to charm Bennett, Gatsby style, into accepting him as his son. His project, conceived in the name of the novel's abused characters, is to humanise and save Bennett: 'I will give him hope, I will extend his reign, I will raise him and do it all so well with such style that he will thank me, thank me for growing in his heart his heart bursting his son' (p. 249).

This is indeed to work within the system. The novel's final entry reveals the depths of his failure: Joe Korzeniowski, aka Joe of

Paterson, becomes Joe Paterson Bennett, war-time secret agent ('face blackened, teeth blackened, heart blacked dropping into blackness': p. 250), CIA Deputy Assistant Director, heir to Loon Lake and the affiliations, patronage, marriages without issue which exactly repeat Bennett's original profile. The system is total and all-absorbing in an analysis gloomier than Foucault or Adorno (for here there is no micro-resistance, nor autonomous art, unless one grants this entirely to the novel's formal complexity).

Joe's (and Clara's) working-class identity is overpowered, we might say, by Bennett's 'class'. Billy Bathgate's roots are, until the very end, no stronger than the neighbourhood orphanage he treats as home when he is noticed by Dutch Schultz. In a sense his Bronx background determines his ambitions, for Schultz is the hero of kids in the area, 'The quality of my longing . . . was a neighbourhood thing', says Billy, 'it was the culture of where you lived.'[87] Still, his apprenticeship to Schultz displaces him. Billy seeks to rise, to move up the levels he perceives on the New York skyline, like a skyscraper ascending from a fixed base. Yet, joining the Schultz entourage takes him out of the city (Schultz's style is on the wane), and Billy is out of place on his return. Only finally, in a fantastical ending (of which there is no sight in the film version of the novel) can Billy be reconciled to his beginnings. After stealing Schultz's mistress, Drew, then saving her from Schultz (both Billy and Joe have sex with their surrogate 'father's' 'girls'), and after Schultz's violent death, Billy returns home to his mother, magically free of Schultz's criminality but possessed of his wealth. A chauffeur presents him with his baby by Drew, and he and his mother 'go back to the East Bronx with him to walk him in his carriage on a sunny day along Bathgate Avenue' (p. 322). In a wash of nostalgia the streets are now full of pedlars, produce and people: 'all the city turning out to greet us just as in the old days of our happiness, before my father fled, when the family used to go walking in this market, this bazaar of life, Bathgate, in the age of Dutch Schultz' (p. 323). Only in this extraordinary way, as the boy becomes the trinity of father, son and ghostly 'husband', can well-being and the wholeness of the family and community life be restored, as if the past were the present, and all things one.

Both novels are extreme statements on the difficulty of sustaining social bonds and the impossibility of social change: a conclusion only confirmed by the manifest contrivance of *Billy Bathgate's* happy ending. In both novels too 'history' is served more by cultural myth than by documentary material, and this too is more romanticised in the later novel. If they contrast in these respects with *The Book of Daniel* we can see their germ in *Ragtime*. In this *series*, therefore, we approach something like the pastiche and nostalgia, the lack of historical depth and social vision associated with postmodernism. Especially if we appreciate the sophistication and knowingness which produces both the greater complexity of *Loon Lake* and the great conventionality of *Billy Bathgate*. Stylistic variation, we might conclude, is the corner late capitalism assigns to the writer of fiction. That this occurs *as a process* and *in spite of* this author's stated ambitions and principles might be in fact all the reply one needs to Jameson and others. Postmodernism does not arrive all at once, but the evidence is there where one might expect it, in the fiction of the decade of high late capitalism. However, Doctorow's two other works of fiction of the mid 1980s, *Lives of the Poets* (1984) and *World's Fair* (1985), question even this assumption.

As we have seen, the destiny of young boys, in relation to their fathers and families, provides the principal metaphor in Doctorow's fiction for the collective fate. If these fathers are not capitalists and criminals, they are artists of a kind, or radicals – whom Doctorow also talks of in terms of their family relationship to the nation.[88] They come thus to represent the promise and failure of dissenting traditions, especially in the passage of the immigrant from European modernity to the United States: the land of individual opportunity, mass entertainment, mass production, new utility goods, which defeats them or redirects their energies. In this America, the individual and collective, the one and the many, are united less in class organisations than in monopoly ownership. Here the ideologue can be reinvented as shopkeeper and salesman, his ideas for a new world channelled into the new media. This is the transformation Tateh undergoes, and is the situation of Julius Issacson (the sensation of his arrest coincides with the arrival of the first TV in his radio shop), and of the father, Dave, in *World's Fair* (the first portable radio appears on the day he loses his record store and Hitler invades France).

World's Fair is set in the Bronx and recalls the family's early life and neighbourhood street culture in a rich, slow and compelling naturalism. Here the younger son Edgar is educated in life's cont-raries. To the mother's order and morality the father poses daring, spontaneity, adventure (the stuff of an earlier bohemian promise) and a magical sleight of hand and know-how (evident still in his getting tickets for a ball game when all seems lost). Dave's life is littered with 'broken promises', yet if he fails in business and perhaps in marriage, he succeeds in retaining a progressive political sense (he sells 'Race records' at his store, he speaks out against fascism, he exposes the pretensions of national ideology exhibited at the Worlds' Fair). We begin to realise that we have met fragments of this father and family, and this New York, elsewhere in Doctorow's fiction and, in a further version, in Doctorow's description of his own upbringing,[89] And we realise too, if we have not before, that in the double life of the novels as displaced autobiography and national allegory, the figure of the son is also the figure of the writer. In *World's Fair*, Edgar writes an essay on 'The typical American Boy' in a competition for the World's Fair. Significantly, he does not win first prize (perhaps because he does not mention 'America' or because of his statement that if a boy is Jewish he should say so), but he does win tickets for a free day for the whole family.

The event of the World's Fair in 1939 (which Edgar visits twice – as one comes to expect in Doctorow) brings this 'era' and novel to its culmination and end. The result is an abrupt closure which gives the novel a curiously boxed sense of the past at odds with the Fair's grand exhibits on America's tomorrow. The father mocks the pretensions of the exhibits, asking why immigrants and the working man are not represented in the Fair's time-capsule, pointing out how the roads of the Futurama exhibit will be built out of Federal taxes and not by General Motors. But the boy finds such constant instruction exhausting. He makes his own time-capsule but does not comment further. And cannot, indeed, while the present time of the novel's first-person autobiographical form remains unspoken. Any expectations we might have, therefore, of Edgar's mature reflections on the clashes or continuities of these utopian speculations and present actuality, of memory and experience, of his father and himself, are frustrated. The personal and historical dialectic of promise and disappointment focused in the father is therefore held at a perplexed standstill, as if the past cannot be moved forward.[90]

World's Fair therefore, reconstructs a strong sense of Jewish cultural and intellectual inheritance, neighbourhood locality and the family, from which Joe and Billy are so estranged. All of this is buried, nonetheless, like the time-capsules in the story, in an eternal, un-wakened prewar era, in a tense, after Jameson, we might call the 'past postmodern'. Unless, that is, we consider this novel in tandem with *Lives of the Poets*. To do so is to appreciate the full ambiguity and tensions in Doctorow's postmodernism. For in a reverse chronology, and the most interesting move in his fiction, we see that *Lives of the Poets* had already accomplished precisely the crucial transition from past to future *World's Fair* cannot make, in a way that no novel had seriously undertaken since *The Book of Daniel*. For in a thread of stories, *Lives* brings that same (as yet unwritten, younger) protagonist, the boy writer of *World's Fair* forward into adulthood. The result is a new kind of mediation between fiction and autobiography, third and first person, and the social and the personal.

Loon Lake, in particular, had shown the power of capital to assimilate all-comers and to reproduce itself unaided. The answer Doctorow's fiction supplies to this severely Foucauldian scenario of little or no resistance is in a sense Derrida, or the deconstructive impulse which accompanied the influence of Foucault through the 1970s and 1980s in US intellectual life. The serial assemblage of *Lives* confirms this, in its own disconnected, fragmentary, interlaced and deferred content, but chiefly in the way the title story revisits earlier novels (and anticipates later). Just as *The Book of Daniel* rewrites the Rosenberg story, *Ragtime* rewrites Kleist's *Michael Kohlhaas*, and *Loon Lake*, if you will, rewrites Dos Passos and *Gatsby*, so *Lives of the Poets* rewrites earlier characters and incidents, concerning the father and family, especially. Two stories in particular, the title story and 'The Writer in the Family' read like supplements and afterthoughts, or 'prethoughts' as the chronology of publication tells us, to *World's Fair* which comes then to present the boy and adult writer, Jonathan, of *Lives* as the youthful writer Edgar. Doctorow's fiction therefore replies to the sameness of capitalism with discontinuity and '*différance*', opposing the montage of the assembly line with the montage of intertextuality.

We begin here to see an answer to the questions both Jameson and Doctorow pose on the authority of the writer, fiction's access to the past and authentic cultural memory, and the possibilities of critique. The perception of a thoroughly textualised world, of mass culture and commodification but of no mass working-class or radical movement of any credibility, has produced in some a self-regarding textual postmodernism which carries out Barthes' 'Death of the Author' to the letter. In Doctorow, the relation of the psychological and social, the individual and the collective is re-posed as a relation of the single text to a world of writing. His figures, and readers, experience a textual enmeshment which Barthes' essay had truly intended as the positive sphere of the Author become scriptor. Texts, we remember, follow 'not a line of words releasing a single "theological" meaning . . . but a multi-dimensional space in which a variety of writings, none of them original, blend and clash'.[91] In 'Lives' the writer-narrator 'strangled in history' (p. 108) is perforce strangled in its writings. To work through to new mediations of the individual in history is therefore to follow its lines and traces, to prise away history's hands, unwind its arms, and so perhaps unfold a 'life theme'. In which case the resulting history will look more like a pattern of circuitry, or cross-city tramline network of the kind which figures in *Ragtime* than a finally reclaimed linear narrative of the facts. Unlike the young boy of less materialist, post-structuralist temperament in that novel, Doctorow sees the skaters as well as the tracks they make, and inks in the 'traces quickly erased of moments past, journeys taken'.[92] He works, moreover, at the patterns they have left, at the points of intersection comprising 'eras', or the scattered parts of 'individuals in whom history intensifies like electroshock' (p. 75); traversing the past, recomposing the parts to produce *situated* retellings. To this degree, in these reiterated, newly-set narratives of person, ethnicity, and nation, Doctorow's fiction can retain the referentiality that makes it still a kind of realism.

If nostalgia is one way of coping with the loss of historicity, situated retellings or rewritings, which both go back and go on, are another. In Doctorow, what is lost, in every novel but *World's Fair*, is the father and all this figure represents. Like 'eras' fathers can come to an abrupt end: they are murdered, electrocuted, rejected; or, more slowly as in 'The Writer in the Family', die of illness, only to return to life in a dream, or in writing, and have to die again. The story 'Willi', where the son contrives the destruction of his parents, is again relevant here. The mixed respect and jealousy of the father, and desire and contempt for the mother, which might shadow the feelings of their sons in other stories, are here at an extreme. So too is the need to be reconciled, or to work through the guilt associated with their deaths (actual or fantasised). This Willi displaces on to the Nazis and the war when 'All of it was to be destroyed anyway, even without me' (p. 35). As elsewhere, Reich represents an outrageous extreme: the disconnected avant-garde, we might say, to the 'modernist-realism' Doctorow produces over the two texts of *Lives of the Poets* and *World's Fair*. In 'The Writer in the Family' the boy Jonathan brings his father back to life (*vide* the theme of reincarnation in *Ragtime*). He learns of his father's radical populist beliefs from his brother, and learns too of his unsuspected navy experience and dreams of sea travel. What is more, he continues the father's life in writing, composing letters from him after his death, from his supposed new store in Arizona to satisfy an aunt and his father's ancient mother. The father is in effect stolen from his immediate family until the boy writes in the 'truthful fiction' of a last letter that he is dying 'of the wrong life' (p. 17). Later, in the title story, as an adult writer and himself a father in contemporary New York (an exceptional combination in a Doctorow protagonist), Jonathan remembers and shares his father's love of the city and subway in an important act of continuity over two lifetimes.

The title story 'Lives of the Poets' is about the disintegrating lives of Jonathan's peers – authors, painters and poets themselves – and all invariably in marriages or heterosexual partnerships in which the couples, in his phrase, are 'not entirely together' (p. 88). That these men are artists and symptoms of the contemporary artist's self-doubt, lack of authority and connection makes this more than a pathetic tale of male mid-life crisis. The artist at the point of dereliction, concludes Jonathan, has affinities with the city's underclass. He wanders the city himself like a vagrant, he feels 'kicked out of the ruling circle . . . deprived of my ancient right to matter' (p. 143) in an affinity with others, such as Linus Pauling and Reich, once more, doomed by their genius or eccentricity. The writer's own position here has a social implication these classic cases do not, however. Jonathan is conscious of new waves of immigration into New York City, and struck by their new, inventive, ways (a Korean who brings a new chair on to the crowded subway, for example – which Jonathan frequents like his father, but unlike his middle-class friends – resolves the problem of space by sitting on the new chair). In the subway particularly he feels 'back in the immigrated universe' (p. 94), an important acknowledgement of both his own Jewish inheritance and the generations of new arrivals to the United States. Rejecting the classic image of the United States as 'the melting pot' encoding the assimilative assumptions of liberal ideology, Doctorow holds to the more difficult idea of 'the absolute multiplicity of us all'. *Lives of the Poets* intuits a new grouping of misfits and marginal social types, along these lines. Its social potential, in a world where standard oppositional unities are discredited, is mooted in a lecture delivered at a seminar of secret service agents or police officers of some kind in the story 'The Leather Man'. The lecturer posits a 'hapless fellow', without a job and frustrated at home who descends to the basement to make a cabinet to retreat into: 'You have them walking into their boxes and locking the door behind them. Fine. But two people do that and you have a community. You see what I'm saying? You can make a revolution with people who have nothing to do with each other at the same time' (p. 70). The 'hapless fellow' might be Nick, one of Jonathan's friends, who has built a himself a sound-proof sub-basement study, or Jonathan himself in his own separate Greenwich village apartment, 'this working retreat I've made for myself in the middle of the electric city' (p. 103). They join the bag-ladies; 'feral children, hermits, street people, gamblers, prisoners, missing persons' (p. 70) the CIA has on file, including a husband and astronaut adrift of their domestic and patriotic bearings. All of these are linked to the 'Leather Man', a mythic figure and untutored sage known to roam the countryside clad in a leather armour. 'So there is a history', we are told (p. 67). There is an aesthetic too, for in his 'essential act' the Leather Man 'makes the world foreign. He distances it. He is estranged. Our perceptions are sharpest when we're estranged. We can see the shape of things' (p. 74).

The key device of modernism is therefore recruited to a poetics of perception and mapping in the postmodern city, one which is committed to reviewing and reinscription as we have seen, neither from a point of assured centrality, nor from a position of absolute exile, but rather from the vantage point of disadvantage, the position of estrangement, self-doubt and marginality.

In the midst of his own impending domestic and artistic estrange-ment, Jonathan comes to the idea of a new sense of self (to rival the reinventions of *Ragtime* and *Loon Lake*), imagining, firstly, a newly grounded and mutually non-repressive relationship with his wife, Angel:

> I'll say there is an evolved being and eventually it declares itself.
> And not just to me but to you too, I am saying we must make
> the whole journey . . . to let go, take the risk, it is the only honor
> and redemption of the last free years. . . . But look, I'll tell her,
> if we do this right we can save of ourselves and our relationship
> what is good about it, we can be colleagues, we are still partners in
> parenthood, we can help each other, relate as real human beings,
> share our thoughts, maintain our regard for each other, maybe we
> can even go to bed from time to time.
>
> (*Lives of the Poets*, p. 122)

Angel is allowed no opportunity to respond to this in the story, but is 'pleased to be asked' later when he tells her of a plan which in a way begins to put his idea into action (p. 144). Her muted latter-day feminism, and Jonathan's attempt to respond to it in this way, themselves read like signs of the political hesitancy, the speculation without clear agency or forms of action afflicting radical traditions in the 1980s. In the context of Doctorow's fiction we might think of the contrasting, earlier and more strong-minded revolutionary feminist Emma Goldman.[93] Her appearance and influence in *Ragtime* had allowed Doctorow to test in fiction the anarchism untried in American history. The result, and Doctorow's judgement, as in the statement quoted above, are, however, ambiguous. The novel closes at the moment of Goldman's deportation in 1919, a narrative decision that would appear to accept the force of conservative opinion, making such ideas, in the mid 1970s, as in 1919, 'so totally utopian as not to be seriously attainable'. Yet Doctorow has consistently cited Emma Goldman's ideas on abortion and birth control as evidence of the way radical ideas can be accepted over a period of time. We might therefore still associate a radical example such as hers, the political alternative that 'stands out clean and shining' with Jonathan's utopian sketch of an 'evolved being'; the 'going on' implicit in the practice of writing as situated retellings. And perhaps we can think further of this 'letting go' and 'taking the risk' as compatible with deconstruction and *différance*. Not, evidently, if these are understood simply to license the liberated play of meaning beyond the constraints of social usage and ideology, for it is exactly an awareness of such constraints which produces Jonathan's thoughts as an *imagined*, and not yet directly communicated alternative. The force of the radical Right and the retreat of the Left in Doctorow's narrative of the American twentieth century have moderated Emma Goldman's revolutionary activity, we might say, into this 'sense of possibility'.

Interestingly, Jacques Derrida himself suggests a connection between Emma Goldman's revolutionary feminism and the strategies of deconstruction. The 'maverick feminist' Emma Goldman, he says,

> showed herself ready to break with the most authorised, the most dogmatic form of consensus, one that claims . . . to speak out in the name of revolution and history. Perhaps she was thinking of a completely other history: a history of paradoxical laws and nondialectical discontinuities, a history of absolutely heterogenous pockets, irreducible particularities, of unheard of and incalculable sexual differences; a history of women who have – centuries ago – 'gone further' by stepping back with their lone dance, or who are today inventing sexual idioms at a distance from the main forum of feminist activity.[94]

In the same interview Derrida speculates ('dreams') further on this new idiom or choreography of sexual relationships,

> what if we were to approach here . . . the area of relationship to the other where the code of sexual marks would no longer be discriminating? The relationship would not be a-sexual, far from it, but would be sexual otherwise; beyond the binary difference that governs the decorum of all codes, beyond the opposition feminine–masculine, beyond bi-sexuality as well, beyond homosexuality and heterosexuality, which come to the same thing. As I dream of saving the chance that this question offers I would like to believe in the multiplicity of sexually marked voices. I would like to believe in the masses, this indeterminable

number of blended voices, this mobile of nonidentified sexual marks whose choreography can carry, divide, multiply the body of each 'individual', whether he be classified as 'man' or as 'woman' according to the criteria of usage.[95]

Jonathan's speech does not dream this far (it is important to realise that Derrida's own thoughts are speculative and utopian), for if he imagines a repositioning or displacement of the common hierarchies of sexual difference his proposal remains marked by them all the same. Nor, given Doctorow's sense that transgressive non-conformity, for all its fascination, is doomed to deportation and exile can he 'go beyond' this attempt to 'go on further'. Here is precisely the position of Doctorow's radicalising postmodern, or new modernist, narrative which is both estranging and grounded, in its realist aspect, in the disadvantageous constraints and conditions of particular moments in a continuing historical narrative. A 'poetics' committed to change, it would suggest to us, must remain 'engaged' with the conditions its seeks to alter.

The poetics of *différance*, as Derrida implies, involves a politics of negotiation with the other: a 'certain dissymmetry,' he says, 'is no doubt the law both of sexual difference and the relationship to the other in general'.[96] I have wanted to single out the story 'Lives of the Poets' partly because it does sketch an idea of newly choreographed sexual relations. At the same time, and less sketchily, it also explores the theme of 'the relationship to the other in general'. It does this through Jonathan's newly alerted sense of immigration, and in a way which in the story takes a more practical political form. Towards the end of the story Jonathan is persuaded to take in illegal Nicaraguan refugees. 'Look, my country, what you've done to me, what I have to do to live with myself', he cries (p. 145). He rides the subway with the family to his apartment, and they move in, occupying his place of retreat from his marriage into his art, and of an anticipated liaison with a younger woman, which he knows now will not take place. This act of illegal 'transgression', this 'good deed', taking the form of a demonstrably political act does not, however, supplant the activity of writing. He sits at his typewriter with this family's young son, already a new-found father of sorts in this new extended family. As news comes on the radio of the discovery of a new infant planetary system, the boy tries the typewriter and they type together the end of what is this story itself: 'I lightly press his tiny little index finger, the key, striking, delights him, each letter suddenly struck vvv he likes the v, hey who's typing this? every good boy deserves a toy boat, maybe we'll go to the bottom of the page get my daily quota done come on, kid, you can do three more lousy lines' (p. 145). If Doctorow does not bring Jonathan to Derrida's 'multiplicity of sexually marked voices' he does here attempt to meet his own commitment to the 'absolute multiplicity of us all, the numbers of us who color the palette from which the society draws its own portrait.'[97]

We remember, finally, all the same, that this story is produced not only in a close intertextual relation with *World's Fair*, but in the same decade as *Loon Lake* and *Billy Bathgate*. Jameson sees Doctorow as 'the epic poet of the disappearance of the American radical past, of the suppression of older traditions and moments of the American radical tradition'.[98] This is true of some, but not all, of Doctorow (and as relevant of course to the European Marxist traditions shaping Jameson's own epic narratives. Certainly, the 'distress' Jameson suggests any reader on the Left will feel at this message in Doctorow might be felt by readers of his own work). Doctorow has been able, in *The Book of Daniel* and *Lives of the Poets*, notably, to access radical aesthetic and intellectual traditions, and to rewrite these into new configurations, even within the American metropolitan postmodern. He does this in *Lives of the Poets* through what is a comparatively neglected and exceptional kind of text in his *oeuvre*: a serial composition of short stories, with a predominantly contemporary rather than historical setting, which itself explores the marginal condition of the artist and drop-out.

The deconstructive impulse, here and elsewhere, in what I want to call his 'modernist-realism', operates most effectively upon assumptions of the priories and truth values of factual and fictional histories. Its further, speculative and more modest extension in *Lives of the Poets* into the realm of sexual difference and encounters with the immigrant other, or other immigrant, helps sustain a 'sense of possibility' where many accounts of postmodernism say there is none. Jonathan's 'modest good deed' at the end is a lesson to the more globalising but thwarted ambitions of such as Jameson, and a small inspiration. For it tells us how things (the situated textuality of writing and relationships) in the here and now of the city in an age when both European and American radical traditions confront their own 'disappearance', might still 'go on'.

In all of this the family remains of considerable importance, whether this is the immediate domestic family or the larger associations this also represents and in which artistic, intellectual, political and national identities are negotiated. Doctorow describes radicals as 'black sheep':[99] outsiders, that is to say, who return home: no more permanent exiles than conformists (as writers, no more uncompromisingly avant-garde than compromisingly realist). Rather, they are in some measure both: estranged family members with an option on a sense of belongingness. This position might be described as that of the dialectic critic who, in Adorno's words, is both participant and non-participant. Adorno is of course Jameson's postmodern philosopher, but Jameson's description of Doctorow's writing as a form of 'homeopathic postmodernism' does not capture the resources he draws on in securing this position from 'outside' postmodernism, namely the ideas of the modern project embodied in the American idea and the perspective of modernist estrangement. In seeking to renew and redirect these, especially in the context of the 'immigrated universe' of the 'marginal' text of *Lives of the Poets*, Doctorow is brought close to the transformed metropolitan perspective of the 'migrant or postcolonial public sphere' discussed, for example, by Homi Bhabha.[100] This is an aspect of the postmodern I want to explore in later chapters.

NOTES

1. Paul Buhle, *Marxism In The United States* (London: Verso, 1991), p. 239.
2. These figures are given in Douglas Tallack, *Twentieth-Century America. The Intellectual and Cultural Context* (London: Longman, 1991), pp. 208–9.
3. John Patrick Diggins, *The Rise and Fall of the American Left* (New York and London: Norton, 1992), pp. 276, 284–5.
4. Ibid., p. 375.
5. Cited in Paul Levine, *E.L. Doctorow* (London: Methuen, 1985) p. 37.
6. Buhl, op. cit., p. 221.
7. Ibid., p. 273.
8. Diggins, op. cit., pp. 348–9.
9. Leslie Fielder, 'Cross the border – Close the gap' in *The Collected Essays of Leslie Fielder*, Vol. 2 (New York: Stein and Day, 1971), pp. 461–85.
10. See my 'Introduction', *Modernism/Postmodernism* (Harlow: Longman, 1992), especially pp. 8–11.
11. Irving Howe, *Selected Writings 1950–1990* (New York and London: Harcourt, Brace, Janovitch, 1990), p. 280.
12. See 'New Styles in "Leftism"', ibid., pp. 193–220, and the discussion below, 'Conclusion', pp. 214–19.
13. Ibid., p. 165.

14. Tallack, op. cit., p. 208.
15. Buhle, op. cit., p. 273.
16. Jameson, *Ideologies of Theory. Essays 1971–1986 Vol 2. Syntax of History* (London: Routledge, 1988), pp. 194–5.
17. Jameson, 'Postmodernism and Consumer Society' in Brooker (ed.), op. cit., pp. 175–6.
18. Jameson, *Postmodernism or, the Cultural Logic of Late Capitalism* (London: Verso, 1991), p. 409.
19. In Brooker (ed.), op. cit., p. 179.
20. Anders Stephanson, 'Regarding Postmodernism – A Conversation with Fredric Jameson', in Douglas Kellner (ed.), *Postmodernism/Jameson/ Critique* (Washington, DC: Maisoneuve Press, 1989), pp. 61–2, 59.
21. Ibid., p. 62.
22. Jameson, 'The Cultural Logic of Late Capitalism' in *Postmodernism*, op. cit., p. 25.
23. Richard Trenner (ed.), *E.L. Doctorow. Essays and Conversations* (Princeton, N.J.: Ontario Review Press, 1983), pp. 25, 26.
24. Jacques Derrida, *Writing and Difference* (London: Routledge & Kegan Paul, 1978), p. 278.
25. E.L. Doctorow, *The Book of Daniel* (1971; London: Pan Books, 1973), p. 293. Following page references to this novel are given in the text.
26. Jameson, *The Political Unconscious* (London: Methuen, 1981), p. 12.
27. Ibid., p. 82.
28. Ibid., p. 102.
29. *Late Marxism, Adorno, or, The Persistence of the Dialectic* (London: Verso, 1990), p. 229.
30. Ibid., p. 9.
31. Ibid., pp. 5, 248.
32. *Marxism and Form* (Princeton: Princeton University Press, 1971), p. xix.
33. Op. cit., p. 241.
34. Ibid., p. 5.
35. Ibid., p. 249. Much the same argument is made in *Postmodernism, or the Cultural Logic of Late Capitalism*, pp. 65 and 264. The idea of an intellectual and artistic vanguard or 'party of Utopia' which Jameson invokes here (p. 180) appears also in his *The Geopolitical Aesthetic: Cinema and Space in the World System* (Indianapolis: Indiana University Press, and London: BFI, London, 1992), p. 110, and in a contemporary interview 'Postmodernism and Utopia', where he talks of the coming into being of 'a new, much larger, much more genuinely international intelligentsia or left network', *News from Nowhere* (Autumn, 1991):11.
36. *The Ideologies of Theory*, Vol. 2, op cit., p. 144.
37. Ibid., p. 146.
38. Terry Eagleton draws attention to the problems of combining Hegel with Macherey, but treats this question fairly lightly. He sees Jameson as neo-Hegelian throughout, 'Fredric Jameson: The Politics of Style' in *Against the Grain* (London: Verso, 1986), pp. 60–2.
39. J.A. Bertoud, 'Narrative and Ideology: A Critique of Fredric Jameson's *The Political Unconscious*' in Jeremy Hawthorn, *Narrative. From Malory to Motion Pictures* (London: Edward Arnold, 1985), pp. 101–15.

40. See on this issue Neil Larson, 'Foreword' to *The Ideologies of Theory, Vol. 1 Situations of Theory* (London: Routledge, 1988), especially pp. xvii–xix, and William C. Dowling, *Jameson, Althusser, Marx. An Introduction to The Political Unconscious* (Ithaca: Cornell University Press, 1984).

41. *Late Marxism*, op. cit., p. 8.

42. Dowling, op. cit., pp. 65, 71–5.

43. *Ideologies of Theory, Vol. 2*, op. cit., p. ix.

44. In one disconcerting move global Capital becomes, in its vast complexity, a word effectively for 'God': the sublimely unknowable we seek to know, 'the ultimate . . . referent, the true ground of Being of our own time', *The Geopolitical Aesthetic* (Bloomington: Indiana University Press; London BFI, 1992), p. 85. For the most part, however, in this study of film as elsewhere, the world system can only be 'mapped and modelled *indirectly*, by way of a simpler object that stands as its *allegorical* interpretant, that object being most often in postmodernism itself a media phenomenon' (ibid., p. 169, my italics).

45. Larson, op. cit., p. xviii.

46. Ibid., p. xix, and see Eagleton's discussion op. cit., especially pp. 72–5. Peter Womack points to the problem in Jameson's concession that this non-narrative and non-representational 'History' is only accessible to us in textual form: Jameson presents us with an object of knowledge which 'can only be accessed by a procedure which effaces its "fundamental" characteristic', 'Noises off', *Textual Practice*, 1, 3 (Winter 1987): 317.

47. *The Political Unconscious*, op. cit., p. 54.

48. Larson, op. cit., p. x.

49. Douglas Kellner (ed.), *Postmodernism/Jameson/Critique* (Washington: Maisonneuve Press, 1989), p. 31.

50. *Ideologies of Theory*, Vol. 2, op. cit., p. 208.

51. Douglas Kellner, *Critical Theory, Marxism and Modernity* (Oxford: Polity, 1989), p. 175.

52. Kellner writes how during the 1940s, Critical Theory became more 'philosophical', distancing itself from practical progressive politics; of how under Horkheimer and Adorno's influence, 'the earlier attempt to integrate philosophy and the social sciences was replaced by more uninhibited philosophical theorizing and speculation'. Their work, he writes, was 'addressed to "critical intellectuals"', and they surrendered the pretense that they were writing for a temporarily defeated revolutionary movement', ibid., pp. 84–5.

53. *Late Marxism*, op. cit., p. 9.

54. Kellner, op. cit., p. 204.

55. See ibid., pp. 208–9.

56. *Late Marxism*, p. 5.

57. *Ideologies of Theory, Vol. 2*, op. cit., p. 196.

58. Ibid., p. 197.

59. It is fair to say that Marcuse could conceive of artistic autonomy in transhistorical and idealist terms, though this is more evident in *The Aesthetic Dimension* (1978) than it is in an earlier essay such as 'The Affirmative Character of Culture' which Jameson cites and which

influenced attitudes in the 1960s. Also, Marcuse attributed a utopian aspect to art which Baudrillard's simulacra do not possess. Baudrillard, it is worth noting too, felt that Marcuse remained too attached to a Marxist notion of political economy. See Kellner, *Herbert Marcuse and the Crisis of Marxism* (London: Macmillan, 1984), p. 404.

60. Kellner, *Herbert Marcuse*, op. cit., p. 210, see also pp. 212, 225, 226; and Perry Anderson, *Considerations of Western Marxism* (London: Verso, 1976), p. 34. For the record, Marcuse had looked to the collaboration of workers and students and seen little prospect of revolution in the United States where there was a radical intelligentsia without a radical proletariat. In answer to a question after the '*événements*' in France in 1968 on the likelihood of revolution in the United States, Marcuse answered that it was impossible 'because there is no collaboration between the students and the workers', quoted in Robert W. Marks, *The Meaning of Marcuse* (New York: Ballantine, 1970), p. 92. It was all the same 'wrong', he said at a later date, to speak of the failure of the New Left. He saw the movement's lasting significance in the 'cultural revolution' it initiated – a 'new type of revolution' which put a programme of radical social change, encompassing the needs of workers, 'oppressed social minorities . . . the women's liberation movement', the struggle for 'the distribution of suppressed information, the protest against environmental pollution, boycotts, etc.' on the agenda of a transformed socialism. (Herbert Marcuse, 'The Failure of the New Left?', *New German Critique*, 18 (1981): 7–9.)

61. *Late Marxism*, op. cit., p. 7.

62. See Tim Wohlforth, 'The Sixties in America' for a contrasting 'internal' explanation which sees the failure of sixties radicalism as lying in its commitment to participatory as against some measure of representative democracy and longer-term structural organisation, *New Left Review*, 178 (1989): 105–23.

63. *Postmodernism*, op. cit., p. 409.

64. *Against the Grain*, op. cit., p. 77.

65. *Geopolitical Aesthetic*, op. cit., p. 163. In this study Jameson presents three non-American films: Sokurov's *Days of Eclipse*; Edward Yang's *Terrorizer*, Kidlat Tahimik's *The Perfumed Nightmare* and the cinema of Jean-Luc Godard as setting some modernist 'residue' or 'survival' against the postmodern world system.

66. Ibid.

67. Ezra Pound, *Drafts and Fragments of Cantos CX–CXVII* (London: Faber, 1970), pp. 26, 27.

68. Trenner (ed.), op. cit., p. 47.

69. *Ideologies of Theory, Vol. 2*, op. cit., p. 208.

70. Trenner, op. cit., p. 65.

71. Doctorow, *Lives of the Poets* (1984, London: Pan Books, 1986), p. 136. In the story 'Willi', which imagines the boy's fantasy of his mother's adultery and his betrayal of her to his father 'in Galicia in the year 1910', the place and dateline propose we think of this archetype as Reich, whose mother committed suicide in this year.

72. Trenner, op. cit., p. 47.

73. Ibid., pp. 64–5.

74. Ibid., p. 55.
75. Ibid., p. 57.
76. Ibid., p. 56.
77. Ibid., p. 53.
78. Ibid., pp. 54–5.
79. In the openly humanist and Enlightenment message delivered to Sarah Lawrence graduates in 1983, Doctorow spoke of every life having 'a theme' and the 'human freedom to find it'. This is the narrative of self-determination, he said, of 'real individualism . . . struggle for a human future and a society unbesieged by terror' undertaken in the name of civilisation ('It's a Cold World Out There Class of 83', *The Nation*, 2 July 1983: 6–7). Its ignoble opponent is represented by Ronald Reagan, a pure product of the 'meld of life and art typecasting we call stardom but which is in fact self-obliteration', in 'Ronald Reagan' in *Poets and Presidents, Selected Essays, 1977–1922* (London: Macmillan, 1993), p. 72. Against the embattled commitment to 'real individualism' stands Reagan's folksy, image-conscious imitation, the nostalgic evocation in 'the same speech' for 'self-reliance, hard work, belief in God, family and flag' (ibid., p. 78). Such thoughts are further evidence that Doctorow would be less than content to represent only the stereotypes and simulations of postmodern culture.
80. Trenner, op. cit., pp. 49, 52.
81. Ibid., pp. 18, 21, 69.
82. Ibid., p. 56.
83. E.L. Doctorow, *Ragtime* (London: Macmillan, 1974), p. 5. Further page references are given in the text.
84. The political ambiguity of the novel is confirmed by the opposite readings Linda Hutcheon and Jameson give to it. See Jameson, *Postmodernism*, op. cit., pp. 22–3.
85. Ibid., p. 23.
86. E.L. Doctorow, *Loon Lake* (1980; London: Pan Books, 1981), pp. 214–16. Following page references to this novel are given in the text.
87. E.L. Doctorow, *Billy Bathgate* (1989; London: Pan Books, 1990), p. 29. Following page references to this novel are given in the text.
88. Trenner, op. cit., pp. 57, 67–8.
89. Ibid., p. 53.
90. In the 'waning of our historicity', says Jameson, 'we seem increasingly incapable of fashioning representations of our own current experience'. He adds, in relation to *Ragtime*, but very pertinently here, that Doctorow seems to have evolved a tense such as the French *passé simple* which 'serves to separate events from the present of enunciation and to transform the stream of time and action into so many finished, complete, and isolated punctual event objects which find themselves sundered from any present situation (even that of the act of story telling or enunciation)', *Postmodernism*, op. cit., pp. 21, 24.
91. Roland Barthes, 'The Death of the Author', *Image Music Text*, ed. Stephen Heath (London: Fontana, 1977), p. 146.
92. *Ragtime*, op. cit., p. 99.
93. The treatment of women and questions of sexual difference in Doctorow's work would merit some closer attention. For the most

part, women characters are mothers or whores (who can be possessed as both in the figure of the surrogate father's 'girl'). In 'Lives of the Poets' they are more evidently wives and partners though a source of men's distress. In *The Book of Daniel* only is there a sister, destroyed by her 'failure of analysis'. Like the mother in *Billy Bathgate* and the grandmother in *Daniel* and *Lives* she is also deranged. With the exception of Rochelle Isaacson (Ethel Rosenberg), Emma Goldman is the only 'historical radical' in the novels and a repeated reference in Doctorow's non-fictional statements.

94. Jacques Derrida, 'Choreographies' in Peggy Kamuf (ed.), *A Derrida Reader. Between the Blinds* (Hemel Hempstead: Harvester Wheatsheaf, 1991), p. 442. Derrida is responding to a question on 'woman's place' which cites the 'maverick feminist' Goldman's riposte to the feminist movement that, 'If I can't dance I don't want to be part of your revolution.'

95. Ibid.

96. Ibid., p. 455.

97. Trenner, op. cit., p. 69.

98. Jameson, *Postmodernism*, p. 24.

99. Trenner, op. cit., pp. 67–8.

100. See Homi Bhabha, 'Conference Presentation', in Philomena Mariani (ed.), *Critical Fictions* (Seattle: Bay Press, 1991), pp. 62–5.

CHAPTER FOUR

New York Nowhere

HIGH TIMES, HARD TIMES: THE 1980s

New York was an archipelago of ghettos seething with aliens
(Bharati Mukherjee, *Jasmine*, 1991)

We think of the 1980s as the period of economic boom and untrammelled consumption, and in this respect, in one of its senses, as the period of high postmodernism, the cultural equivalent of late capitalism identified by Fredric Jameson. For Jameson the key point of rupture initiating this new phase was the 1960s. But other commentators, Mike Davis and Alex Callinicos amongst them, have queried the periodising assumptions directing Jameson's account. As Davis points out, Ernst Mandel (whose *Late Capitalism* provides Jameson's economic markers) speaks of '"the long *postwar* wave of rapid growth". All of his subsequent writings', Davis adds, 'make clear that Mandel regards the real break, the definite ending of the long wave, to be the "second slump" of 1974–5.'[1] Precisely when therefore, as Davis asks, did late capitalism begin: in 1945 or the 1960s; and what part do postwar boom and slump play in accounts of postmodernism? And how, beyond this, are we to view the period of the 1980s, to say nothing of its after-effects and the present contemporary moment? Have the 1990s brought us to the end of postmodernism, or only to the end of one of its forms; an end to a phase in the postmodern?

David Harvey helps answer this first set of questions. He sees a single year, 1972, as the point of epochal transition. Up to this date, he says, programmes of urban renewal and public housing, expanding suburbanisation, economic growth, relatively full employment and a functioning welfare state were common fare in most of the advanced capitalist nations. Whatever the signs of unrest and urban protest these were 'tempered by a certain political commitment to do something about material needs, albeit within the constraints of the efficient and rational planning of urban life and space.'[2] We can in these terms think of postwar urban life and public culture as governed by a predominantly modernist ethos, including the widespread corporate housing and one-off super-skyscrapers like the World Trade Centre and the John Hancock building of the 1960s: examples of a persistent 'International style', berated as late as the early 1980s in Tom Wolfe's *From Bauhaus to Our House* as a snobbish foreign imposition. For Harvey, the modernist aesthetic and associated reformist ethic were replaced, as of 1972, by 'a whole new urban vocabulary':

> Words like 'gentrification' and 'yuppie', styles like postmodernism, the creation of spaces of play and spectacle, the imitation or preservation of past environments, the ceaseless promotion of almost anything that has glitz and glitter are just some of the signs of radical change . . . . The city is no longer treated as an entity malleable for broad social ends, but as a collage of spaces and people, of ephemeral events and fragmentary contacts.
>   We no longer plan the whole, but design the parts. We no longer renew, we rehabilitate and renovate. Aesthetics dominates ethics. Images dominate the narratives of coherent analysis.[3]

The prelude to this change and the end of the postwar social modernism Harvey describes was the recession of 1973–75. Nixon's announcement in 1973 that the urban crisis in the United States was over signalled a shift in state investment away from the inner cities of the North East. The result in New York City was that projects of urban renewal such as the Second Avenue subway, the Kennedy Airport rail-link, improvements to housing, mass transit and the development of New York Harbour had to be shelved or abandoned.[4] In 1975 the nation was awakened to headlines declaring the city to be on the verge of bankruptcy. At the last minute the city was rescued by an emergency federal loan, the stringent conditions of which required heavy cuts in state and city budgets (and thus in public works, services and jobs), as well as higher taxes. At the same time, the planning and development process was granted almost total administrative freedom from federal red tape and supervision. It was against this immediate background that Mayor Ed Koch orchestrated the property boom of the 1980s, offering tax breaks and adjustments to zoning regulations so as to entice business interests. The boom advantaged the old and new rich (the infamous yuppies) in the newly expanded service sector (a category accounting for 85 per cent of all jobs in the city in 1985, and including many part-time and poorly paid typists, shop assistants, cleaners, floorwalkers, burger-flippers and dishwashers as well as the familiar bond salesmen, stockbrokers and lawyers).[5] With the stock market crash of 1987, however – marking the symbolic end of the 1980s – many of the top echelons and newer young financiers themselves felt the effects of financial reversal. As the world was alerted to the new eighties crime of insider-dealing by sensational cases like Ivan Boetsky, playing the market must have suddenly felt like playing snakes and ladders with the ladders taken away.

Over and above these dramatic, fateful workings of late capitalism, the late 1970s and 1980s had also seen the coming and going of Presidents Ford, Carter and Reagan, the rise of the Radical Right in company with a host of TV evangelists, the identification of the AIDS virus, the Star Wars initiative, the Irangate hearings, the invasion of Grenada, the bombing of Libya, and the fall of the Berlin Wall. If the end of Soviet-style communism appeared to leave the field free to the United States, the rising deficit (from $200 billion in 1988 to $350 billion in 1991) threw a dim light on its prowess as a world economic power. Under President Bush, who saw out the numerical 1980s, a show of military might in Iraq was a short-lived distraction from economic and social decline. The earlier period, once more, of capitalist growth and social democracy between 1946 and the early 1970s, was confirmed as America's true period of pre-eminence. Some twenty years later, in 1991, aside from the burden of national debt, unemployment stood at 7.6 per cent; 14.2 per cent of the population were said to be living below the poverty line (measured as a family of four earning $14,000 or an individual earning $7,000); 22 per cent of American children were said to live in poverty; and 29 per cent of the poor and 14 per cent of the population as a whole were without health insurance. For most Americans, the standard of living was lower than that experienced by their parents.[6] In New York City itself, unemployment stood in 1991 at between 9 and 10 per cent, and the number of homeless at 90,000. One million of the population was on public assistance. One-third of the homeless were HIV positive, and one in seven New Yorkers was found to have tuberculosis.[7]

It is clear now if we take this longer view, not only of the mid 1970s to the mid 1980s but over the last two decades of late capitalist postmodernism, that it has been framed at either end by fiscal crises, and that these years have yielded a legacy of increased poverty and social inequality (from 1979–89 the top 1 per cent of families improved their income by almost 75 per cent, the bottom 20 per cent dropped their income by 4.4 per cent).⁸ Such prosperity as existed was highly selective. All that trickled down were the effects of recession.

At the same time, and in New York City particularly, a very real change of another kind has accompanied this persistent economic decline. In the mid 1980s New York ceased to be a majority white ethnic city.⁹ As of 1992, African-Americans and Hispanics comprised one-quarter each of its eight million inhabitants. Hispanic immigrants especially (a variegated grouping including Puerto Ricans, Cubans, Dominicans and Latin Americans), as well as new African and Asian immigrants, have effectively swung the city away from its predominantly European cultural affiliations and modernist identity to that of an ethnically mixed, postmodern cosmopolis. If many look to this development as a further stage in New York's (and the nation's) cultural pluralism, there are strong signs too of new enmities. Richard Gott, for example, points to the nervousness of whites at the Hispanic 'culture of separateness' and 'different path to integration' and to the emergence of David Duke, the Republican ex-Klansman as one vocal sign of popular backlash against this sense of loss of status and national identity.¹⁰ The later emergence of Louis Farrakhan, right-wing leader of the African-American Nation of Islam, and of explicit anti-semitism in the ranks of this movement, is further evidence of the uneasy coexistence of separatism and hybridity under the sign of postmodern difference.

THE STRAITS OF POSTMODERNISM

An account such as the above is assembled, obviously enough, from journalistic and sociological, sometimes statistical sources. This material employs documentary and autobiographical modes, and appeals to the authenticity of fact and direct personal experience, or reminiscence, as ways of establishing the truth. It apparently flies in the face, therefore, of a poststructuralist or postmodern scepticism which finds such methods and assumptions naïve or reactionary and finds notions of truth a superfluous and irrelevant legacy of the Enlightenment project.¹¹ To offer this account here as an accurate picture of changes in the city and as relevant to the fiction of the period would therefore seem to commit me to an outmoded modern project with all its illusions and limitations. Instead, I want, in this very comment, to put the above paragraphs effectively in inverted commas, and to claim that they present 'a' set of truths (in less postmodern fashion a preferred set of truths) rather than 'the' truth. This 'weak foundationalism' is unlikely to withstand the blast of a full postmodernism or to satisfy the requirements of an unfussy modernist commitment. On the other hand, it might provide some passage between the simplified, *papier mâché* Scylla and Charybdis so often labelled modernism and postmodernism: the first dubbed (daubed?) elitist, Eurocentric, dogmatic, teleological; the second rubbed (robbed?) clean of all historicity, reference and claims to truth. (The universalising pretensions of this second, Baudrillardian scenario of the postmodern, and allied dismissal of its deluded, modernist other, is one of the most obviously contradictory features of a mode otherwise unflinchingly critical of binary oppositions and totalising ambitions.)

I want indeed to suggest that the 'post' modern (Raymond Williams's 'present beyond the "modern"') lies in the difficult waters between these obstacles; that it comprises a complex, re-forming set of currents and cross-currents, a dialogic totality in which modern, materialist assumptions and realist practices circulate in and amongst more self-consciously postmodernist forms.[12] It is also clear that these older forms are not always simply innocent of postmodernism, but well versed in and critical of it – or the implications of some of its versions. David Harvey is one such critic. Speaking of changes in the urban environment, he sees the contemporary emphasis on design as providing 'an explanation of the shift from ethics to aesthetics and from modernism to postmodernism. The attention the latter pays to fiction and fantasy rather than function fits that world of voodoo economics'.[13] Harvey speaks on behalf of a continuing and reformulated modernist project, committed to the general principles of social justice, to a materialist method and a flexible class politics as the basis for political solidarity and action in the real world.[14] One would not on this evidence expect him to include his own assessment of the years of postwar boom and decline as an example of postmodernism. Yet his account does compose actions, events and key characters into a narrative, that is to say a 'fiction' of this period. The same might be said of the essays in the volume *In Search of New York*, and other material drawn upon above, as well as the introduction to this chapter itself. These examples quite plainly exist, moreover, in an intertextual relation with other accounts and arguments, or narratives. We come, if we are willing, to appreciate how these accounts employ the discursive conventions of academic or journalistic writing, personal reminiscence and first-person observation and commentary: how they belong, in short, to orders of narrative rather than to either side of an opposition between fact and fiction. In this respect they can be seen as 'postmodernist', even if they do not see themselves this way. It is clear too, however, that these are motivated and rhetorical accounts (employing figures, in the aptly double sense of this word) situated somewhere on the democratic Left. In which respect we might say they remain 'modern'.

The distinction between social and historical fact and fiction needs to be rethought, therefore, in terms of the discursive conventions which employ 'fact' and 'fiction' for rhetorical ends in different kinds of narrative. Like these terms, 'truth' too ought at least to come dressed these days in inverted commas. (One only has to imagine an account of the 1980s from the Republican or Tory Right to appreciate how 'true' accounts are situated, ideological accounts.) E.L. Doctorow's fiction instructs us in just this understanding, and stands as an example of what we can learn in the way of truth and the historical record from literary fiction.

We can progress beyond a disabling 'crisis of representation', therefore, if we rephrase the distinction between fact and fiction, as Harvey indeed does, as a distinction between form and function or aesthetics and ethics. Harvey assumes postmodernism has lost touch with the second (clearly correlated in his view with modernism or the project of modernity). Certainly, one could point to a hermetic preoccupation with a narrowly defined textuality in one version of postmodernism. At the same time, this tendency is itself a cause of concern for those who wish to regain or reformulate an ethical or oppositional position within the postmodern, or contemporary moment. Any attempt to counter 'voodoo economics' and the inequalities of late capitalism, therefore, will necessarily work from within this system and be involved in 'refunctioning' the narratives, or fictions, even fantasies of this world.

Are we to think of this position and practice as critical of postmodernism, or itself a critical postmodernism? Natoli and Hutcheon write how 'the desire to put the postmodern into practice at the level of useful political and social intervention' seems to mean tailoring it to fit a feminist or postcolonialist or Marxist practice, and how 'such efforts often appear to come from within the modern project itself'.[15] The result is an impossible dilemma, they feel, since a modernist belief in universal rights and values cannot be activated in ways consistent with a postmodern critique of such totalising assumptions. Hence the issue, they say, 'that a postmodern "anything" faces: basically how we are going to "do" history, philosophy, sociology, psychology, literary criticism, anthropology, geography, folklore, or any form of art in postmodern ways'; how are we to discover a practice which is 'locally effective' but which makes no claims 'to be universally applicable'?[16]

Their solution would seem to be to slough off the modern. The issue of a contemporary oppositional art and culture looks different, however, if we turn the question around and ask how we are going to do a *modern* anything in a postmodern way. Many would see this as making the universal concepts of democracy, equality or justice responsive and specific to local, provisional situations and communities. The problem with this option is that the resulting postmodern politics, if it successfully avoids the rigidities to which 'identity politics' is sometimes prone, may be confined to local issues or resemble nothing so much as the pavement politics of the English Liberal Democrats; a local influence but a national non-starter. The conditions of postmodernity might prompt us to think, on the other hand, in a quite opposite direction. The advent of democracy in South Africa, for example, surely a key event of the contemporary era, would seem to confirm rather than question the continuing universal vitality of Enlightenment principles. We might conclude that the problem lies not with the universalising claims for ideas of equality, liberty and justice, but with their uneven and unjust application; that the universal has, in fact, not been made universal enough. In these terms, the adjustment the postmodern requires of the modern would be the practical extension and deepening of its principles, not their diminution or abandonment.

An important related factor here has been the changing conception of culture, and thus once more of cultural function. In the liberal and modernist tradition, culture has been seen as a sphere of relatively autonomous form and moral value. It is on these grounds that it has been possible to speak of its 'function', or the function of its handmaidens, literature or criticism, and to see these as a consoling alternative to, or in some way edifying influence upon their opposites: anarchy, civilisation, mass society, commercial culture, or late capitalism – all those things which are inimical to the well-being of an authentic culture, or are simply 'not culture'. Since they are not 'culture' they have often been thought of as 'society'. In the postmodern era, by contrast, where we are told that 'there is no such thing as society' and that textuality or culture 'goes all the way down', a critical culture must work simultaneously within and against an inescapable system of representation. For Hutcheon, and others, this kind of double-life can produce a parodic and subversive deconstruction of ruling linguistic and ideological codes. For Jameson, on the other hand, the postmodern modes of pastiche, recycling and simulation doom critical culture to a purgatory of self-referentiality, forever in danger of losing its footing and object.

Both these commentators accept (Jameson with some serious qualms) that there are no social relations or history, and perhaps no viable universal criteria 'out there', outside of textuality and representation. Their notions of a critical postmodern culture, or its dilemmas follow from this. Whatever else, however, these ideas contrast with the thoughts of others interested nominally in the same broad political project, and who, in the texts cited above, for example, seek a new ethical grounding in postmodernism, or eschewing this term, in the present period after modernism.

This would include those, to return to the particular focus here, who contribute to the volume *In Search of New York*. Their perspective is for the most part that of Left Jewish intellectuals aware of a decline in their cultural influence. In fact, this, as much as the changing economic, social and physical conditions of New York in the late 1980s is the subject of the volume. Irving Howe, a defender in earlier years of literary modernism, a second-generation New York intellectual, tireless campaigner for a democratic America, and leading editor of the journal, writes from deep within the experience of an encounter between modernity and postmodernity and the trials of literary and left intellectual culture. (See the discussion below, pp. 214–19.) Like others, he sees decline and despair, and looks to culture, to the abstract expressionists of the 1950s and to the inspired influence of George Balanchine upon contemporary dance, for signs of hope and vitality in the city. (Unlike others, but in a familiar modernist position, he cites television as a major cause of present woes.) Literary life has produced little, Howe thinks, after the break up of the *Partisan Review* and the end of the Beats. What is lacking, he says, 'is a fresh surge of energy, a new direction or a new idea, a shared and irresistible impulse that could give writers the feeling that they are part of a "movement" or "trend" that might, if only slightly, reinvigorate American culture'.[17] Wesley Brown, in a later, more optimistic contribution to the same volume, finds some cultural hope in the subway (one is reminded of Doctorow's *Lives of the Poets*), where the contradictions of city life are played out on a daily basis: where pluralism dices with paranoia and flamboyant self-assertion meets fear and impacted grievance. At the turnstile of West 59th Street a black guitar player mixes classical and popular styles in a familiar but new way. Brown feels his own breathing and that of fellow passengers relax. 'The remarkable thing about what is happening', he writes, 'is that, separated as we are by the fear of what makes us different, we are joined by our profound attention to this music.' For a brief moment, but no more – significantly Brown says he could not imagine an equivalent political unity – the guitarist provides an example of coexistence, and thus of cultural uplift, affirming 'our common humanity'.[18] A further contributor, Juan Flores, writes in a similar vein of the sustained collaboration of Puerto Ricans and blacks in literature and in music, leading to the creation of hip-hop, rapping and breakdance.[19]

All of these pieces are an answer to the question 'what can culture (or cultural "fictions") tell or do for us?' Howe's sense of cultural emptiness might be read as a sign of the redundancy of the modernist project, though he is not without hope of a future renewal, 'a new "American newness" . . . waiting to be born'.[20] Culture can be enlightening, uplifting, the sign of an alternative communal order or way of being, and in the other essays the critical cultural function Howe feels is dormant is revived, however temporarily. These other examples also show that it is not enough to see these writers simply as beleaguered moderns. The guitarist in the subway mixing classical with popular styles might strike us, for instance, as an example of postmodern hybridity, of how 'to "do"' postmodern art 'in postmodern ways'. We might say too that it is 'locally effective'. In giving this performance cultural meaning, however, Brown himself clearly assumes a universal humanity which derives from a contrasting liberal or modern perspective. Puerto Rican and black graffiti, music and dance styles in the third essay, are more convincingly postmodern: examples of ethnic collaboration in the making of alternative, locally specific cultural practices. But features of this essay too are markedly unpostmodern. Flores talks of a long history that traces these practices back to African dance, for example; he sees them as countering a 'macadamization of the spirit', and as resisting dominant commercial culture. 'Hip hop', he says, 'harbors a radical universal appeal.'[21]

These essays reveal how mixed the resources of an oppositional postmodern culture in fact are, and how this conjunctural moment comprises both residual and emergent tendencies in its passage between the old and the new. They also assume that 'society' exists, and are replete with social and historical reference, as are other essays in the same volume. The authors themselves understand this society, moreover, as divided and uneven; as composed of dominant, dormant and alternative tendencies, and in each case ascribe an adversarial function to culture, whether this is modernist, avant-garde, popular or postmodernist. Coupled with the essays by Harvey, Hutcheon and Jameson, they confirm how unresolved these debates are, how transitional this period really is, and what it might mean to talk of its dialogic totality. We should not be surprised, consequently, if the literary fiction of the period shares, and, in its own ways, comments on these differences. Another answer indeed to the question 'What can fiction tell us?' is that of itself it both illustrates and reflects on the nature and function of 'postmodernist' fiction or a fiction of 'post' modernity. Few examples of more-or-less realist or more-or-less postmodernist fiction in this period are free from this self-consciousness, as we shall see. I want, however, first of all, to comment on another kind of self-consciousness, which bears particularly on the questions raised above concerning developments in the city.

The major recent change in New York City has to do with its transformed ethnic composition. If we want to think of how literature relates to society, or of how its narratives in all their specificity relate to other social narratives, then contemporary New York makes it clear that the 'society' or 'social' in question here has no transcendent unity or common purpose. These changes mean that whites are no longer numerically the majority in the city. Nevertheless – and however embattled some poorer, working-class whites have come to feel – whites quite clearly remain the dominant group in the city's political, economic and cultural order. As Henry Giroux puts it, 'while people of color are redrawing the cultural demographic boundaries of the urban centers, the boundaries of power appear to be solidifying in favor of rich, white middle and upper classes'.[22] This, once more, describes the 'dialogic totality' which a new fiction will be a part of and in some way express. The novels I consider here have for the most part been produced from within this still dominant group: one which in social modernism has defined itself as the norm, the 'self' in relation to various 'others'. What this fiction tells us, therefore, in recording and imagining the lives of the city, will be about its own condition; about the changing social position and consciousness of white in relation to subordinated or emergent groups. The sign of the 'postmodern', therefore, as I have wanted to re-describe it throughout, is the modern in crisis, a moment when its invisible norms become evident, and perhaps impossible, in a more deeply self-conscious way than a postmodernist concern with form alone normally suggests. The novel therefore joins in negotiating the mixed waters of the postmodern. Perhaps on occasion it can also show us what lies beyond. To revert to the Scylla and Charybdis of modernism and postmodernism, Odysseus sails beyond this monster and whirlpool to the island of Helios's cattle, to Phaiaca and so alone to Ithaca and eventual reconciliation with Penelope. The experience of journeying, of exile and homecoming is often very relevant to the stories considered below, chiefly of immigrant groups resettling in the United States. The story of Odysseus might bring us to think too of the 'ocean of story' John Barth speaks of: the vast world library of classical myth, fable, fairy- and folk-tale of which Barth himself and other writers of the postmodern avail themselves. These older, oral and often non-realist narratives also prove a resource for some of the new writers considered here. The postmodern defines itself, one might say, in such writing through the 'premodern'. But again this is not its only resource. We need another description, therefore, of the mixed narrative modes and voices this fiction brings to the changing city. The symbolic entry-point to New York has of course been through the Verrazano narrows and so past the Statue of Liberty to the city harbour. Countless new lives have in that way begun under the welcoming eyes of an embodiment of the modern project. What beckons now, I suggest, as we pass through the straits of postmodernism, must be the 'new modern', a cosmopolis of story fit for its wide and various dialogue.

FALLING STATUES, CLASS AND COLOUR LINES: FICTIONS OF THE '80s

Tom Wolfe is one writer who has responded directly to some of the questions raised above. For years he had expected the appearance of the novel of New York City, 'a big realistic novel' to match 'this astonishing metropolis . . . *where things are happening*' and where the postwar economic boom had produced new wealth, new social stratifications and 'overt racial conflict'.[23] Instead he discovered that contemporary writers had eschewed the realist novel. Philip Roth had persuaded a generation that 'actuality is continually outdoing our talents' and that 'American life itself no longer deserved the term *real*' (pp. xiii, xiv). As he began his own novel, Wolfe found he too had to contend with the marvellous fictions tumbling freely from the cornucopia of daily life. How could the novel compete with the real-life story of Bernhard Goetz or a character like Al Sharpton? Wolfe's own answer was to be a new realism: 'a highly detailed realism based on reporting, a realism more thorough than any currently being attempted' (p. xvii). His illustration is a passage from early in *Bonfire of the Vanities* where he has the Mayor of New York address white middle-class New Yorkers on TV from a stage in Harlem: 'Do you really think this is *your* city any longer?' he asks, '. . . It's the Third World down there!' (pp. xix–xx). The new reality Wolfe means to record is one in which 'within ten years political power in most major American cities will have passed to the nonwhite majorities' (p. xx).

In the event, Wolfe takes Wall Street as the high and the South Bronx as the low point on the New York social scale, and uses one incident – Sherman McCoy's getting lost with his mistress in the 'heart of darkness' of the Bronx – to open a social narrative of racial tension, scandal and disgrace for the white upper middle class. In other words, *Bonfire of the Vanities* shapes and simplifies the unpredictable variety of this society. As the novel progresses, its broad satirical purpose is tailored more and more to the limiting range and focus of the traditional novel; the profound social and political change Wolfe detects confined, in Homi Bhabha's words, to 'the linear and liberal traditions of literary realism'.[24]

Wolfe's novel reveals the plight of fictional realism in a knowing age which has forgotten how to suspend disbelief, and in which the world is too vast and extraordinary for an omniscient perspective to even pretend to comprehend. The distinction between documentary and fabulation which his essay 'Stalking the Billion-Footed Beast' appeals to will not stand up, for the real of this world is already known to be hyper-real. Nor can the 'single, fairly simple story' of realist fiction (p. xxix) hope to encompass this changing society as an epic totality when this is known to be 'more varied and complicated and harder to define' (p. xix).

We might compare Wolfe's 'journalistic realism' with the work of Richard Price. Price's early fiction is based in autobiography and its particular strength, aside from matters of plot and character, is in dialogue. His ear for the spoken word places this work in a tradition of colloquial, regional or urban realism, keen to give authentic expression to the individual and social group. *Clockers* (1992) is driven by a more active social concern, and employs the form of the detective novel to investigate relations between white cops and black kids, the 'clockers' of the title, who deal in cocaine in the projects of the fictional Dempsey in Jersey City. The key relationship is between the weary homicide cop, Rocco Klein, and 'Strike' Dunham, a clocker, who Rocco is convinced is the murderer of a dealer, in spite of Strike's brother having confessed to the crime. Much as in Wolfe's novel, areas of New York are shown as wasted or utterly changed. The Third World has moved next door to the First: JFK Boulevard 'looks like Central America';[25] the Bronx is a 'blasted moonscape . . . every dead building a different nation, a different drug' (p. 69). For Sherman McCoy to lose his way in this New York is to be lost in an alien land and his trip to the courthouse is like a journey to the Congo. In *Clockers*, areas of the City have become threatening wastelands for both black and white, and only the immediate neighbourhood is familiar. Here the Fury (the neighbourhood cops) and the street drug crews are enemies but coexist on the basis of a precarious 'respect' borne of a shared language, set conventions, and common street culture. Rocco and Strike live in the same ruined world. At one point, seeking a witness 'at the bottom of the junkie chain' in the gutted hospital where he was born, Rocco sees 'the dying sun descending over New York' and the Statue of Liberty tracking him. When they find the junkie called 'Almighty' hunched over a wrecked hospital bed, the arm of the Statue of Liberty seems to stick 'straight up out of his head like a prosthetic device' (pp. 215, 220). Liberty herself has symbolically fallen into a huddled, mutant state.

Rocco's only future is another case. Strike has tried to 'envision the future' beyond the three-minute clock time of dealing in the projects (p. 78), and once Rocco discovers his innocence he is granted the longed-for fresh start: a 'See America' book of tickets offers to take him from the Port Authority Bus terminal South to Philadelphia, Washington, Atlanta. 'Maybe he'd try the South for a while, or maybe . . . go out west . . . . He'd just have to see how he felt, think about what he'd be thinking about when he got there' (p. 598).

Price's liberal concern produces a liberal solution, an exit for one, which follows, as inevitably as McCoy's entrapment in his enduring court case, from the conventions of literary realism where a 'social problem' is treated as an affair of individuals. Price's position is paradoxical, however. Though, like Wolfe, he assumes the position of invisible, omniscient narrator, he is also, like Rocco the cop who is deep in crime, the 'insider', the participant observer who researched the neighbourhood for two years and can consequently 'show more', with greater verisimilitude of the postmodern city than Wolfe's binary extremes of white wealth and poor blacks. Unlike Wolfe again, but not yet like a more conspicuously postmodernist writer (such as Auster who uses the detective form for non-realist purposes), *Clockers* is drawn to reflect on the nature of narrative in a way that exposes the assumptions the novel means to protect. Strike's escape from the city derives very obviously from the narrative store-house of American mythology. But elsewhere there are signs of narrative self-consciousness (Rocco is shadowed by a movie actor, and at the scene of the murder feels as if 'he was inside a movie screen', p. 121). And above all, Rocco knows he is a story-teller and story-maker. His job is to work from the stark mystery of a killing. Behind it lies a story of events and motives which at his best he constructs for those involved, scripting what they do not know, or will not tell, out of a fund of experience which has given him a template for the way people in this world will act. He seeks a story which conforms to this existing typology. When this clicks in place, when his story telling meets with the nods and bobbing heads of those he puts it to, he is engaged, fully present, as he brings their narratives into words and form. The lesson of his career, however, is that narratives do not conform to type, that his stories provoke no response or produce their own distorting effects, as in his version of Strike's story.

Rocco is 'at home' on the streets, being an investigator. At home with his young artist wife, Patty and her child, he is uncomfortable. At an anniversary party there ('feeling like the Father', p. 383), one of her friends asks him if 'Rocco *Klein*' is his real name. He responds 'too quickly' – 'What are you, an anti-semite?' (p. 385), and launches into a story of how his grandfather, called 'Sonny Marx', had been blacklisted in the poultry business, had beaten up the boss who had fired him, and how the cop Rocco Aiello had fixed things with the judge in his grandfather's favour. Rocco was his grandfather's hero, and the name, with the grandfather's heroic proletarian credentials, had passed to the grandson (giving 'Klein' some size). The story commands the attention of Patty's friends. And so Rocco tells how as an adult, visiting his grandfather's death-bed, he learns the truth – how his grandfather had been fired for stealing eggs and after two weeks had gone back to the chicken hall to beg, plead, cry for his job back. Only when he was ignored had he struck the boss. 'And I think this was the true story', says Rocco, adding, 'I mean, I'm a detective, right? I should know the truth from the lie when I hear it, right? But with your family . . . the truth is a while in the coming' (p. 387).

Rocco's words describe the slowly revealed truth of *Clockers* itself in his real family of Homicide Dept, big white fathers and black youths in the drug trade of Dempsey. His chosen story for Strike is not a report but a misconstruction, and a trigger to the story's final events. But this self-consciousness on the nature and effect of narrative, an acknowledged instability in Rocco's identity and the claims of truth and falsehood, and thus of the real, is never allowed to directly impinge on the novel's own form. Its main actor, exercising his gifts and talents as an investigator, is an artist who draws our attention to the novel's own narrative artistry. Yet the real narrator, Price, remains caged in the pretence of omniscience and invisibility, unable or unwilling to declare and embody this internal knowledge in what would be a fuller 'realism'.

In the anniversary party with Patty's friends, the conversation is taken up by a woman artist working at waitressing. She screws up orders, but takes it lightly. Unlike Rocco she has 'no sense of identification with the job. Listening to her Rocco felt a stab of resentment at the open-endedness of her life, at her blissful assumption that she could play an infinite number of roles through the coming years' (p. 387). This woman, whose anonymity is a mark of her otherness in this novel, might be a refugee from Tama Janowitz's *Slaves of New York* or Mary Gaitskill's *Bad Behaviour*, and Rocco's resentment looks like an expression of Price's unease at the sometimes indifferent, decentred mobility presented by such fiction.

Janowitz and Gaitskill are amongst those identified by Graham Caveney and Elizabeth Young as members of the eighties 'Blank Generation', a description that includes Lynn Tillman, Gary Indiana, David Wojnarowicz, Dennis Cooper and Joel Rose, and as its principal actors, Jay McInerney and Bret Easton Ellis. Here, so they suggest, is a movement to reinvigorate American culture of the kind Irving Howe seeks but does not find. 'We are in another country', they write, 'where the author is dead' and where 'character' is the pastiched and mutating product of popular media and myth. Against a 'background of consumer frenzy and a fragmented fictional landscape, Ellis and his literary peers took to the streets of America', hoping to render the truth 'through the blizzard of fall-out from an uncertain, nervously apocalyptic world which seemed constantly poised, like a psychotic at bay with no hostages, on the brink of shooting itself in the head'.[26] In this manner they reject academic discourse and English opinion on American fiction, for a street-wise prose, which, as it turns out, is itself full of opinion and – their protestations aside – makes free use of psychoanalytic and feminist theory alongside old-fashioned praise of the creative artist and talk of 'eternal verities'.[27]

Much of 'blank generation' or 'downtown' fiction displays the fragmented, strung-out or hollowed subjectivities and disjointed mini-narratives that have come to be associated with the effects of visual media and the anonymity of the urban postmodern.[28] Often too it shows a self-conscious fictionality of a more open and explicit kind than Price's realism will allow. Caveney and Young's most important claim, however, is that this writing presents a 'revealing critique' of the society of the 1980s (p. viii). In some of the writings of Tama Janowitz, Mary Gaitskill and Catherine Texier, the themes of subjectivity, of the false and the real, are connected with the positioning and repositioning of women in relation to the male control of relationships, property, and forms of domestic and professional employment. Beyond this, however, claims for the critical intent or effect of 'blank generation' writing are unconvincing.

One key example, Jay McInerney's *Brightness Falls* (1992), is clearly a deliberate attempt to write a social novel of the decade. I shall return to its treatment of the 'social problem' of the poor in a later chapter. Its bold intention and literariness (the title from Thomas Nashe, the textual and thematic echoes of Scott Fitzgerald) fail, meanwhile, to disguise its conventionality. Its central couple, the white middle-class Calloways, through whom we witness the 'crack-up' of the 1980s, cannot mediate a comprehensive social view any more than can the individuals and types of *Bonfire* or *Clockers*. Russell 'Crash' Calloway, who battles for control of a publishing company, is heavily implicated in the commercialisation of literary culture. However humbled he is, 'learning to get by with less' after his bout of eighties greed, Russell feels he and Corrine 'could both look down on the culture at large', when in truth their social vision cannot comprehend and in no way impinges on the extremes of plutocracy and poverty which truly define the age.[29]

The most interesting thing about McInerney's novel is who and what falls, and how far. Invariably this has to do with money. The stock market crashes in 1987, avant-garde culture falls with the old-style Corbin Dern publishing house, Propp the modernist fellow-traveller proves a fraud, and Jeff the new white literary hope falls through his manipulated 'tabloid fame' on through a stylish vagrancy into drugs, detox and death (from a condition none 'seemed willing to name'). Corrine who dreams and intuits this general collapse herself miscarries. Yet all of them level out. Even Jeff, the only voice critical of the Calloways' 'goodness', leaves a posthumous novel which rescues his fame and by association his friends, the Calloways, and their author.

Brightness Falls takes far less risk with its own literary identity and middling view of the world than Bret Easton Ellis's *American Psycho* – surely the true sensation of 'blank generation' writing. Ellis's work is itself an intended 'condition of America' novel focused through the fastidious taste and disgusts of a phenomenally wealthy Wall Street yuppie, Patrick Bateman. Bateman's life is given over to shopping, *The Patty Winters Show*, securing reservations at one of the never-ending new clubs in Manhattan and returning videos – the pornographic simulations that inspire his own monstrous maimings and murders of random victims. He is the serial killer as conspicuous consumer, the Manhattan cannibal who, unlike Tama Janowitz's visiting islander, is already there. Bateman's (dis)taste ranges from yuppie acquaintances and rivals, to escort girls, students, taxi-cab drivers, bums and beggars, totalling, he says, 'thirty, forty, a hundred murders'.[30]

At one point after he has taken his psychopathological blood lust on to the streets, Bateman shoots a saxophone player. He is pursued by police and escapes to his office on Wall Street, after killing several other people, and there confesses his crimes in the form of a telephone message to his lawyer. Still he goes uncaught and unpunished. There is no retribution in this world because (unlike the worlds of Doctorow and Auster and unlike *Clockers* and *Brightness Falls*) there are no fathers and no Law. The unrepressed white, wealthy, masculine unconscious roams uncaged, hunting down its 'other', disgusted at the difference. Bateman's killings protect and reproduce a world of one, because the narrow discriminations (dress, music, skin products, springwater) on which his known identity depends count for nothing. He is a cloned freak of late consumer culture who is interchangeable with others of his class. Yet he and this class are not of course whole and one. In Bateman, late capitalism releases its other side, the 'barbarism', which, to adopt Walter Benjamin's famous insight, accompanies this 'civilisation'.[31] The easy mobility this society allows the privileged reveals itself as the licence of becoming anybody, compounded with the fear of becoming another. It is often thought that Bateman hallucinates his activities. Whatever signs there are of this are irrelevant, however, since the novel is itself a fantasy which couples unrestricted desire and contempt with a fear of self-extinction: a fall from white male wealth into the abyss, where, in Bateman's phrase, there lurks at bottom the 'genetic underclass' (p. 266). This 'other' not only threatens the self, but in the logic of the free flow of capital and the highs and lows of the stock market, is a someone the self might become, or is already. *American Psycho* is, so Caveney and Young assume, a satire. Ellis is, 'straightforwardly judgemental and condemnatory', they say, only to concede that the absence of any authorial voice means that 'the onus is on the reader to interject the moral values so conspicuously lacking in the text'.[32] Certainly the novel exposes the barbarism of the 1980s, using Bateman as a limit case of the unchecked and unopposed schizophrenia, loss of affect, and loss of reality of the postmodern. But by that very token it can discover no norms or values of a kind that would make it a satire rather than itself a symptom. The novel's first-person narration cannot employ another figure as a vehicle of consciousness or judgement. (The figure Tim Price, an early model for Bateman, returns late in the novel to express his dismay at the discrepancy between the reality and lying 'normal' image of Ronald Reagan on TV, but cannot complete nor communicate this distinction: p. 397). Ellis attempts to use Bateman himself to this end (switching unconvincingly into third person: p. 349), but Bateman cannot represent a stable social conscience, and is at his most vacuous and contradictory when most 'philosophical'. Thus in the space of one paragraph the would-be liberal relativism of Bateman's 'true' belief: 'every model of human behaviour must be assumed to have some validity' is followed by 'I gain no deeper knowledge about myself, no new understanding can be extracted from my telling . . . . This confession has meant *nothing*' (p. 377). The novel's final words (a sign above a door in Harry's bar) provide a fitting commentary on such knowledge: 'THIS IS NOT AN EXIT' (p. 399).

It is difficult to avoid the hollow feeling that *American Psycho* is a commercial ploy, more a calculated assault on the market than a wilful smack in the face of the bourgeoisie. Like all of the fictions discussed above, it is more a symptom than an analysis of the decade. Either they seek to protect the blank space of the author high upon a narrative shelf while unified selves and economies tumble below them, or they can discover no authoritative perspective. The result is narratives confined by the barely sustained ruse of conventional realism, or sunk in themselves with no exit from a conflation of narrative perspective and social content.

Paul Auster certainly cannot be accused of the first, for in his writing the fall of the author into his fiction is a repeated event. Quite clearly all of Auster's major protagonists are in some way writers. As Auster describes it, writing is an affair of solitude, a compulsion and necessity.[33] But language and the writer are caught in his thinking between the dream of nominalism, a one-for-one fit between word and its thing-like meaning and the arbitrariness and *différance* announced by structuralism and post-structuralism. The individual is similarly thrown between a desire for unity and the play of multiple selves. Often these alternatives are enacted in the individual's location and bearing in physical space, in box-like rooms or in perambulations across the city or journeys across and out of the country: a seeming analogue of the life of a writer's language upon the page and across languages and literatures. Auster's stories reflect on these interlaced concerns of language, literature and identity, seeking moments or types of stability between the extremes of fixity and randomness. Hence his fascination with forms of rule-governed behaviour such as baseball and poker, and the conventional, social form of the family, especially relations between father and son, which figure as a major site both of stability and of unknowingness and fraught disconnection.

Many of these themes appear in Auster's best-known work, *The New York Trilogy*. In the first of these stories, 'City of Glass', Quinn, the academic turned crime writer turned detective, called Paul Auster, trails Peter Stillman across the streets of the upper West Side. Stillman has been released from prison after isolating his son in a darkened room for nine years, his belief being that his son would as a result learn nothing but the pure, natural language of God. Quinn consults Stillman's writings (including a commentary on Milton's *Paradise Lost* and the apocryphal work of one Henry Dark) and discovers there a theory of language and of the utopian society possible in the new world, the sign of which will be the building in 1960 in America of a new Tower of Babel. As he tracks Stillman's daily walks, Quinn sees that his movements in fact spell out the words 'Tower of Babel'. His method of detection as methodical reading fails him, however, and he falls into destitution, possessed by his adopted disguise of a tramp. Learning of Stillman's suicide (he jumps from Brooklyn Bridge – a symbol of connection in the following story between fathers and sons, and with the literary father-figure, Walt Whitman), Quinn occupies the younger Peter Stillman's room, and he himself disappears, part by part.

Utopia, as Henry Dark's *The New Babel* pointed out, is 'nowhere' – 'even . . . in its "wordhood"' (*eutopia*: the 'good place' which is 'no place'). For Stillman it is the paradise that might be regained in America, the dream of a unified self and one language. New York, he feels, is 'the most forlorn of places . . . the brokenness is everywhere'[34] and modern man is like Humpty Dumpty, 'a fallen creature' (p. 82). To build paradise therefore means reversing history, which is to say, reversing the fall. Stillman's is an Enlightenment dream gone mad, repressive and impossible. But there is another 'nowhere', the postmodern nowhere Quinn discovers as he loses himself walking the labyrinthine streets (p. 4), and in his eventual disappearance.

In one of the very few references to Auster in *Shopping in Space*, Caveney feels he does no more than suggest the city's 'barren neon and fragmented psyches'.[35] By contrast, Joel Rose in his novel *Kill the Poor*, Caveney argues, realises the idea of Foucault's 'heterotopia' with greater specificity, presenting the utopian 'nowhere' as now heterogeneous, a world of indifference to difference, since 'each "nowhere" has its own peculiarities, every space differs significantly from any others'.[36] But Auster too presents us with different 'nowheres': Stillman's modern and Quinn's postmodern, and thus two ideas of 'the new' of New York. The first is the longed-for culmination of a long 'masterful' narrative, an assumption of the oneness of God; the second the time of the instant with no connection or continuity. These two broken men are both Henry Dark, both Humpty Dumpty, the egg of Columbus's globe. And both too are like broken statues of America's symbolic liberty. What is to be done? Can the self, the egg, the statue, the tower, the idea and fact of the new world be put back together again, or is there only a heap of broken fragments, the drop into anonymity amid urban disarray?

The question Auster's story poses is also a question, we realise, about stories and the authority or disappearance of the narrator as maker of new worlds. Is the author the superior master or a nobody lost in the text of fiction? In fact, 'City of Glass' holds out a third possibility, a somewhere in-between the high and low of the tower of Babel and scattered limbs. As he walks the streets, Quinn takes notes of beggars and drifters, their otherness, and difference from each other. One of these – amongst 'the elite of the fallen' not yet 'with nothing to do . . . nowhere to go' – is a musician with two wind-up monkeys. Unlike Ellis's Bateman, Quinn is not moved to kill him, nor, like McInerney's Corrine to give him charity. Instead, he notes (in a written prose note which marks a perspective not an identification) how 'the man would improvise endless tiny variations on his instrument', how 'it went on and on, always finally the same' (p. 109). In describing this art of repetitive newness, of difference in sameness and of the many in one, he anticipates a description of the different stories of the *Trilogy* as 'finally the same story' (p. 294) and, more broadly still, the structured 'music of chance' which is Auster's fiction as a whole.

Shopping in Space and Robert Siegle's *Suburban Ambush* present the 'blank generation' as the significant trend in New York fiction of the 1980s. This ignores not only other young writers emerging in the decade but also the new immigrant groups, who in changing the composition of the city have produced a 'literary movement' of a different kind, contributing, as Sam B. Girgus comments, to the emergence over the last twenty years of 'a new ethnic novel [which] compels a reconsideration of what it means to be American'.[37] Girgus includes long-established Jewish and African-American groups in this description as well as Native American, Chinese, Hispanic, Italian and newer South American, Caribbean and Asian-Indian immigrants. I want in what follows to examine the questions of new ethnic or cultural consciousness, and of literary form which this fiction raises.

Girgus suggests that the ethnic novel has shown a 'fluidity and indeterminacy . . . a multiplicity of perspectives and voices', a crossing of boundaries between 'fact and fiction, history and literature, folklore and elite expression, spiritual and sociological sensibilities' which challenges traditional modes of representation and the conventions of 'classic realism'.[38] The fiction of E.L. Doctorow, Toni Morrison and Ishmael Reed, discussed elsewhere in this volume, comes immediately to mind as an illustration of this, and other 'ethnic fictions', as we shall see, also innovate in this way. There are two objections to this account, however. Firstly, ethnic minority writers (Piri Thomas, Oscar Hijuelos, Nicholasa Mohr, amongst others) have also used 'traditional modes of representation' – the forms of autobiography, *bildungsroman*, the picaresque and family chronicle, for example, even the devices of 'classic realism' in writing where the choice of formal mode is determined by or subservient to the expression of a representative social content. Secondly, it is difficult to accept the description 'ethnic novel' as summarising the fiction of the groups Girgus lists when this has been plainly formed in different social histories, and by the differently weighted determinations of class and gender, as well as ethnicity.

We see how this category breaks down if we consider Richard Price and Paul Auster for a moment in its terms, as contemporary Jewish-American authors. Though white and, in broad terms, presently middle-class, neither writer belongs to the 'underground' literary and artistic set comprising the 'blank generation' or 'downtown writing'.

147

Their work relates rather to a tradition of social concern and dissent in Jewish writing (as, more conspicuously, does Doctorow's), and in its own terms joins a highly-prized literary tradition, which though 'ethnic' can hardly be thought of as minoritarian, since it has in many instances occupied the mainstream of American letters. Auster, by common reckoning, is the pure postmodernist to Price's social realist. Oversimplified though this is, the obvious differences in form are clear proof against any belief in a common ethnic or sub-ethnic mode. Also, in this case, the factors of class origin and neighbourhood (blue-collar Bronx and middle-class Brooklyn), as well as marked differences in artistic or cultural affiliation, seem more decisive than a common ethnicity. Auster's philosophical and literary interests connect him with the canonic figures of the American Renaissance as well as the European avant-garde, and he is committed in the tradition of the *atelier* and garret to the idea of writing as lonely artistic vocation. Price's novels, on the other hand, belong to a tradition of dramatic social record and exposé, indebted to writers such as James T. Farrell and Hubert Selby Jnr. The direct, fast-paced realism of this fiction typically absents the author, just as Price is himself distanced, in the exercise of an art of 'honourable investigation', from his working-class background. His writing is both social record and social comment, directing attention to the drugs problem amongst black youth, for example, but is also a personal career move up and outwards – a choice vindicated in one very material sense of importance to the working class, in the production of financially as well as artistically successful film-scripts (*Sea of Love; The Colour of Money*).[39]

There is some reason, all the same, for considering writers such as these alongside other more obviously minority writers. Firstly because, apart from confirming a picture of formal diversity, this combination disturbs the idea of a separated mainstream and avoids ghettoising 'ethnic fiction'. (I want to use Paul Auster to maintain this comparison in much of what follows.) More importantly, if Price and Auster do not employ a common mode or share an idea of the novel, they do respond to a common condition of divided subjectivity. In Auster this is an obvious theme, but it is present in Price too. If his writing has helped him quit the Bronx, he has employed this past as the means to that end and in *Clockers* returns, the figure of the writer who is now both successful outsider and on-the-spot investigator, himself an example of the crossing and recrossing of life-lines, local geographies, class and ethnic territories that has been such a formative influence upon ethnic writing.

At one level, therefore, the ramifications of urban experience produce common effects, in Auster and Price, and in minority ethnic writing. Black, Jewish, Italian, Puerto Rican writers have all commented on the schizophrenic, or stereoscopic experience of being an immigrant or native-born citizen of colour in the United States, especially in its urban centres. Thus Jerre Mangione points to the association of the term 'alien' with 'alienation' and Pedro Juan Soto speaks of his simultaneous hatred and affection for New York City.[40] A third writer, Chaim Potok, coins the term '*zwischenmensch*' for this experience of being between lives and identities: a word for the person who can 'feel at home everywhere and nowhere'.[41] These thoughts echo W.E.B. Du Bois' comments on the 'twoness' of the American negro, and in relation specifically to New York recall Ralph Ellison's essay on Harlem, which he too sees as 'nowhere'.[42] The extreme cultural transition of the twentieth-century passage from feudalism to industrialism experienced 'within negro personality', writes Ellison, and the contrast between Harlem's 'sordid reality' and 'surreal fantasies' has resulted in the simple reply to the question '"How are you?" of "Oh, man, I'm *nowhere*."'[43] This phrase, he says, expresses the Negro's feeling of instability as a '"displaced person" of American democracy', though if this makes Harlem 'the scene of the folk negro's death agony' it retains still the promise of 'his transcendence'.[44] The ambiguity of 'nowhere', once more, the 'no place' which is also utopia, expresses the double sense of a desire for the stability and happiness of belonging and the threat, or actuality, of drifting homelessness.

I want to approach this theme once more in the final section of this chapter. Firstly, however, I would like to consider the broad question of cultural identity, of 'what it means to be American', which Girgus raises above. In general terms it is clear how the question of divided identity might be addressed or resolved. As Girgus reports, theories of ethnicity and culture have looked either to a faith in common values, assuming an underlying or prospective cultural unity, or they have posited a pluralistic mosaic, conceived as either a static grouping of discrete identities or a more dynamic form of polyethnic interaction.[45] There are, in other words, three models: assimilative, liberal pluralist, or dialogic. The first has been most influential, connecting 'descent', in the terms of Werner Sollers' study, *Beyond Ethnicity* (1986), with consensus and the American idea, rather than with dissent, protest or fundamental transformation. An example occurs in Faythe Turner's Introduction to the anthology, *Puerto Rican Writers at Home in the USA*. She reports here on the renaissance of the 1970s, and on its local and traditional roots (at the Nuyorican Poets' Café on the Lower East Side poets read to active audience participation and comment in the tradition of *El Lector*, 'The Reader'). The promise of these years, she says, argued that Puerto Rican literature would be properly recognised as 'a new and vital part of contemporary American literature'. Although this did not immediately occur, Turner sees signs once more at the end of the 1980s that this work is securing 'a permanent place in American Literature'; the inclusion, for example, of four Puerto Rican writers in the *Heath Anthology of American Literature* – 'a good measure', she says, 'of what is recently beginning to be included in the canon'.[46]

Turner's model of culture is an additive, integrationist one, composed of a received tradition and aspiring individual, or minority, ethnic talent. Some of the writers her collection introduces would seem to agree with this, some would not. The New York-born novelist Nicholasa Mohr, for example, who writes, she says', 'very much as an investigative reporter', shares Turner's view. Underlying her sense of difference from Puerto Rican-born novelists and an identification with the cause of 'marginal communities that continue to struggle for equality in the US', lies a faith, she says, in 'the universality that bonds the common human family' and a firm affiliation with the United States and New York. ('This is home', she writes.)[47] Other writers, however, write, in Faythe Turner's words, less as people 'leaving one world and entering another' than as 'people living in two worlds at once'.[48] Her example is from the joint 'Ending poem', by mother and daughter Aurora Levins Morales and Rosario Morales, from *Getting Home Alive*, a text to which I shall return.

> I am what I am
> *A child of the Americas*
> A light-skinned mestiza of the Caribbean
> *A child of many diaspora, born into this continent at a crossroads*
> I am Puerto Rican. I am US American
> *I am New York, Manhattan and the Bronx*
> A mountain-born, country-bred, homegrown jibara child.[49]

Getting Home Alive brings a confident hybridity to the idea of 'Being American'. Traditionally this has meant claiming one's rights as an individual to success and fulfilment: a 'grand narrative' derived from Enlightenment thinking, and often invoked in its most radical aspect to chastise American actuality – by Frederick Douglass, Langston Hughes, James Baldwin, Norman Mailer, Gore Vidal, for example, and by E.L. Doctorow.

In a more recent example, the Asian-American novelist and academic Bharati Mukherjee turns this idealism on its geo-ethnic axis. In her novel *Jasmine* the heroine progresses through misadventures and identities to become a new American in a near classic passage from East to West.[50] Born as Jyoti in the village of Hasnapur in the Punjab after Partition, her identity is already divided. The family has lost its status and fortune after Lahore has become part of the Urdu-speaking Muslim state of Pakistan, and she becomes the focus of a debate on modernity. Her father is persuaded, against tradition, to allow her to continue her education, but she goes further. She marries Prakash, a freethinking 'modern man', who calls her Jasmine ('Jyoti, Jasmine: I shuttled between identities', she says: p. 77). When he is killed she goes alone to America, first to a Punjabi-speaking ghetto in Flushing and then to work as a 'care-giver' to the child of a white liberal couple in Manhattan. 'I became an American in an apartment on Claremont Avenue' she reports. Taylor, the husband calls her Jase. Later, married to Bud Ripplemeyer in Iowa, she becomes Jane, and finally Jase again, exercising her rights in a 'free country' to leave Bud for Taylor and his daughter Duff. Finally she flees for California, 'greedy with wants and reckless from hope' (p. 241). The promise of re-invention in America and her 'very, very *very* Indian' belief in destiny and reincarnation are reconciled. She undergoes a smooth rebirth; a 'genetic' transformation, as she puts it, compared with the hyphenated transformation of Du Thien, a Vietnamese orphan adopted by Bud Ripplemeyer (p. 222).

Mukherjee explains her project in the statement 'A Four Hundred Year Old Woman'. She is, she says, 'an American. I am an American writer, in the American mainstream, trying to extend it . . . . I am an immigrant; my investment is in the American reality, not the Indian. I look on ghettoization – whether as Bengali in India or as a hyphenated Indo-American in North America – as a temptation to be surmounted.'[51]

Mukherjee does not decentre 'America' so much as adjust and reset this centre, changing the names and colours of the same story: the repeated, ever-new story as in *Jasmine* of 'America before it got perverted' (p. 201). This promise of transformation, of a re-invented, newly unified American female subjectivity in her writing contrasts with the anxiety associated with a threatened loss of white middle-class male authority and selfhood in the fiction discussed above. But this 'male' anxiety can itself be transformed, in a connection with ideas of equality and democracy rather than simply loss, to augur a radical and more positive levelling rather than a lowering of status and identity. This possibility flicks through the stories of the *New York Trilogy* and becomes more pronounced in Auster's most overtly political novel *Leviathan*.

In Mukherjee, and many other writers, the American idea of freedom and opportunity is thought to retain its integrity and stand in need only of its practical fulfilment or extension (an 'only' which describes the gulf between the modern project and postmodern experience). In Auster's *Leviathan*, where Ben Sachs decides on a campaign of bombing replicas of the Statue of Liberty, the symbol of this ideal itself – 'hope rather than reality, faith rather than facts . . . the things it stands for: democracy, freedom, equality under the law' themselves come under attack.[52]

Girgus writes of the 'dominant intellectual tradition within academic and cultural centres during the past two decades' as 'demystifying the ideology of America and deconstructing the hegemonic symbols of national identity'.[53] Ben Sachs, however, is more a destroyer than a deconstructor. He does not negotiate with the ideal but explodes it, in an anarchistic, avant-garde gesture, the deliberations of which are arduous and the effects doubtful: an original take perhaps on the unoriginal challenge to America to live up to its ideals. (Peter Aaron in the novel thinks Sachs has helped resurrect the meaning of the symbol when students in Tienanmen Square unveil their imitation Statue of Liberty, p. 218.)

More profoundly, however, Sachs's actions seek to expose these ideals as representing, like his adopted name, the 'Phantom of Liberty'. Sachs also uses the name of the anarchist Alexander Berkman, the colleague and lover of Emma Goldman and the object of a dissertation by Reed Dimaggio (whom Sachs murders before becoming the lover of his wife, Lillian Stern). His wayward, contingent life, and his final political campaign which makes him feel at last 'whole' (p. 228), represent an abandonment both of domestic stability and art (itself an avantgardist decision). His uncompleted second novel, 'Leviathan', becomes the novel Peter Aaron, adopting Sachs's title, writes about him, and which we are reading. But the rejection of the career of writer for a form of creative direct action implies a rejection too of Sachs's first novel *The New Colossus*. As Peter Aaron describes it, this was an experiment in dialogic form: an historical novel of true figures and events blending fiction and fantasy, jumping chapter by chapter 'from traditional third-person narratives to first-person diary entries and letters, from chronological charts to small anecdotes, from newspaper articles to essays to dramatic dialogues' (p. 37).

The title of this novel derives from Emma Lazarus's poem 'The New Colossus' (she is a character in the book), which gave its opening verses – 'Give me your tired, your poor, / your huddled masses . . .' to the Statue of Liberty monument. Emma Lazarus's poem has served the state, expressing a passionate idealism towards America on behalf of generations of immigrants. Sachs's 'angry' novel is already critical of this fallen ideal which has failed its followers, and Auster's adopted epigraph to his novel *Leviathan*, 'Every State is Corrupt', from Emma Lazarus's contemporary Ralph Waldo Emerson, suggests that he shares Sachs's rebellious sentiments towards the type of coercive 'Leviathan' state proposed by Hobbes. Yet if the epigraph is Auster's, he is, and at the same time is not, Peter Aaron, the narrator, who is of course also distinct from Sachs, though he writes 'his' novel. Not only does Aaron comment on *The New Colossus* in the patronising terms of conventional realism ('the novel feels too constructed . . . only rarely do any of the characters come fully to life' – p. 39), he himself continues as a writer when Sachs does not.

Peter Aaron and Sachs are, one might say, options explored by Auster as he reflects on the possible social and political role of the artist. This self-questioning which puts the individual inside and outside fiction, inside and outside the whale and the state, Leviathan, and between language and the social world, is something Auster shares with a writer such as Don DeLillo, to whom *Leviathan* is dedicated, and shares too with other 'ethnic' writers experiencing life on the borderlines.

On 4 July 1986 Sachs falls from an apartment window at a party in Brooklyn Heights to celebrate the 100th anniversary of the Statue of Liberty. Like Humpty Dumpty, 'his entire life fell apart in mid air' and 'he never put it back again' (p. 107). Ten years earlier, on the '200th Birthday of America', Pilar Puente's mural of a punk Liberty is unveiled at the opening of her mother's second Yankee Doodle Bakery, in Cristina Garcia's novel, *Dreaming in Cuban*.

Garcia's novel intercuts two time lines, 1972–80 and 1935–59; the first in its three main sections, the second in a series of interpolated letters from Celia del Pino, the mother of Lourdes, Felicia and Javier and grandmother of their children. Her letters are written to her first Spanish lover from Granada, and follow the path towards the Cuban revolution of 1959. After her estranged husband's death in New York in 1972, Celia devotes herself to Castro's new society. The general narrative meanwhile tracks the contrary allegiances of the three generations of the family to aspects of Cuban and American culture.

In 1975, the date, we remember, of the dawn of the economic boom in the United States, Lourdes walks her new five-block beat in Brooklyn, the first auxiliary policewoman in her precinct. In the area of her bakery she sees signs to reinforce her hard line on law and order – Jews have moved out, replaced by 'black faces, Puerto Rican faces. Once in a while a stray Irish or Italian face looking scared.'[54] The neighbourhood brownstones have become tenements, there is garbage on the streets but America has confirmed her right-wing anti-Communist, anti-democratic attitudes. She thinks herself lucky: 'Immigration has redefined her, and she is grateful . . . she welcomes her adopted language, its possibilities for re-invention . . . . She wants no part of Cuba . . . no part of Cuba at all' (p. 73). Her commitment to Yankee capitalism and sense of civic duty set her against her mother's faith in Cuban communism as the 'greatest social experiment in modern history' (p. 117) and her service there as a people's judge. Lourdes' daughter Pilar snipes at her bigotry, rank materialism and 'dinosaur politics' (p. 27), and feels that she herself inherits a legacy of the love of life, of words and music, a sympathy for the underdog and a disregard of boundaries from her grandmother, over and above the geopolitical boundaries that have separated them for seventeen years.

As one character says, 'families are essentially political' (p. 86). In this political world of affection and discord, ambiguities and crossovers, mother and daughter side with the quite opposite conceptions of liberty embodied in Marxist Cuba and the free enterprise of the American market economy. Pilar, the rebellious daughter and loyal granddaughter is the conduit for these differences; the figure of memory, of record, but also of imagination and originality. The Statue of Liberty she paints for her mother's bakery is a punk Liberty, conceived in the spirit of the Sex Pistols' 'Anarchy in the UK', and with 'enough attitude' to satisfy her patron saint, Lou Reed. At the unveiling the guests are outraged. Yet her mother, in classic pose, obese from overeating at the bakery, falls upon the hecklers, the unexpected protectress of her daughter's licence to paint as she sees fit.

In Cuba, Pilar paints a series of portraits of her grandmother, herself a symbol of liberty, but discovers too the limits of Cuban communism. Can she paint everything she wished, she asks her grandmother. The answer is not if it is against the state (p. 235). Her rejoinder is that Castro (El Leder) must realise that art is revolutionary. She is brought to decide in favour of New York and the United States: 'I'm afraid to lose Abuela Celia again', she says, 'But sooner or later I'd have to return to New York. I know now it's where I belong – not *instead* of here, but *more* than here' (p. 236). New York allows room for dissent and for Pilar's belief in artistic freedom. So she emerges, a transcultural, dialogic personality, speaking and dreaming in Spanish and English, with the potential, like Lou Reed, for being many selves (p. 135). Pilar's identity is responsive and in process, formed by the journey in time across family and national histories, and in space between lands and across borders. Her decision brings neither a babble of tongues, nor postmodern schizophrenia, nor monologic fixity but an emphasis within the still-hyphenated identity of 'American-Cuban'.

Bharati Mukherjee would wish to surmount any equivalent Indo-American identity. She seeks to renew or reclaim a consensual narrative of self and national identity which means reconciling anything 'non' American with this dominant American mythology of self-reinvention, or expelling it. In the meeting of Indian feudalism and the American postmodern, America wins, and had already won in *Jasmine* in the figure of the 'modern man, the city man' Prakash, for whom the future means America. Garcia's story presents us neither with this postmodern nor an earlier modern. She arrives at a sense of continuity which neither cancels nor reconciles the binaries of the Marxist modern and the capitalist postmodern, but absorbs them in the composition of her own self-identity: mobile and hyphenated but decided and dissenting, as if the modern and postmodern were choices within a cultural family connected and critiqued in her. It is a decision, I think, which makes her story 'new modern'.

NO PLACE LIKE HOME: PAUL AUSTER, CRISTINA GARCIA, AURORA AND ROSARIO MORALES

The writings above are often concerned with the experience of displacement and belonging, with what it means to be American, to become culturally evicted or rehoused in New York City. Perhaps we can connect this theme with Freud's discussion of 'the uncanny' which Auster refers to in *The Invention of Solitude*. He, or more precisely the persona 'A' he employs here, accepts

155

Freud's description of the uncanny as the 'revival of the ego-centric, animistic world-view of childhood'.[55] The experience of the uncanny ('*unheimlich*') or 'unhomeness', he writes on 'A's' behalf, is stirred by 'a memory of another, much earlier home of the mind' such as he is experiencing in thinking about his childhood and father (p. 149).

Freud's essay is more relevant to Auster's fiction than this suggests, however, and might point us also to his relation with other 'ethnic' writers. Freud shows there is an ambivalence which connects the apparent opposites '*unheimlich*' (unfamiliar, frightening) and '*heimlich*' (familiar, homely, belonging to the house, but also concealed or kept from sight). '*Unheimlich*', he says, 'is in some way or another a subspecies of *heimlich*.'[56] (Freud connects this through a discussion of Hoffman's story of 'The Sand Man' with a double image of the father, the one who threatens to blind the child – 'that is', says Freud, 'to castrate him', and 'the other, the "good father" [who] intercedes for his sight', p. 353). Beyond this, the uncanny is associated with the experience, or creation of doubles and with coincidence. Thus Freud writes of instances where the subject 'identifies himself with someone else, so that he is in doubt which his self is, or substitutes the extraneous self for his own. In other words, there is a doubling, dividing and interchanging of the self' (ibid.). Further instances depend on the involuntary repetition of the same name, or incident, or numbers, suggesting 'something fateful and inescapable when otherwise we should have spoken only of chance' (p. 359). The '*unheimlich*', Freud is led to conclude, 'is what was once *heimisch*, familiar; the prefix 'un' ['un-'] is the token of repression' (p. 368).

The relevance of all these features to Auster's writing is striking. His fiction returns again and again to the relations of fathers and sons; and *doppelgängers*, substitutes, mirror images, and mistaken identities regularly occur in his stories, as of course do characters with the same name or with Auster's initials. Auster sees the world as a networked series of such coincidences: 'Meeting three people named George on the same day. Or checking into a hotel and being given a room with the same number as your address at home. Life is full of such events.'[57] Examples such as this, and in *The Invention of Solitude* his discovery that the mileage on his father's car corresponded to his life-span, are very close to examples given by Freud (p. 360).

Freud sees this form of the uncanny as resulting from the recurrence of something repressed in infancy and no doubt this suggests one kind of reading of Auster's writing, as itself a case study of the uncanny. We should realise, however, that the uncanny is just as much Auster's conscious subject as he is its example, and that it helps define his purpose as a writer. 'Chance is a part of reality', he says,

> we are continually shaped by the forces of coincidence, the unexpected occurs with almost numbing regularity . . . the world is a place beyond our understanding. We brush up against these mysteries all the time. The result can be truely terrifying – but it can also be comical . . . . As a writer of novels, I feel morally obligated to incorporate such events into my books, to write about the world as I experience it . . . . The unknown is rushing on top of us at every moment. As I see it my job is to keep myself open to such collisions, to watch out for all these mysterious goings-on in the world.[58]

If this type of the uncanny is traceable to infantile psychology, a second class, Freud says, is traceable 'to the old, animistic conception of the universe': the belief amongst 'primitive men', which is 'surmounted' but not surpassed in the life of the individual and educated people, in spirits, ghosts, the return of the dead, and the associated use of magic and sorcery (pp. 362–5). Here the 'uncanny' results, one might say, from the recurrence of the 'premodern' in the modern. Freud mentions here too the idea of being buried alive (a transformation of the unterrifying phantasy of intra-uterine existence) and gives special emphasis to the uncanny effect 'often and easily produced when the distinction between imagination and reality is effaced' (p. 367).

Freud's thoughts lead him here, as it happens, to a description of 'magic realism'. So too do Auster's reflections on his own fiction. As a witness and recorder of the mystery and coincidence of the world he is, he says, 'in the strictest sense of the word . . . a realist'.[59] Moreover, the work which has had greatest influence on him 'has been fairy tales, the oral tradition of story-telling. The Brothers Grimm, The Thousand and One Nights kind of stories you read out loud to children'.[60] He refers to the latter in *The Invention of Solitude*, and tells also in that book of his reading aloud the stories of Jonah and Pinocchio to his son. Pinocchio rescues his father and inventor from the belly of a shark. (One thinks of the motif of being buried alive, referred to by Freud, of Fanshawe's lying in his father's grave in Auster's 'The Locked Room', of characters being enclosed in small rooms elsewhere in his fiction, of the title 'Leviathan', and of other new starts and 'rebirths', including Sachs's in that novel.)

In *The Invention of Solitude* the fable of the son's giving birth to the father in the tale of Pinocchio is an analogue for Auster's own writing in this book and therefore of its own uncanny effect. Also in this text

Auster connects both fairy-tale and reading aloud with his son and cites Freud on the figure of the child as a model of the imaginative writer (p. 164). This is conventional enough perhaps, but for Auster the child, or more accurately, the son, is an example of the writer – of fantasy and fairy-tale and narratives of the uncanny, but also the listener, and thus a doubly vital connection for the writer who is both father and story-teller. In this way, both child and oral story become the means of establishing or re-establishing human kinship and the security of home.

Personal loving relationships between father and son, and man and wife or partners, and thus the social group of the almost nuclear family are the much threatened source of stability in Auster's fictions, a mainstay in their very ordinariness against the unpredictable and random. The 'language of love' and 'of irresistible passions' are, as his character in 'The Locked Room' knows, 'overblown' but still 'accurate' enough to describe his relationship with Sophie. This feeling of centred in-betweenness is little short of paradise, the 'no place' of utopia:

> This knowledge changed me, I think, and actually made me feel more human. By belonging to Sophie, I began to feel as though I belonged to everyone else as well. My true place in the world, it turned out, was somewhere beyond myself, and if that place was inside me, it was also unlocatable. This was the tiny hole between self and not-self, and for the first time in my life I saw this nowhere as the exact centre of the world.[61]

The loss of self, of status, of home and meaning which threatens the couple and small family unit describes Quinn's spiralling decline and disappearance. Quinn has lost his son and wife, assumed first one (literary) identity, William Wilson, already a dummy to his fictional creation, Max Work, then another, that of Auster, the supposed detective. When he encounters the 'real' Paul Auster, the writer, Quinn is offended by what he takes to be a deliberate display of Auster's contented family life. This prompts his decision to stake out the Stillman's apartment and thus his descent to the condition of the 'homeless' when he no longer recognises himself. (He is 'at the end of himself', eventually loses possession of his own apartment and disintegrates to the point of disappearance after occupying Stillman's room.)

We can see a connection here with other ethnic authors who share with Auster a sense of divided, multiple identities and a desire for home. As in his work, the examples discussed above chronicle close personal and family relationships, particularly those of parent and child, and draw too upon earlier oral narrative modes or older beliefs. There are differences, nevertheless, of accent and focus, and these are attributable to gender as well as ethnic and literary or cultural affiliations. *Dreaming in Cuban*, for example, clearly employs an 'animistic conception of the universe' in introducing the figure of the father's ghost, and Jasmine holds, perhaps to the end of Mukherjee's novel, to the 'very Indian' belief in reincarnation. These are quite different from Auster's 'Ghosts' – Blue's disguise which makes him look like Walt Whitman, or the 'ghosts' of Thoreau, Dickens, Lincoln in the story of that title, or the 'rebirth' of characters under other names (Quinn as Auster, Sachs as the 'Phantom of Liberty'). Auster's hauntings are more metaphysical, his investigation of character and subjectivity more introverted and existential. In *Dreaming, Jasmine* and *Getting Home Alive* (of the novels considered here, but generally the case in 'new ethnic' fiction) the plots are more socially situated and referenced; characters cross lands and languages in narratives that mingle the personal and historical (the events of Partition in *Jasmine*, and at the Peruvian embassy in Havana in *Dreaming*). In addition, though Auster writes interestingly of the importance of the figure of the female prophet or story-teller and of the female narrator of *1001 Nights*, the key relationship remains that between versions of the father and son (as is also true of Doctorow's work). Fathers and men are influential in the works by women writers cited here, and in *Jasmine* romantic heterosexual relations are more important than relations with women, but *Dreaming in Cuban* turns most of all on relations between mother and daughter.[62]

In terms of the relevance of Freud, it seems that on balance Auster's uncanny belongs to Freud's first type and the realism, or magic realism, of later ethnic writers belongs to the second. To this distinction these fictions bring the additional insights of layered gendered and ethnic proclivities: by turns male Jewish, female Asian- and Latina-American. Together these forms and perspectives illustrate the angled negotiations marking the passage from the modern to the postmodern, from the anxieties of an individualistic, more centred metropolitan tradition of thinking and writing amongst male Jewish Americans – now experiencing a fresh decentring – to a mode where new migrants, principally women, are caught in the contemporary clash of cultures and traditions. Where the individualist orientation of the one is vertical and abysmal (as in the metaphor of falling), the other is lateral and exploratory.

If there are these mixed affinities and differences of theme and form, at least in inclination, one feels nevertheless that in an important respect these narratives of 'at homeness' and degrees of homelessness, of familiarity and estrangement, do not correspond to the uncanny of Freud's discussion. For while the appearance of the unexpected and unfamiliar, of double and multiple selves, or the return of the dead in these fictions can be destabilising, it is not clear that this is ever 'frightening'. Rather, in the full logic of the association Freud suggests between '*heimlich*' and '*unheimlich*', the unexpected and unfamiliar are regarded by Auster as commonplace, as occurring 'with almost numbing regularity', just as in 'magic realism' the impossibilities of fairy-tale and fantasy are accepted as the everyday. This, we might conclude, is the fate of Freud's modern uncanny in the postmodern, an era notoriously desensitised to the shock of the new, the mysterious, or unfamiliar. If the uncanny has become the order of the postmodern day then the defamiliarising objectives of modernism are, true to report, pre-empted and stymied all at once. For how in a world stranger than fiction can fiction make it strange? We are brought to ask once more whether postmodern fiction can hope to exercise any critical distance upon the postmodern. To respond as Auster does by seeking 'to write fiction as strange as the world I live in'[63] would seem to answer 'no' to this question, for all this 'realism' can do is at best replicate an entirely, and therefore not at all, uncanny world.

This, at least, might be our conclusion if we concur in a homo-genising view of the postmodern as unrelentingly, monotonously new. In fact, the newly compressed space–time relations brought about by postmodern information and communications technologies, by the globalisation of capital and the further penetration of its inherent contradictions, have produced a new source of the uncanny. For what is now strange and unfamiliar, and a source of possible fear in the postmodern city, is the stranger, the social, cultural, or ethnic other made visible by late capitalism: in short, the new immigrant or the new poor. What returns, we might say, is the repressed 'alien' (that especially telling socio-psychic term); the 'other' side of modernity's (and Freud's) white, masculinist, Eurocentred aspect.[64]

Marshall Berman, in the collection *In Search of New York*, comments on the marked new polarities of these years, how the 1980s had made New York into 'a place where capital from anywhere in the world is instantly at home, while everybody without capital is increasingly out of place'.[65] The collapse of civic culture, the deterioration of public services, the combined effects of mass migration and de-industrialisation, the increase in violence and violent death, all, he argues, have contributed to a changed temper and tone in the daily life of the city. The familiar has become shocking, the unfamiliar and distant frighteningly close:

> We were used to shabby, impoverished, neglected neighbourhoods all around the town – some of us worked in them, others drove through on the way out of town; nothing prepared us for the burning down and virtual destruction of many of these neighbourhoods . . . we were used to photographic images of ragged, distressed people down on the Bowery or uptown in Harlem; we weren't prepared to see them face to face, flooding our own streets and doorways and subway stations, and sleeping out in the cold and rain because they had no place to go. We were used to walking through streets full of quiet desperation; we had to learn to negotiate streets full of people shrieking in rage and despair at the top of their voices, and often directing their shrieks at us.[66]

This is the theme explored above in relation to more mainstream New York fiction. The 'other' might be seen as an externalised threat, an enemy, or invader (the feelings of Bronx blacks and Manhattan whites towards each other in *Bonfire of the Vanities*), or, – and perhaps this is the consistently underlying feature – the 'other' is a dangerous potential within the multiple selves that postmodern schizophrenia and mobility make possible and make public. *Brightness Falls, American Psycho, Slaves of New York, A Cannibal in Manhattan, The New York Trilogy* – all in some way treat this fear of what 'other' the self might be, or become, once on the production line of multiple selves that parallels the production of commodities. The 'same' might turn out to be a mere pastiche, a fake, or the cloned horror of *American Psycho*. Hence, in this last novel, the violent mutilation or murder of the 'other' who is the same and who threatens the public self's continued status, and thus his identity.

American Psycho is the most obvious example of the frightful breaking through the veneer of over-familiarity, but a figure such as Auster's Quinn ('rhymes with twin' as Stillman is quick to notice)[67] is again an example. The other (self) is the tramp, the bum, the socially destitute. Where Doctorow in 'Lives of the Poets' seeks an accommodation with this 'underclass', it is always for Auster another 'other self', singular and in retreat, moving towards the end of identity. Auster talks of solitude as a means to the recognition of difference and a sense of connection: of 'moving inward (through himself) and at the same time moving outward (towards the world)',[68] but other, twin male selves in his fiction invariably disappear, and the stories of *The New York Trilogy* are typically empty of people and extraneous activity.

To put this simply, you would not know from this fiction that

New York was a multi-ethnic city. Colour, as it is used for names in the story 'Ghosts' (Black, White, and Blue), is an exercise in the arbitrariness of language, not a designation of skin colour. There are some interesting exceptions, or apparent exceptions, however. In 'The Locked Room' the narrator reports his experience as a census-taker in Harlem. After experiencing the difficulties of obtaining first-hand information from the residents ('for the most part no one was there'; he felt 'like a man from the moon', p. 248), he invents them and the details of their lives, using the names of colours, American presidents, fictional characters, celebrities from film, baseball and so on: inventing Harlem, as it were, out of the cornucopia of language and the roll-call of American heroes. The episode is a revealing instance of the self-protective effects of Auster's fiction in which the 'other' is endlessly imaginable but within a self-generating symbolic and not a social system. At the same time, we remember Fanshawe's anti-racism and Blue's admiration for the black baseball player Jackie Robinson. When on one occasion Blue watches Robinson play, he is 'lured constantly by the blackness of the man's face' (p. 159). At this rare moment he is taken beyond an aesthetic admiration for the field's geometric patterns and surrounding colours to a social and political admiration; and comes to forget Black (which is to say his own solitary blackness) as he gets involved in another('s) identity.

Beneath sentiments such as these there lies in Auster a belief in the democratic tradition of Whitman, Thoreau and Lincoln. In the Plymouth churchyard on Orange Street, Blue studies a statue of Henry Ward Beecher which has behind it a porcelain relief of Lincoln. The statue shows two slaves pleading at Beecher's feet 'to make them free at last' (p. 158). Very little remains stable in Auster's fiction, however, including democracy. By the time of *Leviathan* and Sachs's explosions of America's false replicas of the Statue of Liberty, the inspiration of racial equality Blue derives from this image (the moment is dated as 1947) has given way to scepticism. By the 1980s and 1990s, so this fiction suggests, the Enlightenment heritage has receded and the relations of self and other are played out at the depth of profound solitude.

Jasmine and *Dreaming* offer narratives of the encounter of self and other as a transitional and transformative experience from the migrant perspective. As does Aurora Levins Morales's and Rosario Morales's *Getting Home Alive*. These works are more direct and more socially located than Auster's writing, and more fraught than frightening. Together they may be said to confirm Girgus's view on the way in which new ethnic writing mediates 'the ideological dilemma of achieving a common culture based on difference and heterogeneity'.[69] Homi Bhabha focuses the political implications of this project: 'The historical experience of the Western metropolis', he says, 'cannot now be fictionalized without the marginal oblique gaze of its postcolonial migrant populations cutting across the imaginative geography of territory and community, tradition and culture'.[70] This means, says Bhabha, rethinking 'the very language of cultural community', to establish 'a more equal distribution of power and influence in the cultural conversation among the contentious and competing languages that form the metropolitan canon'.[71] A 'new interpretive community' is needed, he says, 'to bear witness to this experience' and this 'migrant or postcolonial public sphere' he sees now 'posited as a feminised body of memory and imagination'.[72]

These remarks relate very closely to the issues raised here and to the works especially of the Latina writers Cristina Garcia and Aurora and Rosario Morales. To put the issue Bhabha poses in terms of the earlier discussions in this study, the postmodern brings us to the problem of postmodern democracy: how the modern project of liberty, justice, rights and equality might be rethought outside the tradition of liberal consensus or the Enlightenment's distorted heritage. Mukherjee's *Jasmine*, Auster's *Leviathan* and Cristina Garcia's *Dreaming in Cuban* all reflect on this issue. I have focused chiefly on questions of subjectivity and cultural theme in discussing these texts. 'Bearing witness' in 'memory and imagination' to the new metropolitan experience and changed public sphere is also a matter of language and literary form, however, and I want finally to reflect on the contribution these texts make in this respect to the project Bhabha outlines.

A democratic public sphere of hybrid realities in transition calls for a dynamic dialogic form; not, it should be said, in confirmation of its established existence but as part of its imaginary prefiguration. Sachs's *New Colossus* sounds like such a novel: a fiction which exercises the equalising effects of collage across fact and fable, fictional discourses and history. In terms of Sachs's political project the novel is a failure, however, as is its proposed film version, where the form and project would be made popular. The *New Colossus* remains unread by us too of course, and we might draw some consolation from the thought that in truth it remains to be written. Auster himself is on present evidence an unlikely author of this kind of dialogic text. Where then might we look?

It might be thought that the different novels discussed here belong by the very fact of their contemporary existence as novels of the 1980s to some unifying cultural collage; that, taken together, they comprise a kind of dialogised period text. But a dialogic unity implies more of an engaged 'cultural conversation' among 'contentious and competing languages', in Bhabha's words, than an arbitrary miscellany of supposed equals. Nor, if we are to seek a model in individual fictions rather than a period totality will the demands of a new pluralist subjectivity, or new 'feminised' public sphere, be met by the omniscient narrative perspective, character development and closure of the traditional realist novel which this fiction continues in varying degrees to assume.

Richard Price most obviously employs a realist mode which in its very strengths commits the text to an omniscient, undisclosed narrator, allowed to transcend the frictions of social identity lived out between black and white on the New Jersey streets. Where in Auster there is considerable disturbance to the notion of a unified subject, the figure of 'the author, Paul Auster' becomes even more important as a final point of grounded creation and comment. Even in Mukherjee's *The Middleman and other Stories*, where the stories take shifting angles upon new hybrid subjectivities and cultural alignments in America (Asian–Jewish, Hungarian–Indian, Italian, El Salvadorean, Afghan, Filipino, African), and in *Jasmine*, where the chapters alternate initially between Iowa and Hasnapur, there is all the same an assumed or eventual coherence and stability. Her material, says Mukherjee, is immigration; her theme the 'making of new Americans'. To this end she draws upon Indian mythology and the model of artistic structure and excellence given by the tradition of Moghul miniature painting, in which 'there are a dozen separate foci'.[73] The Moghul miniature of her life would contain scenes both from India and the United States, she says, and this is the perfect analogy for the materials and narrative mode of *Middleman*, a varied world of simultaneity and coexistence viewed as if from a newly totalising perspective.

Alone of the more mainstream examples considered above, Tama Janowitz's *Slaves of New York* innovates formally in a way that is consonant with the decentred instabilities of postmodern metropolitan experience, interchanging first- and third-person narrative perspectives in intermittently main, parallel and tangential stories told in both realist and fantasy modes. Its part in the metropolitan cultural conversation is limited perhaps by its white bohemian milieu and casual feminism, but its flexible narrative form helps to disperse, and in the end comically invert, this community's fixed assumptions of woman as slave and man as property-owning master artist.

What *Slaves of New York* lacks, compared with *Dreaming in Cuban* and *Getting Home Alive*, is a historical or public political consciousness of any strength and explicitness. The women of these two texts are enmeshed in the fuller world from which any new public sphere must derive. Both texts are open, that is to say, to the various contending determinations and discourses of this era, and both illustrate how transitional and incomplete this moment is. *Dreaming* employs first- and third-person: letters, dreams and intercalated past and present narrative times to record the dispersed loyalties and conflicts between individuals and families, the twists and turns of branched and contrary histories, the melting and holding of geopolitical borders. It has, as this suggests, an epic reach over personal, social and political histories. Yet it substitutes a multi-perspective composition and montaged sequences of personal and public chronologies for the omniscient, centred narrative view, the continuities and totalising ambitions associated with this traditional form. The result is an affirmative yet provisional accommodation of the antinomies of old and new, the familiar and the strange, the self and other which presents an emergent 'new modern' sense of self in time and place. Pilar feels 'homeless' in Brooklyn, where she has lived all her life, and discovers that she belongs as an 'American Cuban' in New York. She comes in this way to express a critique of fixity and of the melting-pot ideology of totalising national identity, and to suggest instead a *modus vivendi* which is alert to indeterminacy and difference.

Pilar embodies precisely the 'memory and imagination' Bhabha associates with a new 'feminised' public sphere and, as far as fiction and a lone punk girl can express it, stands as something like a new symbol of Liberty and muse of the 'new modern'. It is a mistake to think of even these embryonic signs of a new order of subjectivity and cultural identity as easily established or sustained, however. Pilar cannot control the 'fragments of people's thoughts' and 'scraps of the future' that come to her 'without warnings or explanations' (p. 216). And in the panic at the Peruvian embassy in Havana in April 1980, she comments, 'Nothing can record this, I think. Not words, not paintings, not photographs' (p. 241). The words she sets at the base of her painted Liberty are her favourite punk rallying cry, 'I'm a mess' (p. 141). The scrambled and outlandish contemporary reality is beyond Pilar's powers, and this is in a sense her statement: an expression of new strengths and known limits at a self-consciously transitional moment. Enlightenment epistemology had assumed reason and realism could comprehend reality, and produced as its most common and worst effect the sense of unity and privilege in the observing self. A postmodern 'realism' cannot in its self-knowingness follow this example, for the postmodern is a world in process; in the words of Eliana Ortega and Nancy Saporta Sternbach, it stands 'at the threshold of the unnamed'. The postmodern real and this fiction are therefore at critical points incommensurate, familiar and strange to each other like aspects of the self or self and other. The new that Pilar represents therefore emerges out of a condition of estrangement, indeed is embedded in the very process of self-estrangement, rather than in the new's achieved realisation.

Getting Home Alive is both autobiography and social history. Its coauthored text knits together poetry, narrative, the essay, letters, diaries and photographs, documentary and dream, Spanish, English and Yiddish, in the making of the intimately related, syncretic cultural identities of mother and daughter. The summary figure for its forming subjectivities and relations between women is the quilt depicted on the book's front cover. This signifies, says Lourdes Rojas, the book's *raison d'être*: 'unity within diversity among women'.[74] Once again, however, this should not suggest a settled or finally centred unity, for in working through the dialectic of personal and public histories the book's discourses stretch across open time, geography and identities. 'Home?' Rosario Morales '(shaped on Manhattan Island)' asks herself at one point on a trip back to Puerto Rico, and answers with a statement and question (an apt expression of the borderline postmodern): 'A place where I am never completely at home. But then where am I completely at home?'[75]

The in-betweenness, provisionality and self-questioning of these last two texts instructs us in the crucial role of ethnicity in the making of a new modern. Yet a feminised public sphere that explores 'other forms of social affiliation – those that come to us through pleasure, eroticism, friendship', in Homi Bhabha's words, that re-articulates 'private values and public virtues'[76] needs also to be in dialogue with the extant public realm, and thus with the predominantly masculinised world of work and politics, the social affiliations, pleasure and friendships of the office, the life of the street, of bars, sport, technical know-how and the forms of male sexuality. The discourses of diary, poem, dream, letter, folk-tale employed in *Getting Home Alive* range over the experiences of personal and family life in country and city, the domestic life of the house, the kitchen, the topics of clothes, school, the body, childbirth and child-rearing. It also engages significantly with the more conventionally public themes of political commitment and activity and of national identity. In one remarkable section, 'If I forget thee, Oh Jerusalem', Aurora Morales brings herself to think through the difficulties of religious and political belief and of the prospect of coexistence between Israelis and Arabs. The strengths of the book's gendered, culturally and linguistically hybridised experience remain clear and inspiring. This essay, however, extends its projected unities beyond 'diversity among women'. In involving her in a probing dialogue with herself and her daughter on the questions of religious and political identity, of enmities and peace between nations, of the American perspective on this conflict, it brings us to think of her relation, and the dialogic form this book represents, with the hegemonic discourses of international politics and the masculine discourses of war. In so doing, it reminds us of long-standing borders between the private and public that have still to be crossed in the journey from nowhere to a good place.

NOTES

1. Mike Davis, 'Urban Renaissance and the Spirit of Postmodernism' in E. Ann Kaplan (ed.), *Postmodernism and its Discontents* (London: Verso, 1988), p. 81.
2. David Harvey, *New Statesman*, 30 September 1988: 33.
3. Ibid.
4. For contemporary comment on this crisis citing unsound public borrowing techniques, lack of adequate federal aid, and the inadequacies of the national urban policy, see David Bensman, 'The Problem with New York City', and David M. Muchnick 'Death Warrant for the Cities', *Dissent* (Winter 1976): 4, 21–32.
5. See Jim Sleeper (ed.) *In Search of New York* (New Brunswick, New Jersey: Transaction Publishers, 1989), pp. 59–60.
6. See 'US Poor Get Poorer', *Guardian*, 5 September 1992: 14. The figures reproduced here are taken from the 1991 US census. The *Guardian* report suggests its findings were confirmed by other contemporary surveys linking poverty, unemployment and social malaise with economic problems from the Centre on Budget and Policy Priorities, the National Urban League, the Population Reference Bureau and the labour department. See also Sharon Smith 'Twilight of the American Dream', *International Socialism* 54 (Spring 1992): 37–8, especially.
7. Eric Hobsbawm, 'Harder Times Ahead for Capitalism', *Guardian*, 30 November 1991: 27.
8. Ibid.
9. The academic interest in ethnicity, as Werner Sollers shows, emerged dramatically in the 1970s, when, as he puts it, 'Ethnicity truly was in vogue', Werner Sollers, *Beyond Ethnicity. Consent and Descent in American Culture* (New York and Oxford: Oxford University Press, 1986), p. 21. Key works were Michael Novak, *The Rise of the Unmeltable Ethnics*

(1972); Abner Cohen, (ed.), *Urban Ethnicity* (1974); Andrew Greeley, *Ethnicity in the United States* (1974); Neil Sanburg, *Ethnic Identity and Assimilation* (1974); and Nathan Glaser and Daniel Patrick Moynihan (eds), *Ethnicity: Theory and Experience* (1975).

10. Richard Gott, 'The Racial Price of Life in the Melting Pot', *Guardian*, 11 July 1992: 25.
11. For the expression of this postmodernism, see Joseph Natoli and Linda Hutcheon (eds), *A Postmodern Reader* (New York, State University of New York, 1993), pp. 441–2.
12. David Birch has written of the need to maintain a 'dialogic concept of totality', 'Postmodern Chutneys', *Textual Practice*, 5: 1 (1991): 1.
13. Harvey, op. cit., p. 35.
14. See Harvey, 'Class relations, Social Justice and the Politics of Difference', in Judith Squires (ed.), *Principled Positions. Postmodernism and the Rediscovery of Value* (London: Lawrence and Wishart, 1993), pp. 85–120. Harvey describes his position here as 'a modernised version of historical and geographical materialism'. p. 115. He and other contributors to this volume and project can best be seen as attempting to work through postmodernism to a newly articulated relation between poststructuralism's linguistic and philosophical critique and a practical political critique of late capitalism. See also, Mark Perryman (ed.), *Altered States* (London: Lawrence and Wishart, 1994) and Steven Connor *Theory and Cultural Value* (Oxford: Basil Blackwell, 1992).
15. Natoli and Hutcheon (eds), op. cit., p. 442.
16. Ibid.
17. Howe, 'Social Retreat and the *Tumler*' in Sleeper (ed.), op. cit., p. 5.
18. Brown, 'Where Pluralism and Paranoia Meet', ibid., pp. 76–7.
19. Juan Flores, 'Rappin' Writin' and Breakin': Black and Puerto Rican Street Culture in New York', ibid., pp. 174–8.
20. Howe, op. cit.
21. Flores, op. cit., p. 178.
22. Henry Giroux, 'Postmodernism as Border Pedagogy: Redefining the Boundaries of Race and Ethnicity', in Natoli and Hutcheon (eds), op. cit, p. 453.
23. Tom Wolfe, 'Stalking the Billion-Footed Beast', Introduction to *Bonfire of the Vanities* (1988, London: Picador, 1990), pp. vii, viii. Further page references are given in the text.
24. Homi Bhabha, 'Conference Presentation' in Philomena Mariani (ed.), *Critical Fictions. The Politics of Imaginative Writing* (Seattle: Bay Press, 1991), p. 62.
25. Richard Price, *Clockers* (London: Bloomsbury, 1992), p. 118. Further page references are given in the text.
26. Elizabeth Young and Graham Caveney, *Shopping in Space. Essays on American 'Blank Generation' Fiction* (London: Serpent's Tail, 1992), p. 20).
27. Ibid., p. viii.
28. Robert Siegle's *Suburban Ambush. Downtown Writing and the Fiction of Insurgency* (Baltimore and London: Johns Hopkins University Press, 1989) is the other major study of this writing. It includes discussion of Kathy Acker, Ron Kolm and other performance artists and publishing

outfits, as well as studies of Tillman, Rose and Texier. This fiction, Siegle writes, embodies a 'radical postmodernism' (p. xvi), in which writers cohabit 'the same space with the commodity culture that they critique' (p xv). 'Downtown writing *is* insurgent', he writes, 'but its alpha and omega reside . . . in its status as fiction rather than revolution' (pp. 2–3).

29. Jay McInerney, *Brightness Falls* (Harmondsworth: Penguin, 1992), pp. 415, 403.

30. Bret Easton Ellis, *American Psycho* (London: Picador, 1991), p. 352. Further page references are given in the text.

31. 'There is no document of civilisation which is not at the same time a document of barbarism', wrote Benjamin, 'Theses on the Philosophy of History', in Hannah Arendt (ed.), *Illuminations* (London: Fontana, 1970), p. 258.

32. Young and Caveney, op. cit., pp. 120, 100.

33. See Larry McCaffery and Sinda Gregory, 'An Interview with Paul Auster', *Mississippi Review,* 20, 1 and 2 (1991): 49–62, especially 53; and Adam Begley, 'The Public Eye', *Guardian* Weekend Section, 17 October, 1992, p. 21.

34. Paul Auster, *The New York Trilogy* (1985, London: Faber, 1987), p. 78. Further page references are given in the text.

35. Young and Caveney, op. cit., p. 139.

36. Ibid. Robert Siegle sees *Kill the Poor* as a tale of the contradictions of contemporary American life as lived out by its main character JoJo on the Lower East Side: 'JoJo's real problem', he writes, 'is . . . that he can be neither the socially privileged term nor its oppressed contrary. The repetition in his own life of the national originary experience of immigration and the frontier makes him a function of that primary movement of social *différance*.' op. cit., p. 284.

37. Sam B. Girgus, 'The New Ethnic Novel and the American Idea', *College Literature*, 20: 3 (October 1993): 57. The novels of the 'Blank Generation' do not themselves ignore the presence of the 'other', as the above discussion goes to show. Also, Jay McInerney's recently edited collection of short stories, *Cowboys, Indians and Commuters: The Penguin Book of New American Voices* (Harmondsworth: Penguin, 1994) shows an open awareness of new non-canonic literatures – though he surprisingly lists Afro-American and women's fiction amongst these 'new and marginal cultures' of the 1980s and 1990s. His easy talk of an expanded 'short-story marketplace' suggests a world where white mainstream commercial culture is now calling the shots on 'identity politics'. His idea of the end of the century is, as he says, 'that anything goes', pp. xviii, xxi.

38. Girgus, ibid., p. 59.

39. 'Honourable investigation' is a phrase Price used to refer to his own writing at a reading of *Clockers* (Cambridge Public Library, Cambridge, Mass., 4 June 1992). I am drawing on other remarks made on the same occasion for the comments I make here, including the importance of commercial and artistic success.

40. Jerre Mangione, 'A Double Life: The Fate of the Urban Ethnic' in Michael C. Jaye and Ann Chalmers Watts (eds), *Literature and the*

Urban Experience (New Brunswick: Rutgers University Press, 1981), p. 169; Pedro Juan Soto, 'The City and I', ibid., p. 189.

41. Chaim Potok, 'Culture Confrontation in Urban America: A Writer's Beginnings', ibid., p. 165.
42. Ralph Ellison, 'Harlem is Nowhere' in *Shadow and Act* (London: Secker and Warburg, 1967), pp. 294–302.
43. Ibid., p. 297.
44. Ibid., pp. 300, 296.
45. See Girgus, op. cit., pp. 62, 63.
46. Faythe Turner, *Puerto Rican Writers at Home in the USA* (Seattle, Washington: Open Hand Publishing Inc., 1991), pp. 3, 4.
47. Nicholasa Mohr, 'Puerto Rican Writers in the US, Puerto Rican Writers in Puerto Rico: A Separation Beyond Language', in Asunción Horno-Delgrado, Eliana Ortega, Nina M. Scott, Nancy Saporta Sternbach (eds), *Breaking Boundaries. Latina Writing and Critical Readings* (Amherst: The University of Massachusetts Press, 1989), pp. 114, 115, 116.
48. Turner, op. cit., p. 5.
49. Quoted ibid.
50. Bharati Mukherjee, *Jasmine* (London: Virago Press, 1991). Page references are given in the text.
51. Mukherjee, in Philomena Mariani (ed.), *Critical Fictions* (Seattle: Bay Press, 1991), pp. 24–5.
52. Paul Auster, *Leviathan* (London: Faber, 1992), p. 216. Further page references are given in the text.
53. Girgus, op. cit., p. 67.
54. Cristina Garcia, *Dreaming in Cuban* (London: Flamingo, 1992), p. 128. Further page references are given in the text.
55. Paul Auster, *The Invention of Solitude* (1982, London: Faber, 1988), p. 148. Further page references are given in the text.
56. Sigmund Freud, 'The Uncanny' in Angela Richards and Albert Dickson (eds), *Sigmund Freud. Art and Literature*, Vol. 14 (Harmondsworth: Penguin Freud Library, 1985), p. 345. Further page references are given in the text.
57. McCaffery and Gregory, 'An Interview with Paul Auster', op. cit., p. 52.
58. Ibid., pp. 51–2.
59. Ibid., p. 51.
60. Ibid., p. 57. If we do not immediately think of the 'postmodernist' Paul Auster stories in these terms, it is worth noting that he thinks of *The Music of Chance* as having the structure of fairy-tale and worth recalling the rare moment of fantasy in the story 'The Locked Room' when the father shares the tall tale of going to Boston for a moon rock and an elephant with his son, *New York Trilogy*, op. cit., pp. 302–3.
61. Auster, ibid., p. 232.
62. So too does *Getting Home Alive*, discussed below. Eliana Ortega and Nancy Saporta Sternbach point to the frequent appearance of the 'mother type' and to cultural and generational confrontations being played out on 'the mother–daughter terrain in Latina literature', *Breaking Boundaries*, op. cit., p. 12.
63. McCaffery and Gregory, op. cit., p. 51.

64. For thoughts on modernity's repressed 'other' along related lines, see Wendy Wheeler, 'Nostalgia Isn't Nasty. The Postmodernising of Parliamentary Democracy', in Mark Perryman (ed.), *Altered States*, op. cit., pp. 96–7; and Homi Bhabha in Mariani (ed.), op. cit., p. 64.
65. Berman, 'Looking at our City' in Sleeper (ed.), op. cit., p. 21.
66. Ibid., p. 17.
67. Auster, *New York Trilogy*, op. cit., p. 74. Following page references are given in the text.
68. Auster, *The Invention of Solitude*, op. cit., p. 139.
69. Girgus, op. cit., p. 58.
70. Homi Bhabha in Mariani (ed.), op. cit., p. 62.
71. Ibid., p. 63.
72. Ibid., p. 65.
73. Mukherjee, in Mariani (ed.), ibid., p. 27.
74. Lourdes Rojas, 'Latinas at the Crossroads; An Affirmation of Life in Rosario Morales and Aurora Levins Morales', *Getting Home Alive*', in *Breaking Boundaries*, op: cit., p. 171.
75. Aurora Levins Morales and Rosario Morales, *Getting Home Alive* (New York: Firebrand Books, 1986), p. 76.
76. Bhabha, op. cit., p. 65.

CHAPTER FIVE

Jazz Records

BLACKNESS AND BAKHTIN

Jazz. Black music: also as a verb, to copulate; also as a noun, semen. *See* Jive.

(*A Glossary of Harlem Slang*)

In Jay McInerney's *Brightness Falls*, the author Victor Propp suggests to the young editor Russell Calloway that they are living in an era when anything can happen. He reminds Russell of the incident in Scott Fitzgerald's *The Great Gatsby* when Gatsby drives Fitzgerald's narrator Nick Carroway into the city over the Queensborough Bridge. 'Anything can happen now that we've slid over this bridge', Propp quotes Nick as saying, 'anything at all.'[1] After having already negotiated advances of a quarter of a million dollars for his second promised but non-existent book, Propp has in mind a further new contract with the publishers Corbin Dern. At the same time he wants to encourage the ambitious Calloway to think that he can buy out the company. Propp not only trades on his supposed literary connections and stature (Russell swears he heard him once refer to 'Jim Joyce'), he trades it in, surrendering the literary exhibit to ill-gotten commercial gain. Propp's 'anything can happen' is the greedy adventurism, the 'money for nothing' of the Yuppie era, when 'wishes were Porsches', rather than the romantic dreams of Gatsby. Such is the fate perhaps of the modern classic (Fitzgerald and, in a way, Propp himself) in the money-market of postmodern bestsellers.

No doubt it is part of McInerney's purpose to show just what a fake literary giant like Propp can get away with in an age which so easily confuses aesthetic with commercial values. In his own person as author, McInerney seems to intend a more respectful homage to Fitzgerald's crafted lyricism. For many readers, the story of the Calloways and the more worthy but ruined writer Jeff Pierce will recall the promise and tawdry decline Carroway sees in Gatsby, and that Fitzgerald saw in himself and the America of the 1920s. But these allusions, and others (the characters' names of course, and the title, borrowed from Thomas Nashe, as Fitzgerald borrowed his 'Tender is the Night' from Keats) trail off into the superficial, the neat, and nostalgic, so that the 'echoes of Fitzgerald' in the novel come to function more as design features than as literary or social parallel.

However accurate Propp's quotation the classic modern text is cheapened in his memory of it. However serious McInerney's satiric intent, the tougher ambiguities for both character and author in the earlier example pass unnoticed through the casual weave of his postmodernism. To put this differently, and in terms I wish to employ later, the open intertextuality of McInerney's novel makes it a more dialogic than monologic text. But since Fitzgerald and the 1920s are more knowing allusion than fully engaged precedent in *Brightness Falls*, McInerney does not enter the conversation between author and represented text which Bakhtin speaks of as necessary to a fuller inner dialogisation.

The passage Propp quotes from is an example of what is forgotten in this partial dialogue. For Nick in this incident experiences a full and complex sense of possibility. As the sunlight plays through the bridge's girders upon the moving cars, he first sees the city 'rising up across the river in white heaps and sugarlumps all built with a wish out of nonolfactory money. The city seen from the Queensborough Bridge', he says, 'is always the city seen for the first time, in its first wild promise of all the mystery and the beauty in the world.'[2] For a moment the enchanted, sweet-smelling and sweet-tasting city re-presents the full wonder of the new continent – the 'fresh, green breast of the new world' evoked in the novel's famous closing peroration. Much has been said of the haunting idealism of this ending and its expression of the paradoxically receding yet beckoning goal at the heart of the American dream. But the earlier moment has some of this complexity too. First, immediately prior to the Adamic vision the fairy-tale city inspires in him, Nick sees Gatsby reduce a speed cop to cap-tipping deference by producing a card from the commissioner. Next, as Gatsby's fabulous yellow car, 'its fenders spread like wings', moves over the bridge they pass a funeral procession, 'a dead man . . . in a hearse heaped with blooms', and, following after, the sad faces of the mourners from 'south-eastern Europe'. The incident swirls all at once with the dazzling wonderment, shady connections, repressed immigrant background and the rumour of death that surround Gatsby.

But most important for present purposes is what happens next. 'As we crossed Blackwell's Island', says Nick, 'a limousine passed us, driven by a white chauffeur, in which sat three modish negroes, two bucks and a girl. I laughed aloud as the yolks of their eyeballs rolled toward us in haughty rivalry.'[3] The thought that 'anything can happen' follows immediately on this; not the thought that anybody can make money but that the very order of things might be challenged. Carroway's language is obviously not free of racial stereotype and it is difficult to gauge the tone of his open laughter. (Is it contemptuous or convivial, does he laugh at their presumption, their look, or the absurdity of the world turned upside down?)

The novel does not stop to unravel these attitudes, and blacks are barely present elsewhere (a 'pale well-dress negro' identifies Gatsby's yellow car after Myrtle Wilson has been run down, and Tom is impressed by Goddard's argument in *The Rise of the Coloured Empires* that the white race is in danger of being submerged). These help establish features of plot and characterisation, but are more important in the way they signal a black social presence, shadowing, threatening, witnessing the goings-on of the novel's white middle class. Nick's final thought crossing the bridge, is that 'Even Gatsby could happen', as if a limousine with white chauffeur and black passengers makes even his fiction of himself plausible. And, in fact, we are led during the course of the novel to make some association between their 'haughty rivalry' and the poor boy Gatsby's bid for Daisy. Tom certainly associates the two in the steamy showdown later in a New York hotel room. 'I suppose the latest thing', he storms, 'is to sit back and let Mr Nobody from Nowhere make love to your wife . . . . Nowadays people begin by sneering at family life and family institutions, and next they'll throw everything overboard and have intermarriage between black and white.'[4]

What had happened historically in the United States to stir this anxiety in the white leisured class and to present Gatsby and Nick with the scene on Queensborough Bridge was the migration of blacks from the South to the Northern cities of Chicago (the Buchanans' home) and New York in the late nineteenth and early twentieth centuries. After Emancipation, in the years between 1890 and 1910 the black population of New York City nearly tripled. The area of Harlem had expanded in the same period, and with the collapse of real estate values in the depression of 1904–05 began to provide elegant housing, though still at comparatively high rents, for the growing number of black city-dwellers. As James de Jongh comments: 'No population was less expected – and less welcome – than blacks in the Harlem housing market. The idea of negroes occupying the new upscale area seemed bizarre and outlandish to many residents and property owners.'[5] Whites resisted, predictably, but their actions were ineffective. 'By 1919, the year of the triumphant homecoming of the black 369th Infantry Regiment to Harlem', de Jongh reports, 'Harlem was a firmly established, stylish black community, in an attractive well-built section of Manhattan.'[6]

As such, Harlem gave rise to the idea that this 'city within the city' would become, in Alain Locke's words, 'a race capital'; a hope invested in large part in the intellectual life and cultural expression associated with the Harlem Renaissance.[7] The movement was announced to the world in the anthology of essays, fiction and poetry comprising *The New Negro*, which Locke edited in 1925, the same year of course as the appearance of *The Great Gatsby*. In the first story in the anthology, 'The City of Refuge', by Rudolf Fisher, a Negro, King Solomon Gillis, who is on the run after a shooting in North Carolina, stands amazed, 'eyes opened wide . . . mouth opened wider' at the sights of Negro Harlem, city of plenty and refuge. Most of all he is impressed by the sight of a black policeman directing cars with white passengers and drivers. 'It was beyond belief – impossible', he thinks, 'Black might be white, but it couldn't be that white!' And yet, 'Cullud policemans!' he repeats to himself, half-aloud, and with growing conviction, 'Even got cullud policemans . . . .'[8]

It is as if again, as in Gatsby, anything is possible. Both stories associate a momentous reversal of the established order with the New Negro in what one might call a moment of social estrangement, when the old is amazingly, laughably overturned. The difference between them is marked, however. Where King Solomon Gillis sees 'Negroes predominantly, overwhelmingly everywhere', Nick and Fitzgerald see them only in passing and as background. Nor of course has it escaped black readers and critics than whereas Fitzgerald is canonised, Fisher is forgotten, and the Harlem Renaissance at best regarded as an appendage to American modernism and judged by its standards. King Solomon's wide-eyed amazement has proved no match for Carraway's peripheral vision. 'Black might be white', as King Solomon says, 'but it couldn't be that white.'

Amongst black critics Houston Baker Jr has most directly challenged the hegemony of Anglo-American modernism. He sees in Fitzgerald's Tom Buchanan a brazen spokesman for a generation of modern artists, threatened by 'a new world of science, war, technology, and imperialism', and judges Nick in the above passage 'priggishly astute'.[9] In place of the privileged idea of 'civilisation' and the limiting critical categories of this tradition, Baker proposes a broader discursive lineage of '"renaissancism" in Afro-American expressive culture as a whole'.[10] This brings him to examine a constellation of critical and creative writings (Booker T. Washington's *Up From Slavery*, William Du Bois' *The Souls of Black Folk*, Alain Locke's *The New Negro*, amongst others) in the longer modern period of the 1880s to 1930s. These he reads in terms of their 'mastery of form' and 'deformation of mastery': discursive strategies expressing ironic counter-assimilations of dominant white discourse by African-Americans.

In the second volume of what has become a trilogy devoted to the exploration of this 'renaissancism' Baker explains how 'The discursive history of Afro-American modernism, as I conceive it, reveals the "spirit work" of a racial genius. It reveals, as well, a continuous attempt by Afro-American spokespeople such as Washington, Du Bois and Locke to attune themselves to this genius and to extend its forward motion.'[11] For writers, artists and critics this has involved a double effort at reclamation, the rediscovery of the already given in existing traditions in African-American culture, and of invention, on behalf of a national spirit, or impulse, a 'whole people – a nation of Afro-Americans – coming to democratic birth'.[12] In all instances this project, Baker argues, is rooted in the vernacular, in the 'soundings', as he puts it, of the 'blues geographies' shaping African-American expressive culture.[13]

Baker is entirely aware of the arbitrariness of literary periodisation, of the constructedness of modernism, and of the enlivening 'revisions' comprising a continuing history of African-American culture. Yet he chooses to reject, rather than revise, the Anglo-Irish-American canon of modernism (whose reactionary tendencies, it has to be said, Tom Buchanan at best caricatures), and at the same time to invoke a unified black consciousness and identity, a 'quintessential' Afro-American spirit or 'genius' already in place. Thus he introduces *Afro-American Poetics* as the story of 'perduring *spirit work*. The story of spirit work', he says, 'is a unifying myth. It provides coherence for both the autobiographical self and the general Afro-American cultural enterprise.'[14]

Baker explains here that he is reacting to 'the disappearance of culture and the self announced by postmodernism' One cannot fail to hear in this uneasiness, however (itself common of course, in different forms, to many contemporary black and white critics) an appeal to the psychic and cultural unity characteristic of high modernism. We might say that Baker is himself exercising a 'mastery' or 'deformation' of modernist form, but this would only be to confirm how entangled 'white' and 'black' aesthetics and cultural projects have in fact been. One wonders, that is to say, at the feasibility and radicalism of a claim for an independent and unified expressive culture in the face of a history of complex dialogue and differentiation, and in face of a dominant culture whose hegemony is expressed in just such a will to unity. Baker's statement of transcendent identity and purpose is contradicted, as it turns out, by his own 'revisionist enterprise', and by the tensions he in practice elucidates in the 'spirit work' of African-American art: in the dualities of the Southern heritage explored in Jean Toomer's modernist *Cane*, for example, and between the favoured white literary modes and irrepressible black consciousness he finds in Countee Cullen.

The essay on *Cane*, Baker presents as a demonstration of the infelicitous combination in his own earlier work of black cultural politics with New Critical techniques. He has looked since, he says, for a consistency of critical method and cultural project. Yet his work continues to exhibit the tension in what Anna-Marie Smith has called the 'double game of identities' common to contemporary social movements, caught between strategies based on unfixed identities and assertions of who women, gays, blacks 'essentially "are"'.[15] The real value of Baker's work lies in what might be called its post-structuralist side, in the record of mixed and inharmonious voices, of recontextualised interpretations, including those of his own 'self-in-motion', rather than in its hypothesis or a corrective myth of coherent cultural identity, or consistent African-American 'sound'.

Baker takes the essentialist position he does in reaction to a conception of postmodernism and deconstruction which would undermine all claims to subjective or cultural authenticity. He refuses to join the privileged 'deconstructionist collective'; claiming that African-Americans anyway 'have been deconstructionists *par excellence*', from the first Jamestown disembarkation of slaves to the era of Run DMC.[16] Typically, he fails at such moments to see how the deconstruction which unsettles 'Western discourse' but at the same time homogenises an entire African-American history and exempts it from this critique, is merely the mirror image of the worst in the system of thinking he means to depose.

Henry Louis Gates has been generally more receptive to movements in European theory but wants also to stake out the project for a vernacular black criticism. He has turned consequently from a 'desire to outwit the master by trying to speak his language as fluently as he' (Baker's 'mastery of form') to seek in 'the dark secrets of a black and hermetic discursive universe' a fluency entirely foreign to the master. [17] The times, says Gates, in which black critics felt compelled to imitate the terms of 'white critical theory' are at an end:

> We as critics must turn to our own peculiarly black structures of thought and feeling to develop our own language of criticism. We must do so by turning to the black vernacular, the language we use to speak to each other, when no white people are around. My central argument is this: *black people theorize about their art and their lives in the black vernacular.* [18]

Gates assumes a stark rivalry between, on the one hand, a universalising, distorting, written and white canon and theory and, on the other, an authentic, hermetic, indigenous black vernacular tradition. At the same time he aims, he says, 'to reach out to others in the critical canon', to 'turn outwards to redefine every institution in this profession'. [19] The militant separatism the essay proposes would hardly allow for the dialogue necessary to such reform. It is not surprising therefore that the dichotomies of this essay are problematised in a second where he considers the revision Black Studies has in fact effected within American Studies. 'No longer', he concludes here, 'are the concepts of "black" and "white" to be thought to be preconstituted; rather they are mutually constitutive and socially produced.' [20] In two further, slightly later, essays, Gates argues unexpectedly for a multiculturalist perspective which again seriously questions the earlier argument. 'We are all ethnics', he says, (drawing on the 'canonic' white writer Herman Melville's *Redburn* for this conclusion), 'the challenge of transcending ethnic chauvinism is one we all face.' [21] To be American is to possess a hyphenated, ethnic identity: 'it's only when we're free to explore the complexities of our hyphenated culture', he says, 'that we can discover what a genuinely common American culture might actually look like'. [22] Multiculturalism is therefore endorsed as late twentieth-century Americanism.

Like Baker's 'self-in-motion', Gates has sought to open a route for criticism and theory which has at all points to negotiate the historical and cultural fact of white power. The hazards are plain. To affirm black autonomy apparently means rejecting the idea of cultural difference as the conspiratorial plot of white theory. To affirm black difference means rejecting a hypostatised white hegemony. In the essay 'Goodbye Columbus?', however, Gates steers beyond these reductive polarities. The 'paranoid style' of oppositional theory and criticism, as he here terms it, has failed to articulate the present 'complex, overlapping, disjunctive order'.[23] He comes thus to a quite different response to the signs of postmodernity. 'The globalisation of America and the Americanisation of the globe', he says, have made assumptions of an integrated cultural whole as well as models of the centre–periphery redundant. We inhabit a pluralist, polycentric world, 'a cultural complex of travelling culture'.[24] A more adequate model for this hyphenated self and culture-in-motion, he suggests, would be one which accounted for social and ethnic difference and interchange within regulatory structures of power. 'Perhaps', as he puts it, 'we should try to think of American culture as a conversation among different voices – even if it's a conversation some of us weren't able to join until recently.'[25]

James De Jongh's case study of the 'synapse of historical, social, and cultural forces' represented by the Harlem motif in twentieth-century literature goes some way towards confirming this model. Harlem he sees as a trope, a literary idea or symbolic 'cultural text', at odds from the 1920s with the social reality or 'physical text' of Harlem the emerging ghetto and abandoned inner city. He concludes that: 'The literary motif has evolved in a series of engagements with interpretation: dialogues of a sort – sometimes sustained, at other times sporadic – involving individual authors with the popular reading and literary legacy of the motif itself as well as with the fact and the history of Harlem.'[26] This dialogue has involved successive generations of African-Americans in moods of affirmation and disillusionment since the 1920s, but also Hispanic and Portuguese writers in the broader 'Africana' diaspora, as well as white American and European authors. The latter, De Jongh says, have clung to the perception of the exotic, alien 'human otherness of black life', employing Harlem 'as an occasional signifier of primitivism, in the 1920s; of bourgeois alienation, in the 1940s and 1950s; and radical political idealism in the 1960s'.[27]

In the end, as this begins to suggest, De Jongh sees the shared trope of Harlem as 'embodying two distinct, and largely contrary ideas, of the nature, meaning, and potential of black cultural being'.[28] But the assumption of two 'universes of discourse' (black and white) simplifies the 'complex intermingling', the patterns of convergence as well as divergence across discourses and cultural programmes his book otherwise documents. Nor does it allow for divergences *within* black or white discourse. Both Baker and De Jongh fail, one might say, to take the force of Nathan Huggins's seminal insight in the major earlier study of the Harlem Renaissance that 'the black–white relationship has been symbiotic [and that], blacks have been essential to white identity (and whites to blacks).'[29]

Toni Morrison has with great originality recently taken up the first side of this formulation. Rather than campaign to simply reverse the standard hierarchies of white over black writing, her study *Playing in the Dark* investigates the importance of an internalised black presence for a white literary sensibility. Blacks, she shows, have constituted the Other within the interior racialism (not the racism) of the white paradigm. This, I think, is the way to view Anglo-American modernism, and the way to read the passage discussed above from Fitzgerald's *Gatsby*. The unnamed threesome of two bucks and a girl break temporarily through the text's surface in a glimpse behind its hegemonic racial perspective of the 'unsettled and unsettling population' Morrison speaks of.[30] We might think of the cars in this passage, of the manners, cultures and populations they represent, as going in rival and independent directions. This would be the perspective of an oppositional criticism determined on what Gates calls 'ethnicist affirmation and routinised ressentiment'.[31] But to follow either car and population and not the other, or to track their 'bifurcated progression', as de Jongh invites us to do of black and non-black authors, would be to miss all the complexity of the exchange at the moment of passing and the way that antagonisms, rivalries and a sense of the possible take definition precisely from such symptomatic encounters.

Toni Morrison shows how we might explore the racialism shaping a white literary sensibility. The parenthetical addition in Huggins's statement, 'blacks have been essential to white identity (and whites to blacks)', has of course been the more obvious topic in discussions of racial identity (and hence the more tiresome and obstructive for those seeking alternative, affirmative terms for African-American culture). The complexities of contestation and assimilation which mark the constructions of black identity have followed, undeniably, from the position of this culture within white society. As W.E.B. Du Bois saw most famously and profoundly at the beginning of the century, America 'yields [the negro] no true self-consciousness, but only lets him see himself through the revelation of the other world. One ever feels his twoness, – an American, a negro; two souls, two thoughts, two unreconciled strivings; two warring ideals in one black body.'[32]

The writers of the Renaissance inflected the 'double consciousness' Du Bois described in new ways which were further dramatised by the experience of Harlem, the 'city within a city', in James Weldon Johnson's phrase. Thus Alain Locke spoke of the promise of Harlem as 'a race capital', of 'Negro life . . . seizing upon its first chances for group expression and self-determination', but at the same time saw the new Negro as reaching 'out as yet to nothing but American wants, American ideas', anticipating 'his full initiation into American democracy'.[33] No contribution to *The New Negro* or writer associated with the Harlem Renaissance was free of this sense of division and doubleness. Langston Hughes perhaps gave this dualism its most sustained, conscious and controlled expression, though his allegiance was at the same time quite clear. He spoke, he said, in the influential 'The Negro Artist and the Racial Mountain' for those 'younger negro artists . . . who now intend to express our individual dark-skinned selves without fear or shame'.[34] This programme was provoked, we might remember, however, by the quite different ambitions of a young negro artist who confessed he wanted 'to be a poet – not a Negro poet'. For Hughes this was a betrayal: 'But this is the mountain standing in the way of any true Negro art in America – this urge within the race toward whiteness, the desire to pour racial individuality into the mould of American standardisation and to be as little Negro and as much American as possible.'[35] Hughes was replying to an essay in the previous issue of *Nation* by the black journalist and satirist George S. Schulyer, who argued that a black writer should write within the mainstream of Western European culture since it was this which had shaped his consciousness. Hughes's essay was followed by further letters, including a response from Mike Gold (who began the Marxist journal *New Masses* in this same year), and who, in a third option, urged black writers and intellectuals to leave the cabarets and colleges and 'help the mass of their own brothers in the economic fight'.[36] Hughes's statement is the more remembered but his riposte clearly belongs in a dialogue revealing how a 'double consciousness' was not only individually experienced, but might be negotiated in quite opposite directions by black contemporaries, and further overlaid by different political and class interests.

An example such as this shows how questions of racial identity and destiny cannot be developed or resolved in the language of essentialism or radical externality, when they have been manifestly articulated text by text, moment by moment, in internally fraught and inescapably relational and historical terms. We need then in reading literature, criticism and culture (in the present example and in general) to look and listen for the shaping sounds and silences of an always at least two-way and at the same time unequal dialogue. Gates suggests as much above in the idea of an ethnic America in conversation, adding how easily this can be misconstrued as assuming a free and easy coexistence, a pluralism 'which leaves oppressive structures intact'.[37]

As Du Bois, Hughes and Morrison also remind us, the voices of this cultural dialogue have been internalised to different effect in the formation of literatures, texts and subjectivities. We can look for further theoretical direction on these issues to M.M. Bahktin, whose notion of 'double-voiced' discourse Gates indeed draws directly upon in discussing the relations between Toomer, Brown, Hurston, Ellison, Richard Wright and Ishmael Reed.[38] For Bakhtin's associate, Vološinov, consciousness or 'inner speech' is always 'a social, ideological fact' shaped by 'verbal interaction . . . the basic reality of language'.[39] Every verbal performance, moreover, Vološinov argues, contracts a relation with others in the same sphere. 'Thus the printed verbal performance engages, as it were, in ideological colloquy of large scale: it responds to something, objects to something, affirms something, anticipates possible responses and objections, seeks support, and so on.'[40] This would correspond to the 'double-voiced' intertextuality Gates investigates in African-American writing. This colloquy is in turn powerfully influenced, however, by the hierarchical organisation of society. Thus 'differently oriented accents intersect in every ideological sign', an expression of social struggle, in which 'the social multiaccentuality of the ideological sign' must contend with the ruling class's attempt to suppress its mutability, 'to extinguish or drive inward the struggle between social value judgements which occurs in it, to make the sign uniaccentual'.[41] The 'heteroglossia' (or 'many-languagedness') of texts is always in tension, that is to say, with forces interested in sustaining monologic textual meanings and cultural values, and registers this tension within itself.

Though Bakhtin was concerned especially with the novel, these concepts derive from a general linguistic theory which has since been applied more broadly within cultural studies to the cinema, for example, and the study of sexual difference.[42] They are similarly appropriate, I suggest, to literary and cultural 'conversations' between the self and other; dividing and reforming hyphenated black and white identities. For the forms of patriarchal and racial domination, as well as the class rule Bakhtin/Vološinov highlight, make for asymmetries of power which are played out, and played off against, in language. This perspective would confirm the move Gates and Morrison make beyond a conception of separated discursive and semiotic realms, which at the same time fully recognises the presence and effects of inequality, or of its exposure and subversion.

We need also to understand the formation of cultural and ethnic identity, however, not only as socially and ideologically situated but as in process, as 'in motion', so to speak. Here Baker's self-reflexive 'revisionary enterprise' is instructive. His own readings of the Harlem Renaissance are as much as anything a response to later critical and cultural models, principally the formalism of New Criticism and the cultural nationalism of the Black Arts Movement of the 1960s. The conversation, or dialogue of different voices comprising American culture, is, as this illustrates, a conversation of the present with the past; a 'reclamation' Baker might say, but one which is immediately, if we are to avoid a metaphysics of origins, an 'invention': a constructed and polemical narrative, not a set of facts or voices waiting to speak with unmediated authenticity.

I want in what follows to listen to a selection of voices on one topic of conversation in particular, and that is jazz. In one way this is to draw out and literalise the aural reference and musical metaphors in Bakhtin (voice, utterance, accent, polyphony, orchestration). In another it is to focus a concern with sound and the vernacular, as well as colour, in recent African-American studies. As such it offers a way of assessing positions in the dialogue on racial and artistic identity in the historical period of the Harlem Renaissance in which attitudes towards jazz were a particularly revealing symptom.

Jazz has also been regularly evoked in subsequent periods as a symbolic cultural form, often in association with this earlier period and with Harlem. Music, place and race thus combine in a constellation which we might think of in terms of Bakhtin's 'chronotope': a concept for the related co-ordinates of time and place which characteristically support kinds of narrative (the ruins, vaults and heaths of the nineteenth-century Gothic, the towns and deserts of the Western) and help define particular genres. Claude McKay's *Home to Harlem* and Van Vetchen's *Nigger Heaven* offer controversial and early examples of this new form of the 'Jazz novel'. The later examples I want to examine, *Ragtime, Mumbo Jumbo* and, in a third section, Toni Morrison's *Jazz*, are on the other hand 'historical novels' which review and revise the earlier period and forms for their own 'post-', or new modern times. I want to examine these reconstructions of the 1910s and 1920s, and ask also how in this dialogue they address contemporary readers on questions of colour and cultural value.

JAZZ WITH ATTITUDE: CLAUDE McKAY, E.L. DOCTOROW'S *RAGTIME*, ISHMAEL REED'S *MUMBO JUMBO*

Theodore Adorno notoriously dismissed jazz as 'perennial fashion', the static, standardised product of the mass culture industry, 'always new and always the same'.[43] One of the most decisive answers to this is provided by Ralph Ellison's definition of jazz as an abrasive improvisatory art form.

> There is a cruel contradiction implicit in the art form itself. For true jazz is an art of individual assertion within and against the group. Each true jazz moment (as distinct from the uninspired commercial performance) springs from a contest in which each artist challenges all the rest, each solo flight, or improvisation, represents (like the successive canvases of a painter) a definition of his identity: as individual, as member of a collectivity and as link in the chain of tradition. Thus, because jazz finds its very life in an endless improvisation upon traditional materials, the jazzman must lose his identity even as he finds it.[44]

For Adorno, jazz is monologic, musically and ideologically. conformist, reinforcing the uni-accentual forces in mass society. For Ellison, 'true jazz' – which he tends to associate with Charlie Parker and Bebop – is a situated, dialogic and combative art of self-exploration and discovery. Toni Morrison has recently suggested that she understands black identity differently from Ellison. Ellison 'could project what it was to be a black person', she says, whereas, faced with 'modern flux and fluidity', she cannot. She refers again, however, to jazz, to 'Miles, Louis, Bessie Smith' as well as to the black opera singer Kathleen Battle – 'all these', she says, 'are encompassed in being black'.[45] We can perhaps see these different conceptions of black identity as expressions of a transition from the fated quest for an integrity of self and art work in modernity (Bebop occurring as jazz's modernist moment) to the subjective and cultural mobilities of postmodernity – for which jazz and black music interestingly remains a measure or medium. In a second reference to jazz, in the volume *Playing in the Dark*, Toni Morrison relates the effect of an improvised jazz trumpet solo upon Marie Cardinal, as told in her autobiographical *The Words to Say It*. The book documents Marie Cardinal's madness, therapy and process of healing, and identifies hearing Louis Armstrong in concert as the first moment of her mental collapse, her 'first encounter with the Thing'.[46] As his solo reaches the 'one precise, *unique* note, tracing a sound whose path was almost *painful*, so absolutely necessary had its *equilibrium* and *duration* become, it *tore at the nerves* of those who followed it' (Morrison's emphasis).[47] Marie runs hyperventilating from the concert 'like someone possessed', and Morrison wonders at the 'symbolic figurations of blackness' igniting this panic-striken flight of a young white woman.

If jazz in some way here represents the destabilising 'Other', it has quite clearly at other times been positively valued as a distinctively black cultural form. Armstrong is 'the genius of improvisation' for Morrison in the above discussion, and she wonders not only at the mysterious power of blackness in Marie Cardinal's story, but more simply on her own behalf 'what on earth was Louie playing that night?'[48] Morrison's response reveals how divergent the aesthetic and symbolic encodings given to jazz within black and white culture can be. A prime example of this would be the description of the 1920s as 'the Jazz Age': an expression credited of course not to a black artist but to Scott Fitzgerald, who, in Paul Whiteman's view, knew as much about the jazz age as he himself knew about real jazz.[49] Whiteman's Orchestra played popular dance-hall hits, and by the mid 1920s had made jazz, or a form of it, 'semi-respectable' and commercially successful, while the more adventurous jazz of the contemporary Fletcher Henderson Orchestra, featuring virtuoso black musicians such as Louis Armstrong, already had a more limited following.[50] Whiteman suggests that his own and Fitzgerald's knowledge was superficial if not exploitative. All the same, Whiteman was not ignorant of jazz, and Fitzgerald, somewhat like Gatsby, knew or sensed more than appears, as the memoir 'Echoes of the Jazz Age' shows.

There are two direct references to jazz in this essay: firstly to the word itself which 'in its progress towards respectability has meant', says Fitzgerald, 'first sex, then dancing, then music', and secondly to 'bootleg Negro records' which 'with their phallic euphemisms made everything suggestive'.[51] For Fitzgerald, the 'Jazz Age' meant young (white) people petting and smoking and offending their elders, a

'whole race going hedonistic, deciding on pleasure'.[52] On this
evidence, the associations of jazz with blackness and sex and the
body no more than flicker in and out of the consciousness of
what was a bohemian but still dominant culture, giving a name
to the less respectable antics of well-heeled young white people.
But these brief allusions nonetheless indicate another presence and
vocabulary accompanying Fitzgerald's text and thinking: something
unofficial and lewd that he knows and acknowledges in passing; less
a disturbing solo of the kind Marie Cardinal hears than a distant,
suggestive echo, but a registration of the Other all the same.

Some of Fitzgerald's 'whole race going hedonistic' – in his revealing
phrase – would no doubt have gone slumming in Harlem to discover
the 'black magic', as Claude McKay put it, of the jazz clubs and
cabarets. The number of these clubs grew phenomenally in the 1920s,
particularly on the 'jungle alley' of 133rd Street.[53] Toni Morrison asks
what Armstrong was playing when Marie Cardinal was so affected
by his trumpet solo. It would be just as relevant to know *where* in
the earlier period black jazz musicians were playing. For if it was at
a rent party – an open house party with food, rot-gut liquor and a
25 cent entrance fee to help pay the high rents of Harlem dwellings –
it would have been before an all-black audience. If at the Cotton Club
(where the Duke Ellington Orchestra played from 1927–34), it would
have been in a venue with jungle decor, deliberately reminiscent in its
name of the plantation South, owned by the mobster Owney Madden,
and run for a white-only clientele.

All of this questions any view of jazz as an exclusively black
music, or source of unsullied ethnic identity. To see it this way
is to ignore the mixed cultural and ethnic meanings and conditions
shaping its history (not least in the hierarchies of management and
ownership in the entertainment business and music industry). The
same is true of any claim for the purity of jazz's original music
forms. As Max Harrison argues, jazz has provided a 'matrix' of
'wide racial provenance . . . reflecting the ethnic diversity of the
American population'.[54] As Harrison and others have shown, jazz
derived from a combination of African and European musical forms
and instruments (the field chant and work song, the blues guitar
and banjo developed from Africa, spiritual folksongs, brass-band
instruments introduced by pre-revolutionary British army bands,
the Irish fiddle, the classical piano from Europe). These were used
in the ensemble playing of the early jug or jukebands, which in turn
influenced the forms of Ragtime and Dixieland jazz. Early jazz was
therefore already an expression of the hybridity that has only become

more evident in contemporary neo-bop, jazz-rock, fusion, digital jazz, and the diversified permissiveness of the 1980s and 1990s, a time when, Harrison says, 'all jazz styles remain viable'.[55] Jazz, in short, has been a multi accentual form, drawing increasingly on different cultural-musical traditions, employing an array of instruments to experiment with the patterns of basic call and answer, solo and ensemble playing, popular melody and improvisation, and it has been performed of course by both black and white musicians. As such, jazz is better understood in dialogic terms, as on occasion out-running dominant cultural forms and the drive of commercialism, at others as compromised with or reconciled to them. Peter Wollen has drawn out the fuller implications of this complex and still evolving history. As he argues, jazz has been an inspiration to the other arts, adaptable to different audiences, venues, and media and has criss-crossed the realms of high art and mass culture. This, says Wollen, has made jazz a sign of continuing modernity, and in particular of 'American' modernity:

> Jazz became associated with modernity, with the whole dynamic of
> the period in which the United States industrialised and then, from
> the beginning of the Fordist epoch on, began to overtake Europe.
> It was the epoch in which the skyscrapers were built and in which
> the United States established its dominance within the mass media
> (Hollywood) and industrialised consumer culture. In the 1920s
> and 1930s, jazz became an integral part of America's Great Leap
> Forward, even though the black community was in general left
> behind.[56]

Wollen encourages us to see jazz as one heterophonic topic in the American conversation that goes on defining African-American as well as other hyphenated ethnic identities. One of its most defiant and enthusiastic voices, and one Wollen cites, was Langston Hughes. 'But jazz to me', said Hughes in the famous 'The Negro Artist and the Racial Mountain' in 1926, is 'one of the inherent expressions of Negro life in America: the eternal tom-tom beating in the Negro soul – the tom-tom of revolt against weariness in a white world, a world of subway trains, and work, work, work; the tom-tom of joy and laughter, and pain swallowed in a smile.'[57] Hughes's essay develops as a manifesto for the 'younger Negro artists' who 'now intend to express our individual dark-skinned selves without fear of shame', and he clearly thinks of jazz as a part of this programme: 'Let the blare of Negro jazz bands and the bellowing voice of Bessie Smith singing Blues penetrate the closed ears of the coloured near-intellectuals until they listen and perhaps understand.'[58]

Hughes enlists the excitement, the sound and noise of jazz –
even at the risk, as it seems now, of Africanist stereotype –
against black middle-class sobriety and intellectualism. As much
as anything his statement (the essay, as mentioned above, was a
reply to George S. Schulyer's 'The Negro-Art Hokum') reveals that
the contemporary black community was itself divided in its views
on cultural identity along class and aesthetic lines. In this dialogue,
Hughes's voice as it turned out was an exceptional, protesting and
interventionist rather than hegemonic one. W.E.B. Du Bois, for
example, argued unambiguously for the values of high art, and
exhorted black artists to provide cultural 'uplift'. Alain Locke also,
though he took a close technical and admiring interest in jazz, valued
its 'folk' heritage, and like Du Bois hoped that it would attain
the heights of classical music.[59] In a further revealing example,
J.A. Rogers, in the essay 'Jazz at Home', in Locke's anthology, *The
New Negro*, presents jazz as an authentic and spontaneous expression
of Negro life which, at the same time, 'ranks with the movie and
the dollar as a foremost exponent of modern Americanism'; its
'true spirit', he writes, is 'a joyous revolt from convention, custom,
authority, boredom, even sorrow'.[60] We might think Rogers was
making the same argument as Langston Hughes. In fact in his view
the subversive vigour of jazz's cultural modernism needed to be
moderated and refined if its potential for democratic influence was
to be realised. This process was already underway, he felt, in the big
orchestras which were free of the 'vulgarities and crudities of its lowly
origin and the only too prevalent cheap imitations', amongst whom
he cited the white orchestras of Paul Whiteman and Vincent Lopez
'that are now demonstrating the finer possibilities of jazz music'.[61]
Rogers contrasts jazz's influence upon 'serious modernistic music and
musicians' (the French composers Auric, Satie and Darius Milhaud)
with jazz's 'true home' in the 'none too respectable cabaret' at 'the
mob-level upon which it originated', which presents 'the seamy
side of the story . . . the charm of bohemia, but much more of
the demoralisation of vice'.[62] Hence the need 'to lift and divert it
into nobler channels'.[63] The way of artistic modernism is therefore
preferred to 'modern Americanism' in its 'true' Harlem setting.

The cultural attitudes at work in these responses to jazz were of a
piece with the dialogue engendered by the early 'jazz novel'. Here too
class and race both clearly play an important part in shaping different
projects and positions, but just as clearly these do not line up as black
writers and black culture versus white. The most controversial of
these novels was *Nigger Heaven* (1926) by the white music and drama

critic and later photographer, Carl Van Vetchen. Van Vetchen was a friend of Langston Hughes, James Weldon Johnson and other figures in the Renaissance, a publicist and impressario who presided over lavish soirées for blacks and whites in Harlem and Greenwich Village, and worked strenuously for the cause of black writing. He had written of the need for a black theatre that would be free of the imaginative limitations and commercial ambitions of whites, and warned black writers that the 'squalor' and 'vice' comprising the 'exotic, picturesque material' of negro life would be used by others if black writers failed to exploit it.[64] *Nigger Heaven*, his fifth novel, was in a sense the result. In its simple and symptomatic story an educated and aspiring black writer, Byron Karson, is drawn into a wild affair with Lasca Sartoris and against a lurid Harlem background of drugs, orgies and seduction, shoots her new lover when she deserts him.

The novel sold 100,000 copies. Its form was unselfconsciously that of popular sensation and melodrama: a 'tabloid modernism', we might say, to meet the tone of the new mass society of 'modern Americanism'. As a publishing and cultural event in this new society it helped make the negro a 'vogue' for white intellectuals. For many this attention was a mixed blessing which warped while it opened the market for black writing, and for some the blatant primitivism and bawdy of Van Vetchen's novel was a clear setback and insult. Langston Hughes saw it as 'the first real passionately throbbing novel of contemporary negro life', and was one of the few to appreciate that its title was not a derogatory reference to blacks, but an ironical reference to the segregated upper gallery in a theatre; for Du Bois, however, more typically, the novel was 'a caricature . . . a mass of half truths . . . a blow in the face'.[65]

Van Vetchen's novel was followed by Claude McKay's *Home to Harlem* (1928), the first bestseller by a black Harlem author. McKay had published two volumes of poetry before arriving in Harlem, and in 1917 the poem 'Harlem Dancer', which Arna Bontempts cited as the beginning of the Harlem Renaissance. McKay was sympathetic to Marxism and Bolshevism, an associate editor of the radical *Liberator*, and already by the early 1920s had travelled widely, including journeys to London, where he worked with Sylvia Pankhurst, and to the new Soviet Union, where he met Trotsky, Zinoviev and Bukharin. *Home to Harlem* grew out of McKay's earlier work and radical sympathies, but was inevitably coupled with Van Vetchen's novel and reviewed in much the same way.

The novel follows Jake, a military deserter, home to Harlem from Europe. There he spends his time in sporting houses, clubs and cabarets, in a life of 'pure voluptuous jazzing', devoted to drink, romance, sex and, where necessary, work. The bars and cabarets, where jazz is always playing, the rooming houses, cafés and night-time streets of Harlem form the basic supportive 'chronotope' for the loose plot which takes Jake through various adventures with friends and women to the point where he leaves with his girl Felice for Chicago. 'Jazz' is restored to its fuller subversive double meaning of sex and music, thus enforcing the view of Harlem as 'an erotic utopia' in Osofsky's phrase, or as a 'marginal zone' in Ogren's description of the jazz districts of the major American cities – places of vice and abandon, where in the 'jungle-like worlds' of the jazz joints 'The environment relaxed the restraints of everyday life, and performers and patrons responded by expressing emotions normally held in check.'[66] The time and place of McKay's jazz novel are in this way fused with its action in a carnivalising assault upon the conservative literary and social forms of genteel bourgeois values, whether white or black. The novel's 'hot' music and passion, and excited, unpolished prose present a respectable 'civilised' readership with the embarrassment and seduction of the denied 'other' world of the body, of sensual pleasure and spontaneous emotions with their scattered episodes of love or squabbles and fights. And predictably the scene of this 'other' to the respectable idea of human 'civilisation' is the jungle of animals, the 'savagery' (or Eden) of Africa and the power of blackness in the many fauvist shades it takes in McKay's novel:

> Civilization had brought strikingly exotic types into Susy's race. And like many, many Negroes, she was a victim to that . . . . Ancient black life rooted upon its base with all its fascinating new layers of brown, low-brown, high-brown, nut-brown, lemon, maroon, olive, mauve, gold. Yellow balancing between black and white. Black reaching out beyond yellow. Almost-white on the brink of a change.
>
> . . .
>
> The piano-player had wandered off into some dim, far-away, ancestral source of music. Far, far away from music-hall syncopation and jazz, he was lost in some sensual dream of his own. No tortures, banal shrieks and agonies. Tum-tum . . . tum-tum . . . tum-tum . . . tum-tum . . . . The notes were naked acute alert. Like black youth burning naked in the bush. Love in the deep heart of the jungle . . . . The sharp spring of a leopard from a leafy limb, the snarl of a jackal, green lizards in amorous play, the flight of a plumed bird, and the sudden laughter of mischievous monkeys in their green homes. Tum-tum . . . tum-tum . . . tum-tum . . .

tum-tum . . . . Simple-clear and quivering. Like a primitive dance
of war or of love . . . the marshalling of spears or the sacred frenzy
of a phallic celebration.[67]

Not expectedly, the association of blacks with 'pure voluptuous
jazzing' provoked the criticism of those who sought respectability and
recognition in mainstream American society. Du Bois, for one, found
McKay's *Home to Harlem* nauseating.[68] Du Bois had written how the
'America Negro' in his 'twoness' was 'always looking at oneself
through the eyes of others'. Unwittingly, or perhaps inevitably,
his reaction to McKay's novel bore this out. What he saw was
the stereotypes of the 'old negro' – sensual, carefree, promiscuous
and undisciplined, which would do the 'new Negro' a disservice in
the eyes of white society. In fact, McKay was very aware of this
white stereotype. In *Banjo* (1929), Ray, the educated spokesperson
from the previous novel and now companion in Marseilles to the
roustabout jazz player Banjo, talks of 'the sexuality of negroes –
that strange, big bug forever buzzing in the imagination of white
people'.[69] Du Bois and others associated with the Renaissance were
middle class in education (as was McKay himself), and conservative
in their cultural and moral attitudes. In the character Ray, McKay
looked for some break in this connection; an alliance between mind
and body, modesty and spontaneity, the intellectual and the people.
Ray accordingly takes off at the end of this novel for a vagabond
life with Banjo, because the beachboys of the Marseilles' 'Quartier
Reserve' or 'Ditch' 'represented more than he or the cultured minority
the irrepressible exuberance and legendary vitality of the black race'.[70]
Like Hughes and some others, McKay felt the bourgeois intellectuals
of the Renaissance were out of touch with popular black attitudes and
experience. Though he described Marcus Garvey as 'a curious blend
of bourgeois obsolescence and utopian fantasy', he admired the mass
support of his Universal Negro Improvement Association (UNIA)[71]
and shared with him a sense of the importance of African origins. Like
Hughes again, his stance alerts us to the class differences shaping the
dialogue on black arts and culture, and behind this, to the differences
between Garvey's organisation and the middle-class leadership of the
NAACP and the National Urban League.

All the same, if McKay was more radical and populist than other
black intellectuals and artists, his position could, like Garvey's,
encourage an unworkable separatism which looked naïve alongside
the cultural pluralism of Locke and the accent in the other movements
upon a shared, and differentiated 'Americanness' rather than intrinsic
blackness. (The NAACP and National Urban League were formed

by prominent black and white middle-class individuals in New York, including, most notably, the white social worker and activist, Mary White Ovington.) Nor did McKay himself entirely resolve the tensions between primitivism and civilisation, instinct and education his novels explored. In *Home to Harlem* and *Banjo* the voice of education and sexual reserve lies with Ray, the self-educated aspiring writer. It is he who speaks out against bourgeois minorities in *Banjo*, but he too, in a denial of his own potential, who is brought to express McKay's incipient primitivism at the novel's close. In *Banana Bottom*, the educated Bita returns to Jamaica, and decides eventually to marry the decent but uncouth drayman, Jubban, convinced of the idea that people must remain true to 'their natural unchangeable selves'.[72] This romantic essentialism weakens the effect of the carnivalesque features of McKay's fiction. There is a gregariousness, a joyful free play and air of festival in both first two novels, a code of conduct driven by desire and the body rather than intellect. Yet for all their hedonism and earthy populism, the kind of attitude represented by Ray reinforces rather than overturns conventional distinctions between civilisation and nature – or savagery – with all their class and racial overtones. For the most part too – though the character Bita in *Banana Bottom* redresses their sexism somewhat – these stories confirm the assumed sexual privilege and swaggering independence of black males.

The footloose primitivism of the novels, what is more, and the Jamaican setting of *Banana Bottom* as an entirety, effectively remove them from the urban locales where the strongest social models of cameraderie and, in *Banjo*, of inter-racial group identity and tolerance are represented. (In the setting of the 'Ditch' in Marseilles in *Banjo*, the characters are African, American, and include an Arab woman, Latnah, who lives much the same life as the young male vagabonds.) McKay's largely 'plotless' fiction (*Banjo* is subtitled 'A Story without a Plot'), and the vivid impressionism of his prose style, help to inscribe a social ethic of relaxed, joyful coexistence. But this is associated most strongly with urban life, and urban life in America, not with a return to the land or a life on the road. As Ray declares at one point on the relative freedoms of the United States, when he is stunned by the snobbery and racism he experiences in a Paris restaurant, 'If we can't eat downtown we can eat better in Harlem'.[73] It is in just such a locale, in the 'Ditch' or the 'city within the city' of Harlem, that McKay most successfully envisions a creative, relatively free life for black people as an independent group. In the title to his later study this is the vision of Harlem as the 'Negro Metropolis', a paradoxically enclosed but free, and in some measure utopian, space, a chronotope enabling a synthesis of body and mind and a working solution to the problem of the American negro's 'twoness'.

McKay cannot consistently hold to this urban model and mode of life against the temptations of escape or the uniformities and assimilationist attitudes of the ruling black middle class within this very environment. In a sense too his struggle for spontaneity and group integrity is a struggle against the kind of 'civilisation' represented by American capitalism in the new modern metropolis: a world of increasing standardisation and commercialism governed by both racism and class attitudes. This tension is also precisely what shapes the destiny of the black pianist and protestor Coalhouse Walker Jr in Doctorow's *Ragtime*, written some twenty years later 'about' the earlier decade. The years between the 1890s and 1917, in which *Ragtime* is set, saw the onset of American modernisation, and two of modernity's key symbols – the Model T Ford and the Hollywood film industry – are obviously important players in the novel. 'Ragtime' was the new transitional music of this period, a new marker in terms of skill, entertainment and race pride, coming after the minstrelsy of the later nineteenth century and before 'jazz' (the first jazz recording was made in 1917, approaching the novel's close).

These developments lead Berndt Ostendorf to see the ragtime musicians of this period as a radical cohort of new urban blacks and the music as 'a new revolutionary option'.[74] However, this is to ignore the connections the novel in fact implies between ragtime and the other signs and conditions of modernity. As Ostendorf points out, Coalhouse refuses in the novel to play the 'coon songs' Father expects of him, and instead performs two pieces by Scott Joplin: the then new 'Wall Street Rag' and the more familiar 'Maple Leaf Rag'. But to see this, or the course of action he pursues after his Model T Ford has been vandalised, as 'revolutionary' is to repeat the misreading of Coalhouse made in the novel by Younger Brother.

In joining Coalhouse's gang, Younger Brother surrenders his white identity (he blacks up) to the group name 'Coalhouse'. The potential he sees here for mass support and violent protest behind a charismatic leader contrasts with Booker T. Washington's politics of assimilation (the historical figure appeals to Coalhouse in these terms, mirroring later debates in black politics), but also misconstrues Coalhouse's own intentions. Coalhouse has 'created himself in the teeth' of white prejudice and jealousy,[75] founding his black self on the artistry of ragtime (rather than 'coon' songs), on ownership, and on marriage (denied him after his fiancée's death from police brutality). He seeks neither revolution, nor the equality of sameness, but the right to be black and bourgeois. Thus he seeks the restoration of his Model T Ford (a demand scaled down from the hanging of the Fire Chief, Willie Conklin). The car is accordingly reassembled outside J.P. Morgan's museum, a shrine housing the millionaire's own priceless treasures which the gang have fittingly occupied.

Both Coalhouse and Pierpont Morgan exist by virtue of the status and recognition accruing to property. Coalhouse's stand is doomed (in Doctorow's view the American radical is bound to a sacrificial role), but opens up the relation of individual to mass which figures as a political theme here and elsewhere in Doctorow's writing. The Model T was of course the first mass-produced car, a sign of modernity's technological democracy, at the same time, as it aggravated the alienation of factory labour. J.P. Morgan and Ford are the novel's twins of this phase of monopoly capital, both convinced in a nerveless logic of the theory of reincarnation. For the industrialist, this is only an extrapolation of the potential of the industrial assembly line; for the financier it is the belief in the immortality of a self-evident elite. Coalhouse has no answer to this or to their power. His vehicle is restored by Willie Conklin under the direction of two mechanics. The process therefore reverts from that of the assembly line, where workers work repetitively on the identical parts of autos, to that of a craft industry devoted to recreating the lost aura of the singular vehicle and the personal identity it confers. His car is neither a reproduction, as are Ford's, nor an irreplaceable original, as are J.P. Morgan's treasures. His radicalism therefore lies in his seeking to make and defend an identity which neither defers to old world values on the unique art object or notions of 'genius', nor surrenders to the loss of self in the processes of mass production. His story suggests this is an impossible innovation, however, since on the car's completion he walks knowingly to his death.

The uncomprehending Younger Brother wishes to 'massify' Coalhouse's stand, imagining a 'nation' of identical followers. Significantly, he inherits the Ford but drives it into the ground and walks into Texas to serve Zapata and the Mexican revolution. His special contribution is a knowledge of explosives, but if he thereby aids the cause of national liberation, the blueprints he leaves Father for eleven new ordnance devices are delivered to Washington and come to aid national defence in both World Wars.

It is said of Houdini in the novel that he 'never developed what we think of as a political consciousness . . . from his own hurt feelings'.[76] Coalhouse's radical individualism and Younger Brother's romantic revolutionism represent two courses such a consciousness might take. Both, however, fail to imagine a form of solidarity or mass action which would unite but not eliminate the individual in the collective (providing, in Doctorow's terms, a new mediation between individual psychology and broader social movements). If we are to connect this failure, their futile sacrifice and Younger Brother's compromised inventions with the anarchism that inspires and applauds the two figures, we can only conclude that this political option is tried and found wanting. Certainly it can have no further chance in this novel which at its end, and the end of the era, hands the narrative back to history, the war won and Emma Goldman deported along with other undesirables.

'Ragtime', the music, is entwined in this same social narrative. For Coalhouse to demand the return of his car as if it were a unique object and identical with himself is to fly in the face of the industrial system which had made it available to him. But this was only to repeat the tensions in his situation, and Scott Joplin's situation, as ragtime musicians. Ragtime, that is to say, depended for its popular success on new production processes, just as did the Model T Ford. Both were the standardised products of new modes of industrial production, twin wonders of modernity. The difference being of course that Ford made no claims for the artistic credentials of his product, whereas Scott Joplin and Coalhouse did (or Ostendorf does on his behalf). Joplin was a classically-trained musician and sought recognition as a serious composer. His view of ragtime's status and future was therefore much in line with the thinking of Du Bois, Alain Locke and Rogers. However, his music was produced precisely at the modern moment which obstructed, even contradicted, this ambition as it made it popular. The year of 'The Wall Street Rag', 1909, was the year of the first Model T, and of a law securing income for composers for music played on piano rolls, which of course ragtime was. At a stroke, the player piano mechanised and commercialised the new music in the modern manner. Soon, newer technology making the mass production of recorded music possible would make even this novelty obsolete. To insist, as Scott Joplin did, that his music was not to be played too fast – in a statement Doctorow repeats as the epigraph to his novel, and Ostendorf wants to see as a sign of Joplin's resistance to Taylorism – was really the forlorn plea of the lone artist in a world clattering with pianolas and the wheels of commerce. The fate of his opera *Treemonisha* – rejected and unperformed until 1972 – bears this out.

Coalhouse does not play ragtime in the novel after the first time at the Family's house, but his story is analogous to Joplin's (a press photograph of Joplin which is issued as if it were a picture of Coalhouse illustrates the racial prejudice which standardises all blacks, but says in another way how their protest was the same). Both artists stand on their individual integrity but lose their 'aura' to the new means of mass production and the power of capital which require a subordination of the unique to technical and social uniformities.

Doctorow is of course writing a novel of the 1970s, and the story of Coalhouse Walker's campaign of violence, departing from any correspondence with Scott Joplin's life, is more directly a story for these years. Two obvious contemporary factors suggest themselves as prompting Doctorow's choice of this moment of modernity as a parallel or parable for the later period. One was the popularity of ragtime, especially after the film of *The Sting* (1973). The fact that two awards went to Marvin Hamlish, the film's musical arranger rather than to Scott Joplin only confirms what is said above.[77] For here, at the mid-point of amnesiac postmodern times, the 'aura' of the original artist, as Fredric Jameson would tell us, is one of the first victims of the instant and carefree processes of reproduction. Doctorow's story therefore gives us the beginnings of this process (or, perhaps, in Doctorow's own liberties with texts and time, a contemporary example of it). Secondly, we might see the novel as indirectly addressing contemporary political issues in the 1970s, specifically the issue of strategy which emerged in black politics with the advent of Black Power and a commitment to violent revolutionary action after the civil rights protests and the assassinations of Martin Luther King and Malcolm X in the 1960s. Coalhouse Walker's adopted title of President of the Provisional Government of the United States echoes Marcus Garvey's chosen title of Provisional President of Africa, and as such is a link between this earlier major expression of black nationalism and the revolutionary alternative government of the Panthers. But if Doctorow was thinking about contemporary black politics in this novel, his message is bleak. Coalhouse's sacrifice (one thinks of Huey Newton's *Revolutionary Sacrifice* of 1973) brings no hope, and dissenting opinion in the novel generally is eliminated or compromised. The 'Ragtime era' came to an end with Scott Joplin's death in 1917 and Goldman's deportation two years after. Neither ragtime music nor revolutionary anarchism, the novel seems to say, could outface the standardisation and conservatism of mass society.

Douglas Tallack suggests that the transition from modernity to postmodernity and what this has meant for black politics can be mapped by the 'text' of W.E.B. Du Bois' career. Between the 1930s and his death in 1963 in Ghana (at which point he had given up his US citizenship), Du Bois slipped into what Tallack calls 'his period of marginality'.[78] In the middle of this period, in 1951, he was indicted for treason by the House Un-American Activities Committee. Though he was acquitted, the trial put back the cause of reform in race relations and enforced a discontinuity in black politics to such an extent, says Tallack, that the links between capitalism and racism which this episode had revealed, had to be learned again by the subsequent movement. The eventual outcome, as he sees it, was a form of eclectic, theoretically informed, left counter-cultural nationalism of a kind represented by a figure such as Cornel West.

The sense of discontinuity in this later position has remained strong. West, for example, sees little of present value in earlier traditions of black protest. 'The post-modern period', he writes, 'has rendered the framework of the Du Bois–Washington debate obsolete, but presently there is little theory and praxis to fill the void'.[79] This sense of an empty tradition and present 'void' has become a commonly recognised sign of postmodern temperament, and is the point, in one respect at least, to which Doctorow's *Ragtime* also brings us. The signs of a lack of meaningful dialogue with a usable past or tradition are rarely unequivocal, however, as Doctorow's work illustrates. Many black writers and critics, also, amongst them Toni Morrison, Houston Baker Jr and Henry Louis Gates, have sought to negotiate the present through a reconstructed cultural and artistic relation with the past. The third 'jazz novel' I want to consider, Ishmael Reed's *Mumbo Jumbo*, like Doctorow's *Ragtime* a novel of the early 1970s, is especially pertinent to this project of strategic re-evaluation and the recovery of an African-American cultural history.

As Gates points out, the original dust-jacket of Reed's novel proclaims, 'The Big Lie concerning Afro-American culture is that it lacks a tradition' – if only then to add that '"The Big Truth" of the novel . . . is that this very tradition is as rife with hardened convention and presupposition as is the rest of the Western tradition.'[80] Gates sees Reed's novel as initiating a complex inter- and intratextual dialogue with a host of texts in the Afro-American and Western traditions, 'signifyin(g)' on them in a predominantly parodic mode, which undermines their conventions and false dualisms.[81] The novel's story, to put it at its simplest, is of how 'Jes Grew' seeks its text, pursued by PaPa LaBas and his opponent Hinckle Van Vampton. 'Jes Grew' is the spirit of dance, the unknown 'X factor' liberated by blues and ragtime and jazz, which makes its way in the 1890s to the 1920s of the novel from New Orleans to its first textual expression in New York's Harlem Renaissance and threatens from that base to overrun the country. Already this is to suggest how the novel 'signifies upon' or rewrites earlier texts. The metaphor of ragtime or jazz as an infection or disease was a common one in early writings and appears, for example, in J.A. Rogers' *New Negro* essay and McKay's *Home to Harlem*. 'Jes' Grew', as Reed's epigraphs explain, is 'The earliest Ragtime songs, [which] like Topsy, "jes' grew"', and a term appropriated by James Weldon Johnson.[82] PaPa LaBas has a further complex resonance in Haitian-American culture. He is, Gates explains, 'the Afro-American trickster figure from black sacred tradition . . . the messenger of the gods, the divine Pan-African interpreter' and therefore also 'the figure of the critic', the 'Chief sign reader' of the doubling meanings in the text.[83] Van Vampton, his opponent (his name suggesting, amongst much else, Carl Van Vetchen), is a surviving founder member of the Knights Templar, a force of prejudice and repression throughout history, numbering black and white followers of the path of Aton and of Set, the Egyptian God who banned dancing and music and sex (pp. 172–3).

Whatever their differences the Atonists 'are all together on the sacredness of Western civilisation and its mission' (p. 136). By contrast, in seeking its text, both in writings and in the bodies of dancing African-Americans, 'Jes Grew' would recover the form of The Work, the Book of Thoth – 'the 1st anthology' and 'the original sound' (pp. 164, 178). Thus it would unite the dismembered and dispersed limbs of Set's mutilated brother Osiris, the god of nature and procreation and 'known as "the man who did dances that caught-on"' (p. 162). In the novel's story, Van Vampton and the Knights Templar are foiled but the text is again lost. Nevertheless, PaPa LaBas is hopeful. At the end of the novel when, now a hundred years old, he gives his annual lecture on the Harlem Renaissance in the present time of the early 1970s, he detects a change of mood. The students are interested. After fifty years, they 'knew what he was taking about . . . the 20s were back again. Better' (p. 218), he concludes, as his locomobile turns toward the gleaming skyscrapers on the neoned Manhattan skyline.

Gates follows the novel's punning intertextuality with marvellous care and sympathy (the novel, he says, inspired his own volume of essays, which in its own way therefore joins the criss-crossing weave of rewritten traditions). His conclusion is that this play of and on tradition results in a novel that 'figures and glorifies indeterminacy'.[84]

This follows from the novel's critique of dualism (of the primitive and civilised for example), and has, I think, both a rhetorical and ideological aspect which are worth bringing out. In its doubling narrative *Mumbo Jumbo* plays the narrative of detection in PaPa LaBas' search for 'Jes Grew' off against a variety of sub-narratives and discourses which range widely over time and form, from myth to factual record. To this end Reed employs the essay, newscuttings, signs, notices, posters, telegrams, handwritten letters, poems, songs, drawings, photographs, footnotes and a 'partial bibliography'. A linear narrative of expected closure exemplified by the detective genre is opened to the digressions, slow and fast time of different materials and idioms. The resulting composition of passages of exposition, slangy commentary, the asides, sideways glances, digressions, pips and squeaks of photographs, cartoons, footnotes, headlines, slogans and much else that improvises on its basic narrative line might fairly be described as the making of a bebop novel.[85] At the same time, the novel's critique of dualism is a critique of the conception of 'double consciousness' – the Negro's 'two-ness' which Du Bois saw as a source of strife to be resolved in a blended 'better and truer self'.[86]

There are two additional aspects to the novel, which are worth some further emphasis, however. The first is the novel's madcap chronology, jolts and surprises of structure and discourse which bring a high sense of fun to its principled deconstructive aesthetic. Here, in its compendium of forms as in its content, is something like a sustained spirit of carnival to counter the sobriety of the Atonist path, the unsmiling figure of Jesus, the Marxism which secularised his message, and social realism, the Atonist counterpart in art. Like 'Jes Grew' itself, *Mumbo Jumbo* seeks its form in humour and satire: 'Afro-satire', as Reed puts it, which helps to recover what the African race loses 'In North America, under Christianity' (pp. 96–7). Secondly, it is important to see that in overturning the dualisms of earlier thinking and in its critique of essentialist notions of tradition and identity, the novel presents not simply a rhetoric of indeterminacy but a politics of hope and affirmation. Reed talks elsewhere of the promise, indeed the contemporary fact, of multicultural America – the everyday juxtaposition of Jewish, Chinese, Italian, Vietnamese, Spanish, a blurring of languages and cultural styles that produces 'a cultural bouillabaisse'.[87] 'I'm not going to abandon Western values', Reed says, as quoted earlier, 'I want to mix things up a little. Multiculturalism . . . is becoming the standard. This will be the trend of the twenty-first century'.[88] This dialogic, heteroglossic America Reed opposes, and his jazzy novel opposes, to the monocultural and potentially fascist thinking inscribed in the idea of 'the' Western tradition. Here then is a revised, newly signifying critique of the instrumental and oppressive rationalism of modernity, an alternative that would expand upon the meanings of a world of cultural texts, making them newly modern in the criss-crossing cultures of the United States where such a destiny is possible, because 'The world is here.'[89]

BLACK AND WHITE NOTES: TONI MORRISON'S *JAZZ*

Why is Toni Morrison's novel called *Jazz*? It might seem obvious of course. The novel is set in Jazz Age Harlem and finds in jazz music, so different readers tell us, its 'mode and inspiration' and a language to express 'the free jazz cacophony of the city'.[90] Yet, for another reader, 'the novel bears only a superficial relationship to jazz music' and there is 'little actual evidence that Morrison seriously embraced black music as a fictional device or a source of inspiration'.[91] In fact, there are reasons for thinking that the title, that is to say, the novel's relations with jazz music and culture, is both self-evident and inappropriate or unconvincing. On the one hand jazz is played on the rooftops, in doorways, at parties, in parlours; it is listened to on record, sung along with, and danced to. Jazz seeps through the city and the lives of the characters, and is arguably a strong source, or analogue, for the novel's syncopating narrative, changing registers and virtuoso phrasing. But for all that, jazz is not present in the way that might be expected.

Morrison's novel has in one respect a documentary purpose. In telling us of Joe and Violet Trace and their move from rural South to New York in 1906, it is telling us a typical story of a migrant couple in the first two decades of the century. From makeshift wage labour in the black Tenderloin district they move uptown and so to Lenox Avenue in Harlem, changing jobs and identities as they go, as thousands did. We learn how in New York 'little shaky farms' became 'more and more houses', of high rents, of sub-letting, the resistance of 'light-skinned renters' to new black-skinned neighbours.[92] The novel tells us (twice) of the silent protest parade down Fifth Avenue in 1917, after a series of lynchings and riots, notably in East St Louis; it names key black newspapers of the period, *The Messenger, Crisis, Age*, and *Opportunity*; it tells us (twice) of Booker T. Washington's sharing a chicken sandwich with the President in 1901. And these events are intimately connected to the lives of the novel's characters. Yet *Jazz* makes no mention of Marcus Garvey, W.E.B. Du Bois, or the many luminaries of the Harlem Renaissance. It does not name any black actors or singers or jazz musicians. It does not name any show or revue of the period, not even the enormously successful all-black *Shuffle Along* of 1921 which is commonly thought to have first put the popular new black consciousness on stage. One ballroom, the *Roseland* is named once. Joe works eventually in a Speakeasy but no jazz band is named, aside from a mention of Dorcas's favourite but fictitious band 'Slim Bates and the Ebony Keys'. Joe and Violet live on Lenox Avenue, but as far as we know have never visited any of the hundred and twenty entertainment spots in the immediate ten-block area, nor any of the twenty-five or so clubs in 'jungle alley' along 133rd Street which was within easy walking distance. North on Lenox Avenue the famous Savoy Ballroom occupied an entire block, but again we wouldn't know this from *Jazz*.[93]

This *Jazz*, we have to conclude, does not mean *that* jazz, the jazz of the dance halls and shows, the clubs and juke joints and honky-tonks, of white owners and clientele, of the turkey trot, the monkey glide, the chicken scratch and other new low-down dirty dances. Nor does it mean the 'Jazz Age' of New Negro art and ideas, let alone flappers and bright young things. It is not enough then to say that the novel does or does not relate to jazz, when what it relates to is a particular cultural history, in which, as Morrison well knows, what is left out is as important as what is left in, what counts in fiction as much a matter of value as what counts as fact. We are asked then to see the jazz that is played and written here as a revalorisation, as strategically selected, or in a key word for the characters in the novel, 'chosen'. The more standard history, we come to realise, has not been chosen.

'[T]he choice word, the chosen silence', said Toni Morrison in her Nobel Prize address, 'surges toward knowledge, not its destruction.' Literature, in this account, is thought to be 'interrogative . . . critical . . . alternate' and at risk because of it.[94] What we want to know, therefore, of this novel's critical interrogation is what new alternate knowledge it produces, or in a word Toni Morrison might prefer, what 'wisdom'. The old, but blind wise woman in the tale she told in her Nobel Prize address thinks, 'Word-work is sublime . . . because it is generative; it makes meaning that secures our difference.'⁹⁵ What meaning, or music, then, does the word-title 'Jazz' generate? How, and who for? Whose difference?

Earlier statements by Toni Morrison might have prepared us for the uncommon sense of jazz and the culture of jazz the novel offers. Thus, in the essay 'Rootedness: The Ancestor as Foundation', on the loss especially of the benevolent, protective wisdom of an elder entailed in a movement from rural neighbourhood to the city, she writes:

> But when the peasant class, or lower class, or what have you confronts the middle class, the city, or the upper classes, they are thrown a little bit into disarray. For a long time the art form that was healing for Black people was music. That music is no longer *exclusively* ours; we don't have exclusive rights to it. Other people sing it and play it: it is the mode of contemporary music everywhere. So another form has to take its place, and it seems to me that the novel is needed by African-Americans now in a way that it was not needed before.⁹⁶

Again, in a related essay, 'City Limits, Village Values', which discusses the attitudes of white and black writers to urbanisation, she comments, 'Black music – jazz – may have misled us into thinking of black people as essentially urban types.'⁹⁷ The implication is that there are two black musics: a rural form (blues) and a city form (jazz); that black people have been dispossessed of the healing, story-telling power of the first and falsely associated because of the second with the city. Black migrants, such as those in *Jazz*, therefore, are thought to have severed a vital connection with the village neighbourhood, especially the wisdom of its elders. They do not belong 'essentially' in the city. And they do not have a music to express their condition. Hence the importance of the novel form, which offers to replace the old music, and might be expected, if it is a city novel, to unravel the false associations of the new. The novel *Jazz* begins to sound as if it can only be 'A Blues for Harlem'.

In the event *Jazz* undoes the deceptions of the city and jazz music through the figure of its unnamed but implicitly female narrator who comes to learn that she is as mistaken about them as she is about the lives she narrates. She is 'curious, inventive and well-informed' (p. 137): solicitous like Joe and Violet's neighbour Malvonne, solitary and abandoned like Dorcas's aunt, Alice Manfred, but actually like neither. Above all, however, she is at first an enthusiast for the newness of New York, the city of modernity.

> 'I'm crazy about this City . . . I'm strong. Alone, yes, but top-notch and indestructible – like the City in 1926 . . . . At last, at last

everything's ahead. The smart ones say so and people listening to them and reading what they write down agree. Here comes the new. Look out. There goes the sad stuff. The bad stuff. The things-nobody-could-help stuff. The way everybody was then and there. Forget that. History is over, you all, and everything's ahead at last.

(p. 7)

The music of this modernist consciousness is the new city jazz – likened, anachronistically, to the free-form cacophony of an Ornette Coleman by the reviewer quoted above – which in the novel introduces Dorcas's restive sexuality:

. . . doors to speakeasies stand ajar and in that cool dark place a clarinet coughs and clears its throat waiting for the woman to decide on the key . . . . The City is good at this: smelling good and looking raunchy; sending secret messages disguised as public signs: this way, open here, danger to let coloured only single men on sale woman wanted private room stop dog on premises absolutely no money down fresh chicken free fast delivery.

(p.64)

Towards the end of the novel, however, the narrator reflects:

I ought to get out of this place. Avoid the window; leave the hole I cut through the door to get in lives instead of having one of my own. It was loving the City that distracted me and gave me ideas. Made me think I could speak its loud voice and make that sound human. I missed the people altogether.

(p. 220)

Her error is that she has aestheticised the city, seen it from on high ('All you have to do is heed the design – the way its laid out for you': p. 9), followed the buildings' shapes and shades, and ignored the people.

Perhaps we hear in this a triple judgement, not only on a deluded futurist modernism but on the Harlem Renaissance as a high-flying, disconnected intellectual and cultural minority, and on the cold-hearted hedonism and style wars characterising one version of contemporary postmodernism. The verdict on Dorcas certainly brings a familiar critique of the postmodern to mind. The 'life-below-the-sash' that so troubles her aunt and her cronies, Dorcas thinks of 'as all the life there was' (p. 60). She walks free of the restraints and repressions that her Aunt, in spite of herself, passes on to her. Whereas the uptight Alice struggles to know whether to drop or hold on to the rope braiding sex and sin, jazz and angry protest, Dorcas is 'loose' (we see her unbraiding her hair, shifting her belt buckle), and cannot or will not connect the loud showiness of her own young jazz age with the decorous silent protest of the parade of 1917. She breaks off her serious secret affair with the worthy but besotted Joe because she wants instead to have a 'look' and a 'catch', like the cool youth Acton, to make her the envy of her friends. She and Acton are dancing at a rent party, a place for romance, of 'dazzle and mischief' (p. 188), where 'everything is now' (p. 191) in 'the market where gesture is all' (p. 192), when Joe tracks and shoots her. She 'let herself die', her friend Felice reports; she was hard, 'she used people'. She was 'ugly inside', Violet decides, and Felice agrees (pp. 204, 205–6, 212). Dorcas had shown Joe 'Eden', the Garden in the City; he had 'chosen' her and tasted the apple of herself (pp. 133–5), but she is the victim finally of the women's judgement: condemned as a temptress along with the 'Devil's music' of piano and singer at the party which fades as she expires.

The 'people' (principally Joe and Violet) the narrator has 'missed . . . altogether' have meanwhile missed themselves. The city when they arrive is 'better than perfect', a place of wonder in a world where after Booker T's lunch with the President, 'anything can happen' (p. 107). They find 'their strong riskier selves', but the price of being all new, of broaching one New Negro identity too many, is forgetting the past, the 'little pebbly creeks and apple trees' of the country (p. 34), of forgetting 'what loving other people was like' and starting instead to love 'the way a person is in the City' (p. 33). As the dream palls, and after three miscarriages, Violet loses her footing and her tongue slips: she sits in the street, steals a baby, sleeps with a doll and stops talking. Joe turns to Dorcas to share his 'inside nothing' and motherless childhood (p. 36), only to shoot her when she turns away. He falls into a weeping silence, while Violet, in a burst of urban schizophrenia borne of betrayal and lost connection becomes 'Violent' and takes a knife to Dorcas's body at her funeral, not knowing whether she was 'the woman who took the man, or the daughter who fled the womb . . . bitch or dumpling' (p. 109).

Evidently, both Joe and Violet must reconnect with their pasts. Violet comes, outrageously, to visit Alice, and in the company of her old-time morality and expert working ways finds herself whole again as Alice's scorched ironing sparks the memory of her own laughing, protective, story-telling grandmother, True Belle. Joe must narrate his own past (as if in part to Dorcas) to rediscover in his youth with his guardian Hunters Hunter, his gift of trailing: the intuitive compulsion he had followed in tracking his mother 'Wild', and which he gives himself up to once more in tracking Dorcas across the city. 'In this world the best thing, the only thing, is to find the trail and stick to it', he says (p. 130): a maxim that connects country with city (which looks in this episode 'as uninhabited as a small town', p. 180) and competes directly with the narrator's confidence in the geometric design of the city.

The narrator is mistaken, however, not only in her sense of the relation of people and place, but in misinterpreting their place in time and history. She thinks 'the past was an abused record with no choice but to repeat itself' (p. 220), that one of them would kill the other, that Felice, Joe and Violet are a repeat of Dorcas, Joe and Violet. But they defeat her with their originality. Felice looks like 'another true as life Dorcas' (p. 197), when Dorcas, Felice herself says, was 'nothing like me' (p. 209). She brings a judgement on Dorcas and the happiness to Joe and Violet that her name implies. When she visits them they hear music from another room and they dance. Joe moves his head to the rhythm and Violet 'snapped her fingers in time' (p. 215). They dance as they did to the rhythm of the train and the city when they first arrived. They need a victrola, says Felice; and a bird, they decide. And as they later try to inspire the bird to song they join the jazz musicians playing on the rooftops. They are finally in time once more with the click of the trains and the snapping fingers of the city: 'they are real. Sharply in focus and clicking' (p. 226). The sweet rooftop jazz and rhythmic clicking completes the 'music the world makes' Joe has heard in Virginia, and echoes Wild's scrap of song and snap of twigs (p. 177). The world is in time. To the narrator's admiration and envy they rediscover an understated public love and a private love beneath the quilt, 'way beyond and way, way down underneath tissue' (p. 229) more intimate and profound than love beneath the belt or buckle.

Joe and Violet's lives therefore express a final reconciliation and continuity between the country and city, but not in the end as a 'Blues for Harlem' since the blues story of the novel's plot ends happily. The lone guitar blues Joe identifies with (p. 119) gives way to the jazz sounds of clarinet and brass on the roofs of the city (p. 196). The narrator had thought the city determined lives like the grooves on a record, but Violet learns and passes on to Felice that the world is for you to 'make it up the way you want it' (p. 208). Thus a blues rootedness finds the answering freedom of jazz improvisation in the newly composed lives of the city couple.

The people's voices of *Jazz* syncopate throughout, alternating especially between the narrative bass and a series of first-person solos as the characters speak their own stories. The novel's conclusion, we might think, effectively brings these sounds to a harmonious rest. Yet its most remarkably 'improvised' passages on Golden Gray continue to hang in the air. The narrator here is above all 'inventive', since there is no first person to authenticate the tale. Over the course of twenty-five pages, at moments in a direct dialogue with the reader, she 'imagines' the story, and Golden Gray's own imaginings, through at least three retellings of his journey to confront his black father (Henry LesTroy, or more pointedly, Henry Lestory, who is also Hunters Hunter). Golden Gray journeys through the narration toward the knowledge that he himself is 'another kind' of negro (p. 149) who must choose what he is, white or black. His meeting with the wild, naked pregnant black girl is a symptomatic clash of bewildered identities on this symbolic road. The over-cultivated, foppish city gentleman dares to look with his grey eyes into her 'deer eyes', his whiteness confronting the inarticulate blackness of an abused child of primitive nature. The story is taken up through Henry LesTroy, who names the girl 'Wild', and Joe Trace who seeks her out thinking her to be the mother who left 'without a trace'.

No more is heard of Golden Gray. The narrator who has wanted 'to dream a nice dream for him, and another of him . . . to be the language that wishes him well' (p. 161) appears also at the novel's close to desire to be, or be with, Wild; to occupy her 'chamber of Gold . . . to be in a place already made for me, both snug and wide open' (p. 221). The narrator speaks of being 'touched by her' (as Joe wished to be) and at the novel's end of herself choosing and being chosen and caressed by another ('You are free to do it and I am free to let you because look, look. Look where your hands are. Now': p. 229). The loving dialogue she imagines and wishes to have aloud ('*talking to you and hearing you answer – that's the kick*') is a dialogue with an imagined companion, but also with a 'you' who is the reader.

Toni Morrison has spoken often of engaging the reader in a participating role:

> I have to provide the places and spaces so that the reader can participate . . . . To make the story oral, meandering, effortless, spoken – to have the reader *feel* the narrator without *identifying* that narrator . . . and to have the reader work *with* the author in the construction of the book – is what's important.[98]

Certainly we can feel this intention and its effect in *Jazz*. There are moments, however – paradoxically when this dialogue is most fully engaged – when the created spaces are read as gaps and mysteries or incompletions: moments which readers not only misconstrue but construct differently, finding something wanting, or wanting more.

Deborah A. McDowell, for example, has described the dissatisfaction she feels with the narrative presentation and death of Dorcas, 'the unpunished murder of a woman who dares to desire'. She wants, she says, to know more about Violet, about Joe and 'above all . . . more of his beloved and to mourn her loss, as I do his'.[99] A second reader feels Morrison has not sufficiently aided the national liberation of African people, while for a third she is more and more clearly an 'American' writer, transcending colour.[100] These differences confirm the features of a dialogic exchange. *Jazz* enters a cultural conversation on questions of gender, race, national identity and the writer's political role which is already in progress and in which readers will be already to some degree situated. In this jazzy ensemble readers will discover sympathies and differences, even dissatisfactions as they work both *with* and against the construction of Morrison's text. I want finally to add my own interested voice to this dialogue.

Morrison's investigation of the black presence in white writing in *Playing in the Dark* deconstructs the absolutes of all-black, all-American identity others have assumed. 'We are not in fact "other"', as she says in a complementary essay, 'we are choices.'[101] This is entirely consistent with the conception of *Jazz*. What, we might ask, however, at the end as at the beginning of this discussion, of the white presence, the 'Americanness' in the African-Americanness of jazz as music, culture and novel? The fuller social and sexual world of jazz in the Harlem of the 1920s, with its white musicians, patrons, voyeurs and enthusiasts, is omitted from the novel to a degree that, as Morrison says of the absence of black characters and culture in fiction, calls attention to itself, alerting us to its 'intentionality and purpose'.[102] Whiteness, as she says of blackness, is 'erased from a society seething with its presence'.[103] In so far as Dorcas represents the social–sexual world of live jazz (which is pointedly fictionalised in the novel) it emerges as superficial and self-destructive. Like her this jazz world is apparently expendable.

In the novel's past the 'white presence' lies with Vera Louise and her son Golden Gray. Though her departure for Baltimore with her illegitimate child was 'a renegade, almost suffragette thing to do' (p. 139), she proves to be without principle. Golden Gray, meanwhile, offers the spectacular proof that the result of white joining with black is not grey (Gray is Vera Louise's family name) but golden. His skin colour and curls are a source of delight for both his mother and True Belle – who laughs for eighteen years every day she sees him. Violet remembers that laughter can be serious laughter which sets the world 'right side up' (p. 113), but Golden Gray is regarded as more a freak than a serious carnivalesque disturbance. Certainly he is no wise ancestor.

Joe discovers signs of him in Wild's stone hovel which is all at once womb and kitchen and love-nest. He has to enter head first through its ante-chamber, and there he finds amidst signs of cooking and small ornaments, a green dress and a man's clothes. For Joe, who barely knows that the unseen Wild is his mother, these traces must remain a mystery. Violet, for her part, remembers Golden Gray from True Belle's stories from a time before the most hypothetical, most imagined and improvised episode of the novel which relates his story: 'He was a boy, but I thought of him as a girl sometimes, as a brother, sometimes as a boyfriend, he lived inside my mind . . . the two of us. Had to get rid of it' (p. 208). Golden Gray, her early love and the reason even that she became a hairdresser, proves an intolerable memory and is expelled, a foreign body like her own second Violent self.

Why is this hyphenated golden figure so difficult to include? Because he is neither one thing nor the other, and especially because he is not a black ancestor like True Belle or Henry LesTroy? This, for the most part, is what the novel communicates to us. Yet it also conveys the invention, joy and mystery in the idea of hybridity, passing in Golden Gray's narrative into a jazz improvisation which seeks to express the imagined, the unexpected and unrepresentable. In this complex guise Golden Gray haunts the novel: an eccentric product of African-Americanness (like a 'jolt of black wool and yellow hair', p. 167), who links Joe's and Violet's stories and ancestors, but remains unspoken between them.

Perhaps, however, this difficult hybrid presence can finally be seen another way. Joe and Violet, set 'midway between was and must be' (p. 226), are an expression of ethnic identity in process; a variation on a theme, marking newly composed relations between the city and the country, blues and jazz. Identity is a matter, that is to say, of historical and cultural change, but is felt also in this novel across the generations, in the handing over from old to young in the city. The 'must be' of this new composition in time must therefore belong to Felice, for whom 'Living in the City was the best thing in the world' (p. 207). She remembers how her grandmother cooked catfish yet 'still buys Okeh records'. Her movements are slow, but their 'tempo is next year's news' (p. 222). Felice is the future, this time with a past. In her, perhaps, there lies a new jazz rhythm and identity: one which runs both ways, between past and present, city and village, and even white and black. The novel's selective, revalorised history and music have worked to open out this possibility in the urban new modern. It is a further 'choice' surely, even if in *Jazz*'s present moment this is poignantly wanting.

NOTES

1. Jay McInerney, *Brightness Falls* (Harmondsworth: Penguin, 1992), p. 79.
2. Scott Fitzgerald, *The Great Gatsby* (1926; Harmondsworth: Penguin, 1990), p. 67.
3. Ibid.
4. Ibid., pp. 123–4.
5. James De Jongh, *Vicious Modernism. Black Harlem and the Literary Imagination* (Cambridge: Cambridge University Press, 1990), p. 6.
6. Ibid.
7. Alain Locke (ed.), *The New Negro. An Interpretation* (1925. Reprinted, with Introduction by Allan H. Spear, New York and London: Johnson Reprint Corporation, 1968), p. 7.
8. Ibid., p. 59.
9. Houston A. Baker, Jr,´*Modernism and the Harlem Renaissance* (Chicago and London: Chicago University Press, 1987), pp. 4, 6.
10. Ibid., p. 8.
11. Baker, *Afro-American Poetics. Revisions of Harlem and the Black Aesthetic* (Madison: University of Wisconsin Press, 1988), p. 5.
12. Ibid., p. 4.
13. Baker, *Modernism*, op. cit., xviii.
14. Baker, *Afro-American Poetics*, op. cit., p. 7.
15. In Ernesto Laclau, *New Reflections on the Revolution of Our Time* (London and New York: Verso, 1990), p. 233.
16. *Baker*, op. cit., p. 8.
17. Henry Louis Gates Jr, 'Authority (White) Power and the (Black) Critic; or, It's all Greek to me', in Ralph Cohen (ed.), *The Future of Literary Theory* (London and New York: Routledge, 1989), p. 346.
18. Ibid., p. 338.
19. Ibid., p. 345.
20. Gates, 'Introduction: Tell me, Sir, . . . What is "Black" Literature?' *PMLA*, 105 (January 1990): 21.
21. Gates, 'Goodbye Columbus? Notes on the Culture of Criticism', *American Literary History*, 4 (Winter 1991): 713. In Melville's novel it is thought that the mode of American settlement 'should forever extinguish the prejudice of national dislikes', since 'all nations may claim her for their own', *Redburn* (Harmondsworth: Penguin, 1986), p. 238.
22. Gates, Ibid.

23. Ibid., p. 724.
24. Ibid.
25. Ibid., p. 712.
26. De Jongh, *Vicious Modernism*, op. cit., p. 210.
27. Ibid., p. 216.
28. Ibid., p. 217.
29. Nathan I. Huggins, *Harlem Renaissance* (New York: Oxford University Press, 1971), p. 84.
30. Toni Morrison, *Playing In The Dark. Whiteness and the Literary Imagination* (Cambridge: Harvard University Press, 1992), p. 6.
31. Gates, 'Goodbye Columbus', op. cit., p. 725.
32. W.E.B. Du Bois, *The Souls of Black Folk* (Chicago, A.C. McClurg & Co., 1903). Quoted Abraham Chapman (ed.), *Black Voices. An Anthology of Afro-American Literature* (New York and Scarborough, Ontario: Mentor, 1968), pp. 495–6.
33. Locke (ed.), op. cit., pp. 7, 11–12, 16.
34. Langston Hughes, 'The Negro Artist and the Racial Mountain', *Nation*, CXXII (23 June 1926): 692–4, in August Meir et al. (eds), *Black Protest Thought in the Twentieth Century* (Indianapolis: Bobbs Merrill, 1965, 1980), p. 115.
35. Ibid., p. 111.
36. Gold, quoted Amritjit Singh, *The Novels of the Harlem Renaissance* (Pennsylvania: Pennsylvania State University Press, 1976), p. 144. Schuyler's essay, 'The Negro-Art Hokum' appeared in *Nation* (16 June 1926): 662–3.
37. Gates, 'Goodbye Columbus?', op. cit., p. 714.
38. See Gates, 'The Blackness of Blackness; A Critique of the Sign and the Signifying Monkey' in Henry Louis Gates, Jr (ed.), *Black Literature and Literary Theory* (New York and London: Methuen, 1984), pp. 294–6 and *The Signifying Monkey. A Theory of Afro-American Literary Criticism* (New York and Oxford: Oxford University Press 1988), pp. 110–13.
39. V.N. Vološinov, *Marxism and the Philosophy of Language*, trans. Ladislav Matejka and I.R. Titunik (Cambridge: Harvard University Press, 1986), pp. 12, 94.
40. Ibid., p. 95.
41. Ibid., p. 23.
42. For Bakhtin's main literary studies see *Problems of Dostoevsky's Poetics* (Ann Arbor: Ardis, 1973); *Rabelais and His World* (Bloomington: Indiana University Press, 1984); and *The Dialogic Imagination* (Austin: University of Texas, 1981). For the kind of application mentioned, see Robert Stam, *Subversive Pleasures. Bakhtin, Cultural Criticism, and Film* (Baltimore and London: Johns Hopkins, 1989); and Dale Bauer, *Feminist Dialogues. A Theory of Failed Community* (Albany State: University of New York Press, 1988). Stam, interestingly for the present discussion, defines 'heteroglossia' as 'the interanimation of the diverse languages generated by sexual, racial, economic and generational difference' (p. 17). The concept of 'carnival', he suggests, confirms the broadest social application of Bakhtin's 'dialogics', for in 'carnival' 'everything resulting from socio-hierarchical inequality or any other form of inequality among people is suspended' (p. 21).

43. Theodore Adorno, 'Perennial Fashion-Jazz' in Stephen Bronner and Douglas Kellner (eds), *Critical Theory and Society. A Reader* (New York and London: Routledge, 1989), p. 204. Jameson believes Adorno was thinking of Paul Whiteman's commercialised light jazz, but Adorno's references to jazz's African roots and 'freejazz' make this hard to accept. See Jameson, *Late Marxism* (London: Verso, 1992), p. 141.

44. Ralph Ellison, *Shadow and Act* (London: Secker and Warburg, 1967), p. 234.

45. Toni Morrison interviewed by Salman Rushdie, *The Late Show*, BBC2, 13 October 1992. See also her interview with Paul Gilroy in his *Small Acts* (London: Serpents Tail, 1993), pp. 181–2. Jazz, says Morrison, represents an ideal of cool effortless improvisation, a kind of texture and repetition to which she aspires in writing. At the same time she associates it in more absolutist terms than her comments to Rushdie suggest with something intrinsic, irrevocably black. This description would not fit the music of a contemporary performer such as Cassandra Wilson, who draws on African music as well as Van Morrison and Jimmy Hendrix. Morrison's comments on these two occasions show how she is pulled between notions of essentialist and mobile black identity.

46. Morrison, *Playing*, op. cit., Preface, vi.

47. Ibid., pp. vii–viii.

48. Ibid., p. vii.

49. Arnold Shaw, *The Jazz Age. Popular Music in the 1920s* (New York: Oxford University Press, 1987), p. 42.

50. Ibid., pp. 44–6.

51. Scott Fitzgerald *The Crack-Up and Other Stories* (Harmondsworth: Penguin, 1987), pp. 12, 15.

52. Ibid., p. 11.

53. Gilbert Osofsky, *Harlem: The Making of a Ghetto. Negro New York, 1890–1930* (New York and Evanston: Harper & Row, 1968), p. 185.

54. Max Harrison in Paul Oliver, Max Harrison, William Bolcom (eds), *The New Grove. Gospel, Blues and Jazz* (London: Macmillan, 1986), pp. 230, 231.

55. Ibid., p. 234.

56. Peter Wollen, *Raiding the IceBox* (London: Verso, 1993), p. 110.

57. In Meier et al. (eds), op. cit., p. 114.

58. Ibid., p. 115.

59. Nathan Huggins confirms how black intellectuals' attachment to the values of high art meant that, with the exception of Langston Hughes, 'none of them took jazz – the new music – seriously . . . . They tended to view it as a folk art – like the spirituals and the dance – the unrefined source for the new art.' *Harlem Renaissance*, op. cit., p. 9. Locke, interestingly, wrote on spirituals not jazz in *The New Negro*. See also the discussion of the Renaissance intellectuals' attitudes towards jazz in Kathy J. Ogren, *The Jazz Revolution: Twenties America and the Meaning of Jazz* (Oxford: Oxford University Press, 1989), pp. 116–25. Ogren sees Locke and Rogers as 'defenders of jazz', p. 123.

60. Rogers in Locke (ed.), op. cit., pp. 216–17.

61. Ibid., p. 221.

62. Ibid., p. 222.
63. Ibid., p. 224.
64. Van Vetchen in a response to Du Bois' questionnaire in *The Crisis* in February, 1926, entitled 'The Negro in Art – How shall he be portrayed?', quoted in Amritjit Singh, op. cit., p. 30.
65. Du Bois, *The Crisis*, 32 (December, 1926): 81; quoted in Singh, op. cit., p. 24. For Hughes response, see Singh, ibid., and Langston Hughes, *The Big Sea. An Autobiography* (London: Pluto, 1986), pp. 270–71.
66. Osofsky, op. cit., p. 186; Ogren, op. cit., pp. 57, 127.
67. Claude McKay, *Home to Harlem* (1928, New York: Harper and Bros; reissued Chatham, New Jersey: the Chatham Bookseller, 1975), pp. 57, 196–7.
68. See Singh, op. cit., pp. 44–5, and pp. 42–55 for further discussion of the response to McKay's fiction in the 1920s.
69. Claude McKay, *Banjo. A Story without a Plot* (New York: Harper and Bros, 1929; reissued New York: Hope Mckay Virtue, 1957), p. 146.
70. Ibid., p. 324.
71. McKay, *Harlem: Negro Metropolis* (New York: Dutton, 1940), p. 9.
72. McKay, *Banana Bottom* (New York: Harper and Bros, 1933; Pluto Press: London, 1986), p. 169.
73. *Home to Harlem*, op. cit., p. 298.
74. Berndt Ostendorf, 'The Musical World of Doctorow's *Ragtime*', *American Quarterly*, Vol. 43: 4 (December 1991): 590–2.
75. E.L. Doctorow, *Ragtime* (1974, London: Macmillan, 1976), p. 145.
76. Ibid., p. 29.
77. Ostendorf, op. cit., p. 580.
78. Douglas Tallack, *Twentieth-Century America. The Intellectual and Cultural Context* (London and New York; Longman, 1991), pp. 278–9.
79. Cornell West, *Prophesy Deliverance!* (Philadelphia, 1982), quoted Tallack, ibid., p. 278.
80. Henry Louis Gates, *The Signifying Monkey*, op. cit., p. 220.
81. Reed confirms that he works out of both African and American traditions: 'I'm writing out of a tradition of not only Native American and African American folklore but also out of Mark Twain, especially *Huckleberry Finn*, where you have the trickster and the sense of absurd in life. You find that in African folklore. So I'm writing out of that classical American tradition', in Kevin Bezner, 'An Interview with Ishmael Reed, *Mississippi Review*, 20: 1 and 2 (December 1991): 110.
82. Ishmael Reed *Mumbo Jumbo* (1972; New York: Atheneum, 1988), p. 11. Further page references are given in the text.
83. Gates, op. cit., p. 223.
84. Ibid., p. 27.
85. Gates's view is that 'Reed's mode of writing is perhaps the bebop mode of jazz as exemplified in that great reedist, Charlie Parker', ibid., p. 233. Reed acknowledges this analogy, but tends to suggest more how his work draws upon the popular traditions of vaudeville, cartoon, stage and film. See 'Interview With Ishmael Reed', *Over Here*, 9: 2 (Winter, 1989): 76.
86. W.E.B. Du Bois, *The Souls of Black Folks*, op. cit., quoted Gates, ibid., p. 238.

87. Reed, 'America, The Multinational Society' in *Writin' is Fightin'*. *Thirty-Seven Years of Boxing on Paper* (New York: Athenium, 1990), p. 53.
88. Bezner, op. cit., p. 115.
89. Reed, op. cit., p. 56.
90. Deborah H. McDowell, 'Harlem Nocturne', *The Women's Review of Books*. IX, 9 (June 1992): 4; Alan Rice, The Lady Writes the Blues, *THES* (15 October 1993): 19.
91. Steven Moore, 'Nobel Backlash', *Guardian* (20 October 1993): 5.
92. Toni Morrison, *Jazz* (New York: Alfred A. Knopf, 1992), p. 127. Further page references are given in the text.
93. On Harlem clubs, see Ogren, op. cit., p. 62; and Shaw, op. cit., pp. 59–60.
94. Morrison, 'The Looting of Language', *Guardian*, (9 December 1993): p. 9.
95. Ibid.
96. Morrison, 'Rootedness: The Ancestor as Foundation', *Literature in the Modern World*, ed. Dennis Walder (Oxford: Oxford and Open University Press, 1990), p. 328.
97. Morrison, 'City Limits, Village Values: Concepts of the Neighbourhood in Black Fiction', *Literature and The Urban Experience*, ed. Michael C. Jaye and Ann Chalmers Watts (New Brunswick: Rutgers University Press, 1981), p. 39.
98. Morrison, 'Rootedness', op. cit., p. 328.
99. McDowell, op. cit., pp. 4, 5.
100. See Moore, op. cit., p. 4; and James Wood, 'A Terrible Privacy' *Guardian* 18–19 April 1992: 6.
101. Morrison, 'Unspeakable Things Unspoken. The Afro-American Presence in American Literature', *Michigan Quarterly Review* 28 (Winter 1989): 9.
102. Ibid., p. 11.
103. Ibid., p. 13.

Conclusion: Alphabet City

These phenomena should not lead us, however, into denouncing
the intentions of the surviving Enlightenment tradition as intentions
rooted in 'terroristic reason'.

(Jürgen Habermas)

The nineteenth and twentieth centuries have given us as much
terror as we can take.

(J. F. Lyotard)

'A' IS FOR ANARCHISM

In an article in the late 1960s, Irving Howe suggested how much
of American writing belonged to an anarchist and radical utopian
tradition.[1] In Melville, Thoreau, Twain and Fenimore Cooper this
'social vision' expressed a yearning, he says, for some lost 'stateless
fraternity'; a pastoral alternative of equality and brotherhood to the
inhibiting checks and balances of the Constitution, the restraints
of society and the rule of law (p. 108). Often, Howe adds, this
'Edenic nostalgia' for a 'utopian enclave' has been expressed in a
spatial or temporal displacement, removed from the constraints of
social and political authority in the here and now (pp. 105, 108). The
counter-world of Thoreau's Walden, the forests of Cooper's tales,
the Pequod and Pacific Ocean of Melville's *Moby Dick*, the idyllic
episode aboard the raft in Twain's *Huck Finn* are major examples,
Howe argues, of this attempt to restore the lost American idea.

Howe suggests how the 'stateless fraternity' these works imagine

214

is sited in an ideal place that is 'precarious, transient, unstained' (p. 109); a description which echoes Baudelaire's definition of the dual character of the modern ('the fugitive, the contingent . . . the eternal and the immutable'), while underlining how this literature has served the myth of Adamic innocence before the fall into urban modernity. However strong and questioning this impulse has been, therefore, it is confined, in Howe's reckoning, to a tradition whose imaginative sources and bias are pre-industrial and anti-urban. Significantly too, it is unconnected, says Howe in this essay, with the political tradition of anarchism: 'a movement', in his words, 'with an established ideology and a spectrum of emphases ranging from populism to terrorism [which] has meant very little in the United States' (p. 107).

A number of things might make us think differently about anarchism as a presence in American political culture and writing. Obvious examples to begin with from a later period would extend it, in Howe's own terms, into the twentieth century. One thinks, for example, of Kerouac's quest on the road, the displacements of science-fiction, the allegorical, fabular tales of John Barth, or Robert Coover's and Thomas Pynchon's fictions of a parallel America. Ihab Hassan, indeed, goes so far as to generalise postmodernist fiction's 'Antinomian' attack upon the authority of 'reason and history, science and society' as a united expression of 'Anarchy'.[2] Some of these later examples are also at points explicitly rather than imaginatively or intuitively anarchist in their inspiration. In Pynchon's *The Crying of Lot 49*, for example, the alternative postal system signalled by the acronym W.A.S.T.E. is based, in at least one explanation, upon a clandestine anarchist organisation.[3] Feminist science-fiction, cyberpunk and proto-cyberpunk work has also been frequently influenced by anarchist or countercultural philosophies. Ursula Le Guin's science-fiction novel, *The Dispossessed* (1975), for example, sets the anarchist utopia on the moon Anarres against the capitalist system of Terra, and Joanna Russ's *The Female Man* (1975) presents the planet Whileaway as a utopia beyond the rule of law and men. In the 1980s Bruce Sterling's *Mirrorshades* (1986) introduced cyberpunk as 'An unholy alliance of the . . . underground world of pop culture, visionary fluidity, and street level anarchy',[4] and in Marge Piercy's *Body of Glass* (1992), which draws these feminist and cyberpunk trends together, the political organisation of the town Tikva, which has to defend itself against the multinational corporation Yakamura-Stichen is run as a jolly, rough and tumble affair whose foundation is 'libertarian socialism with a strong admixture of anarcho-feminism, recontructionist Judaism . . . and greeners'.[5]

In addition, and more significantly for present purposes, many of the urban-based figures or movements examined in previous chapters show a sometimes loose, sometimes committed affiliation with the main forms of philosophical or political anarchism. Examples would include Randolph Bourne, The Wobblies, Emma Goldman, John Dos Passos, William Burroughs, E. L. Doctorow, as well as Sacco and Vanzetti, and the characters Sachs in Auster's *Leviathan* and Pilar in Cristina Garcia's *Dreaming in Cuban*. Amongst Howe's fellow New York intellectuals, Paul Goodman was an unwavering and influential libertarian anarchist and Dwight MacDonald came to adopt an anarcho-pacificist position in the postwar period.

If it is a mistake to think of these individual examples as comprising anything so solid as a tradition, there are nevertheless strong links between them. Often too the political affiliations of more recent examples are routed back to a common base in currents of thinking in the 1960s. Here indeed America witnessed both types of anarchism Howe identifies – on the one hand, in the activities of the militant cadres of the Students for a Democratic Society (SDS), including a terroristic offshoot such as the Weathermen, and, on the other, in the mass-based, amorphous and sometimes pastoralist protests of the counter-culture.[6] The New Left was a sign of a shift to a new political–cultural agenda in the postwar, postmodern period, and it is clear that Howe was strongly opposed politically and personally to its attitudes and activities. His writings express less an eccentric, individual position, however, than the embattled beliefs of a postwar literary and political formation, specifically that of a New York-based Jewish intelligentsia committed to the 'complexity' and 'ambiguity' of writers in the modernist canon, the achievements of bourgeois liberalism and the cause of liberal or democratic socialism in the United States. This project Howe sees a new generation as rashly abandoning. In 'New Styles in "Leftism"', for example, written in 1965 (two years before the article on anarchism in American literature), he attacks the dogmatic style of a minority committed to 'kamikaze radicalism . . . white Malcolmism . . . black Maoism'.[7] This 'fringe' element, it turns out, comprehends a swathe of 'leftist' types': old Stalinists, Marxist-Leninists, Maoists associated with *Monthly Review*, Malcolm X, the 'guerilla tactics' of Leroi Jones, dropouts, black and white desperadoes, supporters of Castro, followers of Frantz Fanon, who looked for political change to students, the poor, the peasantry, blacks or the Third World rather than to American workers.

What these diverse movements and styles share in Howe's account is a spirit of rejection: whether of Communism, bourgeois revolution, white society, or the Old Left. He does not in this essay associate these tendencies with anarchism – in fact he has difficulty naming them, which is itself symptomatic – but he does do so in a further contemporary essay on 'The New York Intellectuals'.[8] Here he talks of the 'innocence' of those who would seek to reject the past and, most revealing, of their embracing precisely the populist and terroristic tactics he has said counted for little in American political life. Thus 'in reality', he writes of the New Left, 'a deeper divergence of outlook has begun to show itself. The new intellectual style, insofar as it approximates a politics, mixes sentiments of anarchism with apologies for authoritarianism; bubbling hopes for "participatory democracy" with manipulative elitism: unqualified populist majoritarianism with the reign of the cadres'.[9] What is this but the 'spectrum of emphases . . . from populism to terrorism' Howe had attributed to anarchism? The political reality of the 1960s evidently contradicted his belief that this 'meant very little in the United States', and he found himself battling with its diverse styles and strategies as if confronting a many-headed, virtually unnameable Other.

Many commentators and writers since the 1960s – including notably Pynchon, Doctorow and Marge Piercy, of those mentioned above – have of course viewed this decade in more positive ways. In one example, Murray Boorchin has in particular applauded the anarchist side of the 1960s as having initiated later progressive tendencies in feminism, anti-militarism, eco-politics and munici-palism.[10] A further figure who has consistently drawn upon the inspiration of the 1960s, and to whom I refer later in this discussion, is Noam Chomsky. Douglas Tallack describes Chomsky's work as 'the most important legacy of New Left thought' and interestingly sees an affinity between his interventions and Randolph Bourne's earlier views on the role of the radical intellectual.[11] Chomsky has emerged as the most prominent critic of American foreign policy from the years of the Vietnam War to US involvement in Central America and the Middle East. Significantly, too, what explicit political allegiance he has expressed has been with anarchism or libertarian socialism. In the essay 'Notes on Anarchism', published in the early 1970s, he speaks of these positions as equivalent, or more precisely, of anarchism 'as the libertarian wing of socialism'.[12] In this mode, he says, anarchism does not imply a specific theory of society or 'doctrine of social change fixed for the present and future' but a vigilant concern to dismantle outmoded and oppressive forms of authority as 'appropriate to the tasks of the moment' (p. 152). A 'truely democratic revolution' to ensure 'liberty, diversity, and free association' (pp. 155, 157), will be opposed therefore both to capitalism and to forms of centralised state control. Instead, and here Chomsky has drawn consistently on the model of mass protest in the 1960s, it will insist on direct popular or workers' appropriation of capital and the means of production, in councils or communes.

In the tradition Chomsky describes, anarchism is a non-authoritarian, provisional and collaborative political mode, sceptical of fixed aims and of 'grand narratives'. At the same time, it is, he says, the inheritor of Enlightenment principles: 'it is libertarian socialism that has preserved and extended the radical humanist message of the Enlightenment and the classical liberal ideals that were perverted into an ideology to sustain the emerging social order'.[13] Nothing suggests that Chomsky has departed from these views, though the historical and political context for them has of course altered. The later period of the 1980s and 1990s has been marked by wide debates within the traditions of American liberalism and the Left, prompted by the anti-Rationalist and anti-Enlightenment arguments of postmodernism and deconstruction, the rise of the New Right, the political crisis of Irangate, the Gulf War and other US foreign engagements, as well as the ramifications of the fall of state socialism from the late 1980s. The effect of these events has been what might be described – echoing earlier discussions – as an intensification of difference, producing a multiplication of 'left' political vocabularies, on behalf of, amongst others, post-Marxist, new liberal, neo-pragmatist, democratic Left, multiculturalist, green, queer, lesbian and post-feminist positions, as well as the ambiguities of 'political correctness'.[14]

The tone and direction of these debates has been governed at the very least by a self-consciousness towards the universalist claims of the modern project. In these circumstances the anarchist belief that Chomsky represents in an anti-statist, non- or post-Marxist libertarian democracy has appeared as a newly viable answer to the contemporary search for an anti-foundationalist ethics, critical of but continuous with Enlightenment principles. As a result, trends in the 'Lyrical Left' of the 1910s and the New Left, and individual figures such as Bourne and Chomsky, can appear, as in Tallack's assessment, in a new alignment, skirting the orthodoxies of both Left and Right in the 1930s and immediate postwar years.

This is one side of the legacy of the 1960s. The contrasting and widespread sense that the 1960s failed in its political and cultural initiatives, that its 'new sensibility' was a recipe for cultural indulgence or narrow dogma has nonetheless persisted. In Irving Howe's judgement, the New Left's uncompromising rejection of the past and of a reformist programme amounted to a betrayal of liberalism, and so, it sometimes seems, to a kind of anti-Americanism. From this perspective 'anarchism' and the synonymous 'leftism', with its spectrum of emphases, was the name for a perverse and destructive turn in American Left politics.

Howe and Chomsky represent different constructions of the New Left and of the meanings of anarchism in American political life. In the recent period the expressions of countercultural protest and terrorism associated with this term have acquired new social and political references: 'anarchist' being used to refer, for example, as we shall see, to the lifestyle and militancy of the new inner-city poor, and 'terrorist' in a more familiar attribution to America's enemies abroad. Despite the changes in political reality and rhetoric, however, this discourse evidently serves now as then as a way of describing the social and political 'other'. At one level, therefore, we might conclude that the deep 'divergence of outlook' Howe reacted to at the earlier cultural and political watershed of the 1960s has continued into the 1980s and 1990s, if in newly inflected forms. This sense of separation and of unbridgeable extremes, of a dominant consensus and American way for the Left as for the Right, and thus of unrecognisable, even unnameable forces and tendencies outside of it remains, I suggest, a leading feature in the continuing irresolution of the 'postmodern' period, and, indeed, a main challenge to any movement beyond it.

MEET ME IN TOMPKINS SQUARE: JAY McINERNEY'S *BRIGHTNESS FALLS* AND DON DeLILLO'S *MAO II*

I want in what follows to discuss examples of New York art and literature of the late 1980s and early 1990s which refer to, or draw some subject matter or inspiration from 'the spectrum of emphases' Howe suggests the term 'anarchism' conveys. Whether in a loosely stereotyping or more developed sense, anarchism in these examples is associated with the new poor of New York's Lower East Side, and specifically the squatter groups of the East Village. Often this theme is explored in relation to events in Tompkins Square which I also trace below. One work, Don DeLillo's novel, *Mao II*, engages both with the spectacle of the homeless in Tompkins Square and the question of terrorism. I treat this in conjunction with other texts to suggest how this vocabulary has been both articulated, and disarticulated, in recent years.

Both 'anarchism' and 'terrorism' designate uncompromising and militant opposition. From one perspective they name the external threat of extreme sectarian violence against the state or the internal threat of mass protest and misrule. From another they project a utopian enclave or revolutionary alternative achieved through violent or non-violent means. In the broadest terms they therefore trigger a concern for national security and law and order. More particularly, as here, in their association with an urban area and population they draw our attention to the question of the stability or otherwise of the contemporary public sphere. This, and the writer's relation to it, is my principal concern, though, as elsewhere, this is a way of asking about the transition from modernism to postmodernism, and about what lies beyond this contemporary transitional moment. 'Whatever the explicit political content of the great high modernisms', says Fredric Jameson, they were always in some way 'dangerous and explosive, subversive within the established order'.[15] Jameson's language suggests that modernism posed an almost classical anarchistic threat to the status quo. To ask how a later literature relates to this political form, to the contemporary social problem of homelessness, to the metropolitan public sphere and national identity is to ask what oppositional role it can now play.

It is commonplace to think of the postmodern city as decentred, and to mean by this something like the physical rhizome of Los Angeles or Tokyo, or the amoebic 'sprawl' of cities and suburbs one into the other that has occurred everywhere. Older cities have presented a different experience of decentring, however; concentrating this within more or less settled limits, to create, as in New York, a palimpsest of densely packed change and differentiation upon the city's graph-paper page. As any tourist guide will tell you, you can view the range of postwar architecture along one short section of 53rd Street. (On 53rd and Park Avenue, The Lever Building, which was the first glass-box skyscraper in Manhattan stands at the opposite corner of the Raquet and Tennis Club, which in its turn faces the Mies Van de Rohe/Philip Johnson Seagram Building. City Corp and Philip Johnson's late eighties Lipstick Building are a block away.)

Elsewhere, where there was once Little Italy, there is an expanding China Town, the population of which includes a rising percentage of Asian and Filipino immigrants. The immigrant identity of other areas of the city and the Boroughs is also changing. The Lower East Side is less Jewish than Puerto Rican, the Corona district of Queens, once Italian, is now Hispanic – a description that includes Puerto Ricans and those from the Dominican Republic, but also more recent immigrants from Peru, Columbia and Ecuador. Areas of the city become unsafe – for women, for white males, for those who don't belong – in the space, as we say, of the same day.

Times coexist; places merge and separate. Still we, or novelists and characters in fiction, seek a stabilising centre. Thus, with all the romance of a remembered passage from Scott Fitzgerald, Russell Calloway in Jay McInerney's *Brightness Falls* believes that in New York he will penetrate the veils of the world to come to a ballroom of 'irresistible music' in the sky, or the source of 'mad energy' at the city's centre.[16] With more sophistication, Victor Propp, the non-producing, very late modernist sees the city as a Derridean text, 'words collapsing underfoot . . . surfaces giving way suddenly' before him (p. 71); while, in another conception in the same novel, Bernard Melman and the new Titans of capital imagine themselves at the control panel of the city, gathered 'within half a mile of Park Avenue and 72nd Street' (p. 163). In the event, Propp's over-writing produces a black hole of suicidal gibberish and Melman falls after the Crash of 1987. The centre proves less a place, unless it is the air through which brightness falls, than a force, the wayward mechanisms of the market that, like Gorky's gold devil spinning at the city's hub, whip the characters through these dramatic turns of fortune. Some accordingly rise but most fall; some are 'haves' and most are 'have-nots'. The Calloways occupy a higher-middle rung in all this; the 'happening couple' who are the novel's narrative centre. While Russell wants to climb to have and do more, Corinne is concerned to help the 'have-nots' below. After the Crash they settle at a new level, a little below their starting position, admonished by the slight bump, but still with a good view. And they have a novel to read, by their dead friend Jeff Pierce, which is 'sort of about all of us' (p. 411).

There is another more horizontal way of thinking about the city, however, as there has been since the first sense of contrast between rising skyscrapers and the monumental style representing civic life. The central places in this view are not the private corporations, or the financial district or invisible market forces, but the civic buildings, the public utilities and public places, like the significantly named Grand Central Station and Central Park. But these landmarks centre the city less convincingly now than they once did. (Commuters move *en masse* through the station at set times on a limited radius; the population takes exercise and leisure in popular sections of the Park at the end of working weeks and at the free and safe ends of working days.) Also, the physical nature and conception of public places have altered. Since zoning laws have required architects and developers to 'buy air space' and to 'give back' to the city in return for taller buildings, a generation of newer public places has appeared in the shape of atriums, plazas, arcades and foyers, sunken entrance ways extending to new subway entrances, or pocket-size, stone-clad alleys called 'parks'. Meanwhile, other kinds of places; niches on the street, abandoned buildings, caves below bridges, and the older squares and parks have been occupied by the city's poor. The more these people are on public view, the more they have disturbed the idea of who the public is and what public places are for.

The occupation of Tompkins Square between Avenues A and B, in the so-called 'Alphabet City' area of the Lower East Side, during the 1980s and early 1990s, by hundreds of homeless people raised precisely this issue in the city.[17] The East Village has long been a radical, plebeian and latterly bohemian quarter of New York. Auden lived on St Marks Place, Ginsberg on 7th Street. Abbie Hoffman and others addressed anti-Vietnam protest rallies in Tompkins Square. The Weathermen blew up a house, killing three of their members on West 10th Street; Warhol introduced the Velvet Underground in the East Village; the Fugs, the Grateful Dead and Charlie Mingus played at the Tompkins Park bandshell; and countless other bands performed at the Fillmore East – almost as if a cable connecting underground politics with underground culture were set to detonate at key points across Manhattan's middle. In the 1980s this radical counter-cultural past, increased poverty, and an undisguised heroin trade vied with a process of gentrification which brought young middle-class professionals into the area as neighbours to squatters, activists and drug dealers. In 1983, in 'Operation Pressure Point', the police began a campaign to clean up the area. Around 300 homeless people nevertheless established themselves in 'Tent City' in the Park. In August 1988 an attempt by police to clear the Park resulted in the 'Battle of Tompkins Square'. On Memorial Day 1991 a concert in the name of 'Housing as a Human Right' became a ragged skirmish between police and the homeless, amongst them what the *New York Times* described as 'self-styled anarchists' and *The Village Voice* as 'green-haired anarchists', noting too that their symbolic presence was being 'used by the media to epitomise the growing lawlessness of New York City'.[18] A week later at 5 a.m. on 3rd June, following a weekend of negotiations between Mayor David Dinkins's office and homeless representatives, 350 police in riot gear moved in with bulldozers to clear the area. The Park was closed, and a renovation plan of $2.3 million put in force, resulting in railed-off areas, the removal of the bandshell which had become the centre of drug dealing, the introduction of two playgrounds and regulations on the Park's use. 'This park is a park' said Mayor Dinkins, explaining the action, 'not a place to live'.[19] The homeless moved to encampments they called 'Dinkinsville' on Avenues B, C and D, which were themselves cleared the following October. They were 'like an army' said one squatter, of the police and bulldozers, 'like the one that went to Saudi Arabia'.[20]

In a study of the history and recent events in the Square, Janet Abu-Lughod describes the new social, generational, and ethnic differences in the area as forming a new kind of the inner-city neighbourhood where diversity and friction are both high and co-ordination and unity fragile. The East Village has become in this account the quintessential expression of a decentred urban area, with all its potential for difference and dispersal, brought now, says Abu-Lughod, to a 'temporary hiatus'.[21] Amongst those battling against the police and the city and in internal power struggles for some shared or self-determining interest in the public realm of the Square, Abu-Lughod identifies white working-class residents, community housing activists, counter-cultural squatters and, to a lesser degree, African-American and Latino residents in the Loisada housing projects and the homeless of the Park themselves.[22] The 'self-styled anarchists' in this social *mélange* have been associated with various squatter groups and communes who had occupied, repaired and maintained houses while campaigning against eviction and on behalf of the homeless for the provision of affordable accommodation. But as Andrew Van Kleunen has shown, these groups were themselves an internally diverse composition of New-Agers, environmentalists, craftspersons, alienated professionals and drop-outs. The anarchist groups he describes as 'punk/cultural "anarchists"' and 'political anarchists', a term designating 'Communists, Yippies, general anti-authoritarians, radical populists, liberals, and others on the factionalized left'.[23]

The evictions from the Square gave these various groups some unity against the police and city officials. The novelist Sarah

Schulman, commenting as a local resident on the ubiquitous police presence in the neighbourhood after the mass eviction also drew the more general implication of particular interest here that 'The definition of who constitutes The Public is rapidly changing. Now homeless people – that is, people with no private space, people who must live in public space – are being told that their homelessness is their *private* problem. That they are no longer part of the "general population".' This she extends to the situation of others – women seeking abortion, nude dancers made to wear pasties, and AIDS sufferers – deprived of information, subject to petty controls and, in the words of *The New York Times*, as 'not a concern for the "general population"'.[24] In her novel *After Delores*, the homeless of Tompkins Square are thought to be unreal, the whole scene, in a familiar postmodern topos, to be like a TV fiction. In the later non-fictional statement, Schulman declares her continuing commitment to political activism, to a 'politics of repetition' which will keep such issues alive, 'knowing that no large social gains can be won in this period'.[25]

In Schulman's view, the poor are ejected from the public sphere. But we might see this the other way round, and suggest that in occupying the Square the homeless had inverted the idea of the public realm which Dinkins and the police subsequently, with some duplicity and embarrassment, sought to restore. Patrick Wright's account of the events of Tompkins Square and of the work of the designer and inventor Krzysztof Wodiczko suggests this way of viewing the contemporary instability of the public sphere and the artist's social and political role.[26] Wodiczko sees developments in cities such as New York as entirely undercutting the idea of the bourgeois public sphere as an open physical space for the free expression of opinion, since now this symbolic expression of bourgeois democracy is occupied by those who 'are utterly bereft'; 'aliens' expelled from the city's life to the nowhere of public space.[27]

Dinkins's method as a representative of this democracy was to reclaim this space by force. Wodiczko's is to use his art to reveal a problem and the need for a different solution. To this end he had produced a customised homeless vehicle based on the shopping trolley, and, following this, a so-called 'Poliscar' with sleeping and washing facilities, a TV monitor, a video link, and CB radio as parts of a 'Homeless Communication Network' intended both for communication and defence. The 'Poliscar' – which for Patrick Wright evokes Kafka, the Tatlin tower, and the first British tanks called 'cubist slugs' – had been photographed against the backdrop of the 'Dinkinsville' shanty towns, but was otherwise exhibited and not used. Its cost, Wright reports, would be $60,000. In practical terms, therefore, it was clearly an absurd proposal; yet another example it might seem of postmodern style, the artist doodling in a world of evasive play above any real social reference. Its real effect, however, had less to do with its practical potential than its impact as an idea or experiment, even an absurd experiment, or as Wodiczko puts it, 'the concretisation of a present problem'. As a conceptual device the 'Poliscar' brought advanced technology and the primitive conditions of the homeless together to reverse assumptions, exactly in the way a radical art work in a gallery or book-store might be asked to do. His 'Poliscar', that is to say, associated design, private space and property with the poor not with the rich. And though apparently a commodity, it was not for sale or mass production.

This new view of things reinforced Wodiczko's pointed designation of the homeless as people 'without apartments' but with different histories, cultures and outlooks. Categories of thought and received distinctions such as those between the private and public, art and commerce, the rich and poor, those with and those without, were turned around, with wit, but with an awareness too that this kind of provocation was no substitute for a long-term solution. Wodiczko was not 'offering a grand design for a better future', he said, but a 'transitional device', on the 'realistic assumption that it could take 30 years to get beyond all this misery'.[28]

Wodiczko's device goes off like a Dadaist squib while Schulman dedicates herself to unrelenting protest. As much as anything, these examples illustrate the frustrations and limits of art's political repertoire, prowling the borders, now outside, now inside the spectacle of a public realm in crisis or at a 'temporary hiatus'. Two other works help to bring out the extremes of hopelessness and of a deep commitment to radical change which play around Schulman's and Wodiczko's statements. Joel Rose's novel *Kill the Poor* is set in 'Alphabet City', where Rose lived and helped produce the magazine *Between C & D*. The novel has been praised by Graham Caveney and by Robert Siegel for investing all the personality which shapes the lives of the story's actors in the physical environment of the neighbourhood rather than in the characters themselves. The human actors, that is to say, are known by where they have lived in the city's narrative and geography. Thus, using cocaine and heroin becomes 'going uptown and downtown'; 'between C and D' means 'between Coke and Dope'. The effect of this conflation is that there is no distancing perspective from which to view the characters or events, or to name this condition. Instead there is a reverse process of interiorisation, an implosion into the circles of fiction where everyone is an actor or an extra. The sets of a film which Steven Spielberg is making in the neighbourhood are accordingly greeted as more real than the three-dimensional buildings of brick and stone they represent, just as these give substance to the characters' drifting, empty lives. Simulacra triumph over their dim referents. Rose's novel presents the postmodern condition as an all-embracing, inescapable system of fictions which Jameson and others, following Baudrillard, describe as the character of life under late capitalism. Yet no transformative social action can follow from this. The figure Jo-Jo Peltz, whose divided and dissolving identity the novel follows, feels he is contending daily with the hassles of Alphabet City, surviving, as Caveney puts it, in streets where there is 'the constant fear of mobocracy . . . the menace of anarchy waiting to happen'.[29] An apartment block is burned down and Jo-Jo is arrested. He is innocent, but this is no matter to the police, to himself or his cell-mate, since all are sunk in the fatalistic gloom that Caveney describes as 'desperate indifference'.[30]

The second work is *Penniless Politics*, a long poem by the British poet Douglas Oliver, living at the time of writing in St Mark's Place, off Tompkins Square.[31] In the poem, the figure of the poet Will and his Haitian partner, Emen, enlist Voodoo and the help of a local black woman activist, a Cuban–African boxer who donates his prize money, and an Asian shop-owner to form a new party called 'Spirit' which will radicalise the apathetic non-voters of Brooklyn, the Lower East Side and the Bronx. After various money-making scams, they slip police surveillance and at a televised assembly in Morrisiana in the Bronx announce their decision to secede as Section AI under a new Constitution. The poem speaks in the people's many voices, as does Emen, when possessed by the Loa she delivers the terms of a new Declaration of Independence and Constitution. Its series of amendments ensure that Section AI will be a participatory, non-militarist and ecologically sound democracy, a new libertarian enclave in which the white male poet, at a cross-roads of conscience and power, writes his own deconstruction into a subordinate, clerkly role; the scrivener to the people's party.

The imagined utopia of AI is consistent both with Irving Howe's anarchist literary tradition and with the principles and prospects of Chomsky's libertarian socialism. The new future will be multi-culturalist, feminist, anti-racist, critical of the abuse of Enlightenment principles but explicitly derived from this tradition. And if all this sounds too politically correct, we realise that it is in fact self-mockingly correct. The story ends briskly with the announcement that 'All has happened in a breath/and now it has ended, not a trace left behind . . . 'What', the poet Will asks, 'did you expect?'

> . . . You, hypocrite reader, etcetera?
> You want some opiate, a poetic abracadabra
> so your ordinary responsibility for our ordinary political failure
> can be charmed away? No, America, that jackass soiled with its
> ordure
> its continued braying of freedom, knows half its own people
> block their ears and don't vote . . .
>
> (*Penniless Politics*, p. 76)

The poet knows that not even one proposal of the new Constitution – to cut out private cars and save world oil – would have any chance of success, for in the real world of political blinkers and vested interests 'We wouldn't know Spirit, if Spirit on top, it fucked us up the ass' (p. 77).

The poem ends as an accusation, a satirical, utopian accusation perhaps, which recognises the distance of its own ideals from popular apathy and the need instead – which it can at best hope to activate – for ordinary political responsibility.

Rose's novel is a fiction of fictions which writes doom and passivity across the face of any social vision. *Penniless Politics* is an inspirational fancy which knows it is unreal. *Kill the Poor* has been praised for its realism, while *Penniless Politics* has been welcomed as a contemporary epic, a *Waste Land* or *Paradise Lost* for our times.[32] Together these works present the two faces of anarchism and the two sides of postmodernism: their brief episodes of desperate violence and principled libertarianism corresponding, on the one hand, to a self-conscious fatalism induced by a world of vacant fictionality, and, on the other, to a self-aware art of the crossroads, combining the traditional with a multivoiced popular in an inflated, self-deflating desire for change. Which is more effective art? I side with *Penniless Politics*'s utopian pluralism rather than *Kill the Poor*'s dystopian flatness,[33] but this is really only of importance in a public forum where such things can be discussed. At the time of writing this would be a difficult and at best partial debate, since only *Penniless Politics* is currently available in Great Britain in a recent reprinting. In circumstances such as these the difficult questions of art's role and function I have wanted to raise throughout this study become very simple. Out-of-print books are poor homeless things, whatever they say.

There are two implications to this. The first is that a criticism interested in a transformed public sphere cannot limit itself to the internal forms and philosophies of individual texts or to their supposed ideological effects, since an improved public realm must, first of all, be one in which these different voices are heard. At the same time we cannot view publishing as a simple channel of communication, a gatekeeper providing access to the public sphere. More manifestly now than ever, publishing is a player in the market place. Increasingly the 'public' knows books as simulated products with massive sales and serious money advances, or as prize-contenders or specials of some kind or another, in limited hard-back runs at cut-down, trial-run, read-and-return-it prices.

Kill the Poor expanded on a story in *Between C & D*. It was published as a Paladin paperback in 1990 and has suffered the fate of a first novel. Douglas Oliver's *Penniless Politics* first appeared as an interim publication of 200 copies set from the author's typescript in a card cover. Oliver read parts of the poem at the St Mark's Poetry Society and the Nuyorican Poets' Café on the Lower East Side. Its public life therefore was deliberately that of a poem in progress, composed in dialogue with a small, committed, local audience. Its appearance in a limited edition, joint publication in New York and as a Bloodaxe paperback in Great Britain three years later continues its life as a minority publication. But there is a point to this. For Oliver, we realise, has seceded from the dominant literary public sphere in the very nature and form of his work as much as in its internal argument. Like the new Party in the poem which is begun through a chain-letter, this grass-roots upwards-and-outwards system of communication is reminiscent of samizdat and underground publications from the 1960s, through punk to the present – and in another 'anarchist' echo, of the Trystero letter service in Pynchon's *Crying of Lot 49*. This is in a part a joke, but the joke is part of a debunking cultural style which understands the public sphere as composed of mainstream and alternative and oppositional networks, or to put it differently, which actively dissents in its very mode of production from homogenised notions of 'the' public. As Pynchon and others confirm, the ownership and control of ideas and information are crucial to advanced capitalist societies. Writers need to be published to be made public, but publishing is a commercial, ideologically interested sector in this now global public sphere: one which in the United States has consistently refused Noam Chomsky's political writings an outlet in any major newspaper, magazine or mainstream publishing house. Questions about the dissenting role and public responsibility of writers therefore run into questions about the publishing system and about late capitalist postmodern society at large. Is it always and entirely compromising? Is it open to transformation? Can it be tricked and evaded like a stupid giant by a small, local alternative?

Brightness Falls and *Mao II* are books with extensive print-runs by internationally known writers. Any questions of their influence upon ideas and attitudes are therefore questions about writing within the networks of an existing public sphere. Both novels directly treat the figure of the author and the surrounding world of publishing and publicity with a self-consciousness I take as confirming that the writer's role and responsibility comprises a pressing contemporary theme. In fact both novels deal with this through two writers or artists: Victor Propp and Jeff Pierce in *Brightness Falls*, and Bill Gray (the writer) and Brita Nilsson (the photographer) in *Mao II*. The figure of Propp, who renegotiates his contract ever upwards on the strength of one novel and a promised manuscript, makes *Brightness Falls* in this respect more openly satirical. Whatever the artistic pretensions of the house of Corbin and Dern who in the old days published Breton and Co., publishing in the 1980s is a high profit-making business, and the author an expensive image. But satire requires a standard of better judgement. Propp might cheat the system, but he too is a cheat, his manuscript an illegible text.

In a sense this final nothingness represents the truer logic of McInerney's social analysis, though it is not one he follows, or can follow, either internally or in the production of his own book. Jeff, the second author, is supplanted by the 'image' of a writer at a photo-shoot. In the novelist's metaphor of falling he subsequently drops furthest of all, out of the social circle of the Calloways and the world of photo-calls, public readings, publishers' dinners and deadlines through the poverty and drug culture of Tompkins Square into a detox centre and death through an AIDS-related illness. In the true logic of his disaffection there would be no product, no text, no writing. A posthumous novel is announced, however, one which ratifies and unites the Calloways, saves the idea of the author's identity and integrity, and transfers unstoppably to McInerney's own text.

Nothing is done to redeem the degraded world of publishing in the novel; nor is anything done to remedy the poverty of the homeless. Corrine is effectively Jeff's thematic partner in the novel's probing of society's lower levels. She works one day a week in a soup kitchen on the Bowery, and later gets caught up in the aftermath of a police attack on Tompkins Square on a night when anarchism is abroad and she imagines 'an orgy of rage and destruction' is about to consume the entire city.[34] She befriends Ace, a black man who lives in Tent City, here called 'Reagantown' or 'The New Jerusalem' after the title of a street mural, but backs away from him in her apartment on the night of the riot. Ace, we hear later, has died of AIDS. Corrine's cause is sentimental and individualised, and her life basically unaffected. Things happen to people rather than people influencing events, but then these things level out as pretty much the same. Great wealth and dire poverty remain; there is unreported police brutality and the threat of AIDS, but, in spite of everything, there can be novels of integrity, like Jeff's, and like McInerney's, which reflect the survivors back to themselves. What else does this imply but that nothing really needs to change?

Mao II, I believe, asks more testing questions of itself. DeLillo's novel was reviewed in the United States in precisely the week of the evictions from Tompkins Square, and it takes the situation of the homeless there into its view of contemporary America and America's future. Karen, who is the novel's witness to the life of Tompkins Square, is an unsuccessfully debriefed Moonie, spell-bound by the figure of the charismatic leader. The novel opens with the spectacle of mass weddings, including her own, in the Yankee Stadium, and so introduces its concern with the loss of the individual in the crowd, a theme confirmed in Karen's blank and fascinated viewing of the soundless TV spectacles of the Hillsborough disaster, the despairing crowds at Khomeni's funeral and the crushing of the student revolt in Beijing. She is recruited as secretarial help to Bill Gray by Scott, the novelist's self-appointed aide and protector, who has decided that Bill's reputation depends on perpetuating the myth of his authorship not on the fact of a new novel. Scott arranges a photo-shoot with Brita – who, after a career photographing urban suffering, has turned to writers – as an interim taster to the waiting public. Bill is in retreat from his writing and the world but is concerned about the writer's public role which in the novel's main premise he sees as usurped by terrorists and gunmen. A Maoist group in Beirut takes a French UN official and minor poet hostage, and Bill is drawn into the public world this entails, drifting away from Scott, America, and his publisher, first to London where a bomb explosion cancels a planned reading of the poet's verse, thence to Athens, and so towards Beirut in an attempt to close with the writer's contemporary rival. Bill is lost *en route*, while in New York Scott works ever harder at the traces of his image and Karen discovers Tompkins Square. People stand around saying the Square is 'just like Beirut, it looks like Beirut'.[35] And she tells them 'to prepare for the second coming' . . . for 'the total power of our true father' for 'total control' (p. 179).

At an earlier moment Scott gives Karen a poster of Warhol's *Mao II*, struck by its indifference, the way it is 'unwitting of history' (p. 21). Like her, he is drawn to the dream of absolute control, imagining a future in long shot of faceless 'crowd on top of crowd' (p. 70). Warhol and Mao stand as the icons of this transcendence in Western pop and Eastern communism and are brought together in the novel, fittingly enough, in the sphere of the Middle East where the culture of pastiche, anonymity and mass art signalled by Warhol's name finds a perverse echo in the cult of the unseen leader and mass obedience associated with Maoism. Like Western artists and authors, the historical Mao Zedong has become a recycled image, revisited in Warhol's mass produced *Mao II*, and in Abu Rashid, an Arab terrorist leader whom Brita goes to photograph in Beirut. 'All men one man', Rashid believes: himself an image repeating Mao and repeated into the future in his son and followers (p. 233). In the streets of Beirut, Brita sees towering red 'Coke II' signs that run together the iconography of American consumerism with echoes of the cultural revolution. Somehow, the suggestion is, the Lebanon and America, and Beirut and New York's Tompkins Square in particular, exist not as opposites but inside one another, their desires and fears intercut like TV programmes.

What also approaches the surface in this swim of artistic, political and urban forms is the image of a new 'Maoism' in the United States. The only salvation for America's own Beirut of Tompkins Square is embodied by Karen, the backsliding disciple of the Reverend Moon and prophet of his coming 'total power'. But if Moon is America's Mao II, who then was its Mao I? The novel's intercutting of East and West conveys an anxiety over a future represented by Karen's terroristic oneness and Scott's robotic devotion, but suggests too that this scenario, in the United States as in the Lebanon, is a repeat of an earlier political moment. Does this mean that the Reverend Moon, Karen and Scott are the disturbed inheritors of the New Left Maoism of the 1960s, so fearful to Irving Howe? Do the 1980s repeat the 1960s, the second time as enveloping pastiche, and is this a form once more of the deadlock and hiatus, the marking-time and back-tracking in the anamnestic mode of the postmodern, before a decisive move forward?

Mao II is of interest, I believe, because it both registers this mood and tone and signals some advance towards a 'new modern'. The anxieties it expresses relate to long-standing themes in the

231

postmodern condition. Essentially in the book's own terms this concern is that the loss of the artist's social authority, the deprivations of Tompkins Square, including the loss of a common language and sanity in the incoherent spluttering of its inhabitants and Karen's parrot-like Moonie talk – in a word the 'decentredness' of subject, language and city – will be answered by a new deadening centredness. Already this appears in the impersonal regimentation of new buildings with their watchful security men, in Scott's possessive, self-generating classificatory systems, and above all in the coercive power of ideological dogma. Where earlier fiction had re-imagined a lost America as an anarchistic utopia, *Mao II* reads off the signs in America's desolate present as a terroristic dystopia with little consolation. The code words 'Beirut' and 'Maoism' summon up this nightmare; like foreign agents which encroach upon and, all but in name, invade the United States in the broad light of day via television satellite.

As these references begin to tell us, these anxieties belong in particular to events of the 1980s, to the affair of the American hostages in Iran, the Beirut bombings of the early and middle 1980s, and, as DeLillo has said, to the implications of the *fatwa* issued upon Salman Rushdie.[36] The novel does more, first of all, therefore, than repeat earlier anxieties: it presents a changed world which has escalated and deepened them. For these signs of the increased internationalisation of the writer's field of influence have brought new and unexpected enemies and a real threat of extinction. DeLillo's book therefore underlines, even globalises, Howe's sense of the continuing alternative disasters of unrelieved chaos and mass uniformity, of anarchism and authoritarianism, but interprets this as the prelude to a profound psychic as well as political disorder. Any remaining integrity in this analysis, at its most articulate in Bill Gray, appears to lie still in the individual conscience of the writer and intellectual looped into society. As Bill puts it, the writer competes with those plots and fictions which drain the world of meaning as when, for example, a hostage is taken. The 'other fiction' of the novelist, he believes, pushes 'out toward the social order, trying to unfold into it', a writer 'creates a character as a way to reveal consciousness, increase the flow of meaning. This is how we reply to power and beat back our fear' (p. 200).

Yet it would be a mistake to think that *Mao II* appeals simply and vainly to a traditional liberalism in the face of these new dangers. The TV pictures of Tiananmen Square Karen watches show not student terrorism but state terrorism, a battle between crowds, rather than the individual and the system, which is for no less than the public sphere: 'whoever takes the great space and can hold it longest. The motley crowd against the crowd where everyone dresses alike' (p. 177). On the other side of the world and TV screen, the motley, many-voiced and homeless hundreds of Tompkins Square are vulnerable to 'the Master's total voice' (p. 194), as is the centreless, drifting Karen, but so far as we see they are not yet lost. Even Bill Gray is brought out of his isolation to defend his position and his idea of the social order in conversation with a Maoist sympathiser, and goes finally to his death seeking talks with his terrorist counterpart. Howe had reduced the forms of anarchism to a non-negotiable threat from the Other. The alternative is to look more directly in the face of terrorism, to investigate its meanings, to pursue a dialogue beyond the borders of liberal America, and this the characters of *Mao II* begin to do.

Noam Chomsky and Edward Said have done most in recent years to question the binary thinking by which America has maintained a subordinating and demonising view of the foreign Other necessary to its official ideology, economic wealth and military supremacy. Chomsky argues that America has conducted proxy terrorism in a number of countries for a number of years, notably in Vietnam, Laos, Cuba and in Nicaragua through the Contras. He writes of the US bombing of Libya as 'the worst single act of international terrorism in 1986';[37] an event that, as Said has pointed out, was orchestrated so as to be available for evening news schedules.[38] The facts and analysis which Said and Chomsky have presented of American foreign relations and the workings of American ideology reveal a more complex array of positions and motives than models of terrorism or massed uniformity and fanaticism, on the one hand, and liberal democracy and the lone individual artistic or intellectual conscience, on the other, will deliver. However, we do not need to consult such outright critics of American foreign policy to see that the meanings of terrorism change with our cultural and political perspective. In *Terrorism and Democracy* (1991) Admiral Stansfield Turner, former Director of Central Intelligence under President Jimmy Carter during the Iran hostage episode is concerned with how the United States – which represents the democracy of his title – can effectively defend itself against the menace of terrorism after failing to do so in the 1980s. Even this orthodox division of the world into us and them cannot suppress its own ideological motivation, however. At one point Turner reflects:

As Americans we feel we are defending the rights of the individual
to a safe, humane, and unmolested life. The Shiite fundamentalists
in Tehran and Lebanon feel they are awakening individuals to the
spiritual values of life . . . There are those who insist that what
we call terrorism is not that when it is carried out to liberate
people from cruel domination – the African National Congress's
struggles against apartheid; the Romanians' overthrow and killing of
Ceauşescu.[39]

Once we are inside an identity, its meanings change: 'the contras
were freedom-fighters', says Turner, 'because we shared their political
aims, but the Shiite fundamentalists were terrorists because we did
not.'[40]

Said calls for a cultural dialogue of equals to further break down
such fixed assumptions. We need ways, he says, of 'imagining other
non-European societies and peoples in a non-dominative way'.[41]
Mao II, as I have suggested, embarks on this difficult imagining
through the figure of Bill Gray. It goes furthest in this direction,
however, not through his eccentric mission, but through Brita. In
her one-sided dialogue with Abu Rashid, he argues that terror is
an enabling strategy which 'makes the new future possible' (p. 235).
She listens and decides his new Maoism is 'eloquent macho bullshit'
(p. 236), until finally she transgresses the rules of the meeting and
removes the hood over Rashid's son's head. In photographing his
face she photographs the face of the future, but can only see there
a staring hatred. Later she stays in East Beirut and learns more,
against her expectations. A tank passes underneath her balcony but
its appearance is the prelude to a wedding, not more fighting, and she
toasts the couple in four languages. In the distance she sees flashes,
not from gunfire but from a camera. The camera shoots like a gun,
but they are not the same. Perhaps therefore the artist can deliver
an interpretive, multifaceted record to counter the cyclopic hatred
of dogma. Perhaps. DeLillo's own text includes five news photos,
and to some degree therefore his own record openly combines the
discourses of fact and fiction, word and image. This again signals
a move 'out towards the social order' beyond the constraints of
a single 'total voice'. But the novel's discourses, like its dialogues
across cultures and beliefs, are in the end limited, or obstructed. Nor
is the experience of dialogue or wished for dialogue outside America
turned back upon the homogenised public sphere that awaits the
writer's contribution or the photographer's assignment. Bill's idea
of the writer's social role assumes a receptive and unquestioned
social order the writer seeks to 'unfold into', and the novel offers
no considered advance on this. Worse, it offers no other future than

Karen's Moonie, new Maoist scenario for the warped metropolitan realm of Tompkins Square.

When asked in 1969 to comment on the role of left students or intellectuals, Chomsky said they must think of themselves as responsible for the people of Vietnam, Guatemala or Harlem.[42] In this view the role of the dissenting intellectual and writer is to secure information, to reveal the unspoken, to uncover the repressed and so, with circumspection, to open not add to the bulk of an accepted language. One such task is surely to disperse the homogenising stereotypes of 'anarchist' and 'terrorist', to 'increase their meaning', to adapt DeLillo's phrase. But who twenty-five years on is the writer responsible to: what people and what public, when as the texts I have examined and the social life of the inner city show, these notions and identities are at once contested and shapeless?

Edward Said's answer is that a dialogue of equals between cultures will come from 'the negative and unofficial, or perhaps anti-official sphere, the politics of exile, immigration, the crossing of borders, heterogeneity, hybridity'. He conceives of an 'exilic wanderer going across forbidden territory with sympathetic adaptation rather than stubborn assertions of identity'.[43] This is to commit the dissenting writer to an intensification of modernist alienation, free in this later era of modernism's assumptions of order and hierarchy, but given to seemingly permanent opposition and dislocation. In *Getting Home Alive*, examined earlier, Aurora Morales calls similarly for a dialogue of East and West, of Jew and Arab beyond stereotypes, but knows that to realise this imagined 'look of the future' in a world of 'hatred and terror and factionalism' is 'the most difficult task'.[44] *Mao II* sets first Bill and then Brita along this path. That they do not cross all borders, that there is no alternative to Karen's 'terroristic' vision for Tompkins Square, shows the further difficulty of completing this journey and of a return home, in the movement so characteristic of modernism. In their different ways, *Brightness Falls* and *Penniless Politics*, of the other texts examined here, also show how resistant the conformities of the present remain. Yet still a multi-voiced, multi-discoursed New York narrative moves in and out of sight and hearing across this group of texts. *Mao II* projects a fearful new totalitarianism out of present chaos but also begins to articulate a diversity of forms and discourses. It is in the second that hope for a 'new modern' lies in a 'future beyond the present' to extend Raymond Williams's phrase. Some stories, *Penniless Politics, Mao II* and *Getting Home Alive* amongst them, show us that an alternative is imaginable in the midst of the many impediments to it. Their

New York Fictions

double view, neither close-up nor long-lens, neither individualistic nor massifying, competes with the fundamentalist simplicities of a 'total politics, total authority, total being' (p. 158), and reveals, at its most confident, how a 'new modern' will emerge, as it must, from the crowded and constraining motley of the old.

NOTES

1. Irving Howe, 'Anarchy and Authority in American Literature' (1967) in *Selected Writings 1950–1990* (New York and London: Harcourt Brace Jovanovich, 1990), pp. 103–18. Further page references are given in the text.
2. Ihab Hassan, 'POSTmodernISM', *New Literary History*, III, No. 1 (Autumn 1971): 27, 29.
3. Thomas Pynchon, *The Crying of Lot 49* (London: Picador, 1979). See pp. 82–3, 91, 119. For some discussion of Pynchon's 'mystical' anarchism, see Paul Maltby, *Dissident Postmodernists* (Philadelphia: University of Pennsylvania Press, 1991), pp. 162–4.
4. *Storming the Reality Studio*, ed. Larry McCafferey (Durham and London: Duke University Press, 1991), p. 345. In this volume the editor and Richard Kadrey list William Burroughs, Kathy Acker, The Velvet Underground, The Sex Pistols, and Sonic Youth – amongst many other cult and countercultural icons – as major influences upon cyberpunk. Sterling describes himself as a 'self-professed eccentric Bohemian' whose values are those of the counterculture – but who also, interestingly, sees 'civil rights, knowledge, power, freedom and privacy' as 'timeless issues', 'A Statement of Principle', *Science Fiction Eye*, 10 (June 1992): 14–18. Amongst cyberpunk authors, Lewis Shiner's fiction draws most explicitly upon anarchist ideas. See, in relation to his novels, *Frontera* and *Deserted Cities of the Heart*, Robert Donahoo and Chuck Etheridge, 'Lewis Shiner and the "Good Anarchist"' in George Slusser and Tom Shippey (eds), *Fiction 2000. Cyberpunk and the Future of Narrative* (Athens, London: University of Georgia Press, 1992), pp. 183–90.
5. Marge Piercy, *Body of Glass* (London: Michael Joseph, 1992), p. 383.
6. By 'both types of anarchism' I mean the forms of populist and terroristic anarchism Howe describes. Usually three main forms of anarchism are identified: individualist anarchism in a tradition from Benjamin Tucker to the right-wing 'Anarcho-Capitalism' of recent years – including George Wallace, Barry Goldwater and the 'Young Americans for Freedom' (YAF) organisation, founded in 1960 – which denounces the interference of Church and state, but endorses private property; secondly, the communist–anarchist tradition, deriving from Kropotkin and Bakunin (and including Emma Goldman in the United States), which believes in spontaneous popular action and

236

common ownership; and thirdly, the anarcho-syndicalism, notably of the IWW, which rejects private property and believes in the revolutionary role of trade unions and other workers' organisations. See Marian J. Morton, *Emma Goldman and the American Left. Nowhere at Home* (New York: Twayne Publishers, 1992), p. 2. For a discussion of 1960s radicalism as strongly anarchist in character, including the expression of anarcho-capitalism, see David Deleon, *The American as Anarchist. Reflections on Indigenous Radicalism* (Baltimore and London: Johns Hopkins University Press, 1978), especially pp. 117–31. Deleon cites increased state interference, the unpopularity of the Vietnam War, and the defeat of Liberal reform represented by Eugene McCarthy as the chief reasons why 'all forms of American anarchism . . . made a startling reappearance in major expressions of youth culture, black protest, the New Left and dozens of explicitly anarchist papers and groups' (p. 119). Both left and right-wing libertarianism, as he points out, looked to figures such as Jefferson, Tom Paine and Thoreau as forebears (pp. 121–22, 125–31). His discussion confirms that the right-wing, anti-communist libertarianism of a figure such as Dos Passos in the postwar years was not the absolute about-face it might at first seem.

7. Irving Howe, 'New Styles in "Leftism"', *Selected Writings*, op. cit., p. 193.

8. David Deleon's description of the splintering of SDS 'into various decentralist and authoritarian elements' effectively summarises Howe's taxonomy. He adds that the Maoist control of SDS liberated decentralised fronts for women, gays, Chicanos and others, as well as research and publishing groups and the 'explosion of explicitly anarchist journals', op. cit., pp. 121, 123.

9. 'The New York Intellectuals', in *Selected Writings*, op. cit., p. 268.

10. Murray Boorchin, 'New Social Movements. The Anarchic Dimension' in *For Anarchism. History, Theory, and Practice*, ed. David Goodway (London and New York: Routledge, 1989), pp. 261–74. Boorchin sees Howe as having moved to the political centre (ibid., p. 264).

11. Douglas Tallack, *Twentieth-Century America. The Intellectual and Cultural Context* (London and New York: Longman, 1991), p. 209. Tallack is thinking of Bourne's 1917 essay, 'The War and the Intellectuals'. I have cited Bourne above in the list of those who showed some affinity with anarchist thought. This is not to my knowledge explicit in Bourne's case. Deleon, however, writes of his 'almost visceral anarchism' (op. cit., p. 82). Elsewhere, Thomas Bender sees Bourne as a model for a later Left intelligentsia, and cites the continuing relevance of his cosmopolitan and pluralistic vision to New York City, 'Looking at Our City' in *In Search of New York*, ed. Jim Sleeper (New Jersey: Transaction Publishers, 1989), p. 28. Alan Wald also, in *The Responsibility of Intellectuals* (1992) writing as a 'Marxist historian' committed to socialism and the primacy of class struggle, expresses a triple debt to Raymond Williams, Bourne and Chomsky. Chomsky himself recalls Bourne's early criticism of the role of the university in his 'The Function of the University in a Time of Crisis' (1969), and points to its similarities with the rhetoric of the contemporary student movement, *For Reasons of State* (London: Fontana/Collins, 1973), pp. 91–2. Chomsky's own

acknowledgement in his essay 'The Responsibility of Intellectuals' is to Dwight Macdonald who, as mentioned, adopted an 'anarcho-pacifist' position in the postwar period. MacDonald in turn has been a strong influence upon Norman Mailer, a figure who Howe felt mounted the most serious challenge to the assumptions of the New York intellectuals (see *Selected Essays*, op. cit., pp. 278–9).

12. Noam Chomsky, 'Notes on Anarchism' (1970), in *For Reasons of State*, op. cit., p. 157. Further page references are given in the text.

13. Chomsky evokes Bakunin, von Humbolt, and the early Marx in this argument, as well as the writings of Rudolf Rocker and Daniel Guérin. His formulation, as I suggest, is pertinent to arguments which seek to retain Enlightenment principles while acknowledging the force of post-structuralist and postmodernist critique. In terms of the writers surveyed in this volume, aside from Randolph Bourne, his thinking seems most immediately relevant to E. L. Doctorow. For some further discussion and illustrative comment see Ralphael Salkie (ed.) *The Chomsky Update. Linguistics and Politics* (London: Unwin Hyman, 1990), pp. 186–96.

14. The use or eschewal of the term 'socialism' alone in this process of political stock-taking and reconstruction would repay study. Howe concluded in the essay 'Thinking About Socialism' in 1985 that if the term was abandoned its substance would have to be reinvented, *Selected Essays*, op. cit., p. 489. Chomsky, as noted, views socialism as an integral part of anarchism. Elsewhere, Fredric Jameson struggles between the classical Marxist view that socialism emerges from within capitalism and the sense of the inescapability of the market, the 'culture of consumption' which says 'socialism does not work', *Postmodernism* (London: Verso, 1992), pp. 205–8, 335–6; Stanley Aronowitz in an essay of 1994 on 'The Situation of the Left' in the United States feels the term and its associations must be dropped for a programme of 'radical democracy', *Socialist Review*, 23 (3), 1994: 5–79. Meanwhile, Natoli and Hutcheon's 508-page *Postmodern Reader*, containing essays by Hutcheon, Cornel West, Jane Flax, bell hooks and Houstan Baker Jr, does not index the term once.

15. Fredric Jameson, 'Postmodernism and Consumer society' in *Postmodernism and its Discontents*, ed. E. Ann Kaplan (London: Verso, 1988), p. 27.

16. Jay McInerney, *Brightness Falls* (London: Penguin, 1992), p. 389. Further page references are given in the text.

17. Geoffrey Biddle points out in the Preface to his collection of photo-graphs, *Alphabet City*, that the population of the area was Puerto Rican. The Puerto Rican name for the Lower East Side was 'Loisada'. It was renamed 'Alphabet City', says Biddle, when developers saw the chic potential of the name and began to 'gentrify' the housing.

18. *New York Times*, (4 June 1991), A1: 1; *The Village Voice* (11 June 1991): 16. *The Village Voice* also reported that the 'riot' by anarchists which followed the concert 'was provoked by police overreaction' (ibid).

19. *New York Times*, ibid. The eviction, it should be noted, occurred in the same week that the City Council approved a new Civil Rights Bill to prohibit discrimination in housing, employment and public accommodation. David Dinkins, the City's first black Mayor, had been

elected in 1989. By 1991 he was out of favour after showing indifference to a subway murder the previous summer. Under his Mayorship the City slipped into renewed recession. Its budget deficit, which stood at $500 million in 1989, had increased by 1991 to $1500 million. One in four New Yorkers were at this time classed as poor, and there were reportedly 100,000 homeless on the streets. The closing of Tompkins Square appeared to Sherletta McCaskell, President of the Clients' Advisory Board at the Lexington Avenue Women's Shelter, who had been engaged in negotiations for an alternative to the eviction, as a 'betrayal from an administration they thought would stand up for the rights of the poor' (*The Village Voice*, 11 June 1991: 16).

20. *New York Times*, 16 October 1991: 1.
21. Janet L. Abu-Lughod and others, *From Urban Village to East Village* (Oxford: Basil Blackwell, 1994), pp. 4–5.
22. Ibid., pp. 258–60.
23. Andrew Van Kleunen, 'The Squatters: A Chorus of Voices . . . But is Anyone Listening?' ibid., p. 294.
24. Sarah Schulman, 'Why I Fear the Future', in *Critical Fictions. The Politics of Imaginative Writing*, ed. Philomena Mariani (Seattle: Bay Press, 1991), p. 192.
25. Ibid., p. 193.
26. Patrick Wright, 'Home is Where the Cart Is', *Independent on Sunday* (Review section), 12 January 1992: 12.
27. Ibid.
28. Ibid.
29. Graham Caveney, 'A City on the Kill', in *Shopping in Space, Essays on 'Blank Generation' Fiction*, ed. Elizabeth Young and Graham Caveney (London: Serpent's Tail, 1992), p. 131.
30. Ibid., p. 130.
31. Douglas Oliver, *Penniless Politics* (Hoarse Commerce, 28 Albion Drive, London, 1991; reprinted Newcastle: Bloodaxe Books, 1994). Page references in the text are to the later edition.
32. Howard Brenton in the *Guardian*, 7 April 1992; reprinted as the 'Foreword' to the later edition of the poem, pp. 11–12.
33. In case it seems I am dismissing Rose's book and this postmodernism out of hand, the film of *Die Hard New York* was being made when I visited the Square in 1994. A bystander said of Bruce Willis that he 'looked like a bum'. Confusing simulations multiply around us. I don't think the commercial fiction of Willis's film overtook the social narrative of the Square, however. Someone shouted insults at the director for being there and for the delay. A small group of other bystanders wondered at the power of a film company to simply move in and close off Avenue A and the side-roads for a whole morning, and there was talk of how much money Willis earned and what the local people would do for a grand a day.
34. Jay McInerney, *Brightness Falls* (London: Penguin, 1992), p. 398.
35. *Mao II* (London: Jonathan Cape, 1991), pp. 146, 173. Further page references are given in the text.
36. DeLillo, profiled in *The New York Times*, 9 June 1991, Section 7, *Book Reviews*, p. 10.

New York Fictions

37. Noam Chomsky, *The Culture of Terrorism* (Boston: South End Press, 1988), p. 80. See his analysis of the Western world's selective use of the term 'terrorism' in *ibid.* (ed.), op. cit., pp. 154–8.
38. Edward Said, 'Media and Cultural Identity' in *Information and Misinformation in Euro-Arab Relations* (The Hague: Euro-Arab Dialogue Lectures III, Lutfia Rabbani Foundation, 1988), p. 36.
39. Admiral Stansfield Turner, *Terrorism and Democracy* (Boston: Houghton Mifflin, 1991), p. 181.
40. Ibid.
41. Edward Said, op. cit., p. 45.
42. Noam Chomsky, in C. P. Otero (ed.), *Radical Priorities* (Montreal: Black Rose, 1983), p. 205–6.
43. Said, op. cit.
44. Aurora Levins Morales and Rosario Morales, *Getting Home Alive* (New York: Firebrand Books, 1986), pp. 208–9.

Index

241

Index